An Explanation of the Bayqūnī Poem
In Hadith Terminology

شرح المنظومة البيقونية في مصطلح الحديث

Sharḥ al-Manẓūma al-Bayqūniyya
fī Muṣṭalaḥ al-Ḥadīth

By Imam ʿAbdallah Sirājuddīn al-Ḥusaynī

Translated by
Imran Rahim

Edited by
Abdassamad Clarke

LOOH PRESS
SUNNI PUBLICATIONS

ISBN 978-90-79294-30-5

An Explanation of the Bayquni Poem
in Hadith Terminology

Imam ʿAbdallah Sirajuddin al-Husayni

Translation by:
Imran Rahim

Edited by:
Abdassamad Clarke

Cover Design by:
Vehemence

Printed by:
IngramSpark

Published by:
Looh Press
Leicester, United Kingdom
www.loohpress.com
info@loohpress.com

Sunni Publications
Rotterdam, the Netherlands
www.sunnipubs.com
info@sunnipubs.com

بسم الله الرحمن الرحيم

Dear reader,

When you read any of my books, please recite Sūra al-Fātiḥa, and donate the reward of your recitation to the renowned scholar and great Gnostic, carrier of the banner of the authority of the Qur'an and Sunna, the Qur'anic exegete and scholar of Hadith—with sound chains of narration from many great scholars of Hadith in Aleppo, Damascus, Morocco and elsewhere in the Islamic world, complete with written authorisations which I have kept with me—my Shaykh and noble father, Shaykh Muḥammad Najīb Sirājuddīn al-Ḥusaynī, may Allah, the Exalted, have mercy upon him, and reward him well on behalf of the Muslims; Indeed, He is All-Hearing, All-Knowing. Āmīn

—ʿAbdallah b. Muḥammad Najīb Sirājuddīn al-Ḥusaynī

TRANSLITERATION TABLE

ا/آ/ى	ā	ظ	ẓ
ب	b	ع	ʿ
ت	t	غ	gh
ث	th	ف	f
ج	j	ق	q
ح	ḥ	ك	k
خ	kh	ل	l
د	d	م	m
ذ	dh	ن	n
ر	r	ه	h
ز	z	و	w/ū
س	s	ي	y/ī
ش	sh	ة	a
ص	ṣ	ء	ʾ
ض	ḍ	أ	a/u
ط	ṭ	ا	i

HONORIFIC PHRASES

Exalted and Sublime is He
Allah's prayers and salutations
 be upon him
Allah's prayers and salutations
 be upon him and his family
Peace be upon him
Peace be upon them
May Allah be pleased with him
May Allah be pleased with her
May Allah be pleased with them both
May Allah be pleased with them

TABLE OF CONTENTS

ABOUT THE AUTHOR — 11

THE ARABIC TEXT — 16

THE ENGLISH TRANSLATION — 17

INTRODUCTION — 25

CHAPTER ONE
CLARIFYING THE SCIENCE OF HADITH — 26

THE SCIENCE OF HADITH NARRATION [*RIWĀYA*] — 26
    The first to compile
      in the science of Hadith narration — 28

THE SCIENCE OF HADITH COMPREHENSION [*DIRĀYA*] — 30
    The codification of this science — 33

CHAPTER TWO
A CLARIFICATION OF SOME OF THE TERMINOLOGY
  AGREED UPON IN THE SCIENCE OF HADITH — 36

THE DIFFERENCE BETWEEN A HADITH *QUDSĪ* AND THE QURʾAN — 38
    Formulas used to narrate a Hadith *qudsī* — 40

THE *BASMALA*, THE *ḤAMDALA*,
  AND SENDING PRAYERS UPON THE PROPHET ﷺ — 43

CATEGORIES OF HADITH — 47

WAYS OF CATEGORISING WITHIN THE SCIENCE OF HADITH — 48

CHAPTER THREE
ACCEPTED HADITH [*MAQBŪL*] — 50

SOUND [*ṢAḤĪḤ*] — 50
    Concerning the restrictions to the definition
      and what is excluded from it — 51
    That which establishes the integrity of a narrator — 53
    That which establishes accuracy — 54
    Levels of *ṣaḥīḥ* — 55
    Reasons for the superiority of
      Ṣaḥīḥ al-Bukhārī over *Ṣaḥīḥ Muslim* — 57
    Types of *ṣaḥīḥ* — 59

The ruling on the ṣaḥīḥ Hadith
with regard to it being used as proof 61
The statements of the scholars regarding the effect
that the ṣaḥīḥ Hadith necessitates: certainty [qaṭ']
or high probability [al-ẓann al-qawī] 61
The rulings for classifying Hadith as
ṣaḥīḥ, ḥasan and ḍa'īf 64
A benefit 65

FAIR [ḤASAN] 66
Types of ḥasan 67
Degrees of ḥasan 69
The ruling on the ḥasan 69
A principle 70
A benefit 70

TERMS FOR THE ACCEPTED HADITH 71

CHAPTER FOUR
REJECTED HADITH [MARDŪD] 73

WEAK [ḌA'ĪF] 73
Types of ḍa'īf 73
The ruling on acting upon weak Hadith 75
Conditions for acting upon weak Hadith
according to the verifying scholars 77
The ruling on narrating weak Hadith
without clarifying its weakness 77
The manner of narrating weak Hadith 78

CHAPTER FIVE
**THE CATEGORIES OF HADITH WITH REGARD TO THOSE
TO WHOM THEY ARE ATTRIBUTED** 79

RAISED [MARFŪ'] 79
Examples 79
Types of marfū' 80

CUT-OFF [MAQṬŪ'] 80
The ruling on the maqṭū' 81

HALTED [MAWQŪF] 82
Types of mawqūf 83

SUPPORTED [MUSNAD]   89

CONNECTED [MUTTAṢIL] WHICH IS ALSO CALLED MAWṢŪL   90

CONCATENATED [MUSALSAL]   91
    The ruling on the *musalsal* Hadith   94

CHAPTER SIX
THE CATEGORIES OF HADITH WITH REGARD TO THEIR PATHS   95

UNUSUAL [GHARĪB]   95
    The ruling on the *gharīb*   97

RARE [ʿAZĪZ]   97

WELL-KNOWN [MASHHŪR]   98
    Reminder   99

ABUNDANT [MUSTAFĪḌ]   100

MASS-TRANSMITTED [MUTAWĀTIR]   100
    Types of *mutawātir*   102
    The ruling on the *mutawātir*   102

CHAPTER SEVEN
THE CATEGORIES OF HADITH WITH REGARD TO THE CHAIN OF
NARRATION BEING CONNECTED OR DISCONNECTED   103

SEVERED [MUNQAṬIʿ]   103
    The ruling on the *munqaṭiʿ*   105
    A benefit   105

PROBLEMATIC [MUʿḌAL]   105
    The ruling on the *muʿḍal*   106

MISLEADING [MUDALLAS]   106
    Types of *tadlīs*   106
    The ruling on *tadlīs al-isnād*   107
    The ruling on *tadlīs al-shuyūkh*   109

INITIALLY DISCONNECTED [MURSAL]   110
    The ruling on the *mursal*   111
    The *mursal* of a Companion and its ruling   113
    A principle   114
    A benefit   114

SUSPENDED [MUʿALLAQ]   115
    The ruling on the *muʿallaq*   116

TRANSMITTED USING 'FROM' [*MU'AN'AN*]   117
    The ruling on the *mu'an'an*   117
TRANSMITTED USING 'THAT' [*MU'AN'AN*]   118

CHAPTER EIGHT
UNCLEAR, UNKNOWN, ANOMALOUS AND INVERTED   119
UNCLEAR [*MUBHAM*]   119
    Types of *mubham*   120
    The ruling on the *mubham*   120
UNKNOWN [*MAJĀHĪL*]   121
ANOMALOUS [*SHĀDH*] AND ITS OPPOSITE: PRESERVED [*MAḤFŪẒ*]   122
INVERTED [*MAQLŪB*]   124
    The ruling on the *maqlūb*   126

CHAPTER NINE
INVESTIGATION [*I'TIBĀR*] AND ITS OUTCOMES   129
SUPPORTIVE [*MUTĀBA'A*]   129
CORROBORATION [*SHĀHID*]   130
SOLITARY [*FARD*]   130
    The ruling on *fard muqayyad*   133
    A benefit   134

CHAPTER TEN
DEFECTS, ALTERATIONS, DISCREPANCIES AND INTERPOLATIONS   135
DEFECTIVE [*MU'ALLAL*]   135
    The ruling on the *mu'all*   138
ORTHOGRAPHICALLY ALTERED [*MUṢAḤḤAF WA-MUḤARRAF*]   138
INCONSISTENT [*MUḌṬARIB*]   139
    Examples   141
    The ruling on the *muḍṭarib*   142
INTERPOLATED [*MUDRAJ*]   143
    Idrāj in the wording   143
    Idrāj in the chain   144
    How to recognise *idrāj*   146
    The ruling on *idrāj*   147

CHAPTER ELEVEN
COMPLEMENTARY AND CONTRASTING — 148

RULINGS ON ADDITIONAL RELIABLE NARRATORS
[*ZIYĀDA AL-THIQĀT*] — 148

ELEVATED AND DESCENDING CHAINS [*ISNĀD ʿĀLĪ WA-NĀZIL*] — 150
    Elevated [*ʿālī*] and its types — 151
    Descent [*nuzūl*] and its types — 154
    The ruling on *ʿālī* and *nuzūl* — 155

MUTUAL NARRATION [*MUDABBAJ*] — 156

RESEMBLANT AND DIVERGENT [*MUTTAFIQ WA-MUFTARIQ*] — 158

SIMILAR AND DISSIMILAR [*MUʾTALIF WA-MUKHTALIF*] — 160

DENOUNCED AND AFFIRMED [*MUNKAR WA-MAʿRŪF*] — 162
    A benefit — 163

CHAPTER TWELVE
ABANDONED, FABRICATED,
    CONTRADICTION AND ABROGATION — 164

ABANDONED [*MATRŪK*] — 164

FABRICATED [*MAWḌŪʿ*] — 165
    Ways of recognising fabrication — 165
    Reasons for fabrication — 168
    A benefit — 170
    The ruling on fabrication — 170
    The ruling on the *mawḍūʿ* — 171
    The ruling on narrating fabricated Hadith — 171
    Books of fabrications — 172

CONTRADICTORY NARRATIONS [*MUKHTALIF AL-ḤADĪTH*] — 173
    The most important works — 176

ABROGATING AND ABROGATED [*AL-NĀSIKH WAL-MANSŪKH*] — 176
    How abrogation is identified — 177
    The importance of knowing this subject — 179

Chapter Thirteen
Narrators, Scholars and Students   180

Knowing whose Narrations are Accepted
  and whose are Rejected   180

      Narrating from people of creedal innovation
        [*ahl al-bid‘a*]   181
      Levels of *jarḥ wa-ta‘dīl*   181
      Expressions used by particular scholars of Hadith   184
      When is *jarḥ wa-ta‘dīl* accepted?   185
      Contradictions between *jarḥ* and *ta‘dīl*   186
      Aspersions that have been transmitted
        about some of the Imams   186

Bearing Hadith and Relaying them   192
      The conditions for bearing Hadith   192
      The age at which receiving a Hadith is accepted   193
      Ways of bearing and transmitting Hadith   194

Ways of Studying Hadith   203
      The ruling on reading Hadith with *tajwīd*   204
      Etiquette of the scholar of Hadith   205
      Etiquette of the student of Hadith   208

Conclusion   211

Bibliography   213

Index   217

ABOUT THE AUTHOR

ONE OF THE GREATEST SCHOLARS that the Syrian city of Aleppo—known in the Levant as "the city of scholars"—has ever known was the friend of Allah ﷻ, Imam ʿAbdallah b. Muḥammad Najīb Sirājuddīn al-Ḥalabī al-Ḥusaynī ﷺ, an extraordinary saint who dedicated his entire life to the service of Islam. His qualities were many and his skills outstanding. Imam ʿAbdallah, known as "the Light of Aleppo," was a renowned spiritual master of the Rifāʿī path, an expert in Ḥanafī jurisprudence, a *ḥāfiẓ* and brilliant exegete of the Qurʾan, as well as a scholar and *ḥāfiẓ* of Hadith, having memorised more than one hundred thousand traditions. He was most famous, however, for his immense and intense love for our master Muhammad ﷺ, the Messenger of Allah.

A descendant on his father's side of the Prophet's grandson ﷺ, our master Ḥusayn b. ʿAlī b. Abī Ṭālib ﷺ, Imam ʿAbdallah was born into an honourable and pious family on the verge of the collapse of the Ottoman Sultanate in 1923 CE. During his childhood, Imam ʿAbdallah was surrounded by the love and care of his father, the esteemed Shaykh Muḥammad Najīb Sirājuddīn al-Ḥusaynī ﷺ who was himself a spiritual master, and a leading jurist, exegete of the Qurʾan and scholar of Hadith.

Imam ʿAbdallah began his pursuit of knowledge at an early age and memorised the Qurʾan when only thirteen years old under the guidance of his father. At that time, he was studying Hadith at the Islamic school of al-Khasrawiyya. There he studied under leading scholars of the time such as the great Imam Muḥammad Ibrāhīm al-Salqīnī ﷺ, the saintly Shaykh ʿĪsā al-Bayānūnī ﷺ, Shaykh ʿUmar Masʿūd al-Ḥarīrī ﷺ, Shaykh Fayḍallah al-Ayyūbī al-Kurdī ﷺ, Shaykh Aḥmad al-Shammāʿ ﷺ and several other prominent scholars. Imam ʿAbdallah also frequented other scholars who who did not teach at his school, such as Shaykh Aḥmad al-Kurdī ﷺ and Shaykh Muḥammad Saʿīd al-Idlibī ﷺ. As he remained in their proximity, the great scholar of Hadith and leading historian of Aleppo, Shaykh Muḥammad Rāghib al-Tabbākh ﷺ, noticed his intelligence and intense devotion to the pursuit of knowledge and he decided to become his mentor.

He continued his studies under the supervision of his father, Shaykh Muḥammad Najīb Sirājuddīn who always attracted large crowds to his lessons. In this environment Imam ʿAbdallah was given the opportunity to further develop his skills and increase his knowledge and his fame as a scholar soon spread throughout Aleppo. He began teaching Islam in various Mosques, such as the Ḥamawī Mosque where he tutored one hour in the morning, four times a week. Soon he was asked to teach at various colleges including the Shaʿbāniyya School. He also taught many courses and lessons in various Mosques including his own where he continued to impart knowledge upon the masses even when the funds that provided his payment were stopped. Then came one year in which his father's age prevented him from continuing his classes. Imam ʿAbdallah, still only twenty-two years old, carried the heavy load of succeeding his father as a scholar. The demands of the public and the high level of his father's classes made this a great test for him, but by the grace of Allah ﷻ he succeeded in it, and honouring this responsibility caused the admiration of the public for him. Following the vacuum caused by the closing of the Shaʿbāniyya Islamic school, Imam ʿAbdallah felt the need to found a large Islamic school in Aleppo that would take charge of training future scholars and preachers.

He decided to revive religious teaching by founding the School of Islamic Teachings in 1958 CE. Its program combined legal courses, Islamic spirituality, the life and qualities of the Messenger of Allah ﷺ as well as the sciences of Hadith. In addition, he founded a Qur'an school whose mission it was to teach its students the Majestic Qur'an. Generous scholarships were granted to the pupils in order to encourage the preservation of this knowledge.

Imam ʿAbdallah was known to be generous and helpful towards the poor, lenient towards the pupils of his school, and famed for his humility and devotion. As Imam ʿAbdallah became the leading scholar of Aleppo, he conveyed in his classes the quintessence of Islamic legislation and spirituality. In a moving voice, he often spoke of love towards the Messenger of Allah ﷺ and the duty to follow his excellent manners. He promoted love for the Sunna and revived it in his behaviour and exhortations. His foremost student, son-in-law and biographer, Shaykh Nūr al-Dīn ʿItr, mentions that he was "extremely scrupulous and avoided any doubtful thing."

Imam ʿAbdallah ﷺ was truly in love with the Messenger of Allah ﷺ. He did not cease pointing out his qualities, his ethics and the nobility of his status in nearness of Allah ﷻ, and did not accept anyone to be given the same importance as our master Muhammad ﷺ. In light of this incredible love Shaykh ʿAbd al-Raḥmān al-Shāghūrī ﷺ called him "the Pole of Prophetic love of our times." Shaykh ʿAlawī al-Mālikī al-Ḥasanī ﷺ—the father of Shaykh Muḥammad b. ʿAlawī ﷺ—used to say about him: "This man is walking towards him [the Prophet ﷺ], even if it would be on his eyelashes." Shaykh Aḥmad Hārūn ﷺ used say to him: "You are surrounded by the vision of our master the Messenger of Allah ﷺ." Ḥabīb ʿAbd al-Qādir al-Saqqāf ﷺ used to say about him: "It is obligatory upon every eye to see him."

Imam ʿAbdallah ﷺ wrote more than thirty books dealing with Islamic spirituality, creed, ethics, and the noble manners of the Messenger of Allah ﷺ, the sciences of Hadith and exegesis of the Qurʾan. One of his famous works is the book of which we have the translation before us today: *An Explanation of the Bayqūnī Poem in Hadith Terminology.*

- *Ḥawla Tafsīr Sūra al-Fātiḥa*
- *Ḥawla Tafsīr Sūra al-Ḥujurāt*
- *Ḥawla Tafsīr Sūra Qāf*
- *Ḥawla Tafsīr Sūra al-Mulk*
- *Ḥawla Tafsīr Sūra al-Insān*
- *Ḥawla Tafsīr Sūra al-ʿAlaq*
- *Ḥawla Tafsīr Sūra al-Kawthar*
- *Ḥawla Tafsīr Sūra al-Ikhlāṣ*
- *Hadī al-Qurʾān al-Karīm ilā Ḥujja al-Burhān*
- *Hadī al-Qurʾān ilā Maʿrifa al-ʿUlūm wal-Tafakkur*
- *Tilāwa al-Qurʾān al-Majīd*
- *Al-Taqarrub ilā Allah Taʿālā*

- ***Shahāda Lā Ilāha Illā Allah, Muḥammad Rasūl Allah ***
  (*The Testimony of Faith: There is no god but God,
  and Muhammad is the Messenger of God*)
- ***Sayyidunā Muḥammad Rasūl Allah***
  (*Our Master Muhammad the Messenger of Allah*)
- *Al-Hadī al-Nabawī wal-Irshādāt al-Muḥammadiyya*
- *Al-Ṣalāt fī al-Islām*
- ***Al-Ṣalāt ʿalā al-Nabī***
  (*Sending Prayers upon the Prophet*)
- *Ṣuʿūd al-Aqwāl wa-Rafʿ al-ʿAmāl*
- *Al-Duʿāʾ*
- *Tarjama al-Shaykh Muḥammad Najīb Sirājuddīn al-Ḥusaynī*
- *Al-Īmān bi-ʿAwālim al-Ukhrā wa-Mawāqifuhā*
- *Al-Īmān bil-Malāʾika wal-Baḥth Ḥawla ʿĀlam al-Jinn*
- *Al-Adʿiyya wal-Adhkār al-Wārida*
- ***Sharḥ al-Manẓūma al-Bayqūniyya fī Muṣṭalaḥ al-Ḥadīth***
  (*An Explanation of the Bayquni Poem in Hadith Terminology*)
- *Adaʿiyya al-Ṣabāḥ wal-Masāʾ*
- *Manāsik al-Ḥajj wal-ʿUmra*
- *Al-Ṣiyām*
- *Mawāqif Sayyidinā Muḥammad Rasūl Allah maʿa al-ʿĀlam*
- *Durūs Ḥawla baʿḍ al-Tafsīr Āyāt al-Qurʾān al-Karīm*
- *Al-Isrāʾ wal-Miʿrāj*
- *Hijra Rasūl Allah*
- *Al-Īmān bil-Qaḍāʾ wal-Qadar*

Imam ʿAbdallah's students were numerous, many of them becoming prominent scholars themselves, such as his son Shaykh Aḥmad Sirājuddīn, his nephew and son-in-law Shaykh Nūr al-Dīn ʿItr, Shaykh Sāmir al-Nass, Shaykh Muḥammad ʿAwwāma and Shaykh Muḥammad al-Nīnowy, may Allah preserve them.

Following a surgical operation carried out towards the end of his life, the health of Imam ʿAbdallah deteriorated. On the 4th of March 2002 CE [1422 H.] he returned to his Lord. The news of his passing was announced throughout the Muslim world and covered it with a veil of sorrow. Imam ʿAbdallah b. Muḥammad Najīb Sirājuddīn al-Ḥalabī al-Ḥusaynī was buried in the Shaʿbāniyya complex, next to the graves of its Ottoman founders.

May Allah sanctify the noble Imam's secret

بسم الله الرحمن الرحيم

ابتدأ بالحمد مصليًا على نخبة خبر نبي أرسلا

وذا من أقسام الحديث شعبه وكل واحد أتى وشدّه

أولها الصحيح وهو ما اتصل إسناده ولم يشذ أو يُعَلّ

بروايته أيضًا بطعن مثله معتمدًا في ضبطه ونقله

والحسن المعروف في طرق وشذت رجاله لا كالصحيح اشتهرت

وطاب ما عن رتبة الحسن فضربه فهو الضعيف وهو أقسامًا كثر

وما أُضيف للنبي المرفوع وما انابجَ صوا المقطوع

والمسند المتصل الإسناد من راويه حتى المصطفى والمربيّن

وما بين كل راوٍ يتصل إسناده للمصطفى في المتصل

وما أضفته إلى الأصحاب من قوله فدا فصوم وقوي ركن

وموصلًا منه الصحابي سقط وقل غريب ما رواه راوٍ فقط

وكل ما لم يتصل إسناده إسناده منقطع الأول لا

والعضل الساقط منه اثنان وما أتى مدلسًا نوعان

الأول الإسقاط للشيخ وإن بيّنة من فوقه بعن و من

والثاني لا يسقطه كمن أصفا أو ما فيه ما به لا ينعرف

وما خالف ثقة به الملا قال ثان والمقلوب قسمان ثلا

أبدا له راوٍ وما أبرا وقسم وقلب إسناد لمتن قسم

والفرد ما قيّده تر بثقة أو جمع أو قصر على راوٍ ثقة

وما بعلة غموض أو خفا معلل عندهم قد عرّ وشا

وذو اختلاف سند أو متن مضطربه عند أهل الفن

والمدرجات في الحديث ما أتى من بعض الألفاظ أروا أتصلت

وما روى كل قرين عن أخه مدرج ثناء فيه حوا وأنها

تفق لفظًا وخط انف وهبته فيما ذكر يا المفترق

ومتلف

بسم الله الرحمن الرحيم

(١) أَبْدَأُ بِالْحَمْدِ مُصَلِّيًا عَلَى مُحَمَّدٍ خَيْرِ نَبِيٍّ أُرْسِلَا

(٢) وَذِي مِنْ أَقْسَامِ الْحَدِيثِ عِدَّهْ وَكُلُّ وَاحِدٍ أَتَى وَحَدَّهْ

(٣) أَوَّلُهَا الصَّحِيحُ وَهْوَ مَا اتَّصَلْ إِسْنَادُهُ وَلَمْ يَشُذَّ أَوْ يُعَلْ

(٤) يَرْوِيهِ عَدْلٌ، ضَابِطٌ عَنْ مِثْلِهِ مُعْتَمَدٌ فِي ضَبْطِهِ وَنَقْلِهِ

(٥) وَالْحَسَنُ الْمَعْرُوفُ طُرْقًا وَغَدَتْ رِجَالُهُ لَا كَالصَّحِيحِ اشْتُهِرَتْ

(٦) وَكُلُّ مَا عَنْ رُتْبَةِ الْحُسْنِ قَصُرْ فَهْوَ الضَّعِيفُ وَهْوَ أَقْسَامًا كَثُرْ

(٧) وَمَا أُضِيفَ لِلنَّبِيِّ الْمَرْفُوعُ وَمَا لِلتَّابِعِ هُوَ الْمَقْطُوعُ

(٨) وَالْمُسْنَدُ الْمُتَّصِلُ الْإِسْنَادِ مِنْ رَاوِيهِ حَتَّى الْمُصْطَفَى وَلَمْ يَبِنْ

(٩) وَمَا بِسَمْعِ كُلِّ رَاوٍ يَتَّصِلْ إِسْنَادُهُ لِلْمُصْطَفَى فَالْمُتَّصِلْ

In the name of Allah,
most Gracious, most Merciful

1   *I begin with praise, / sending prayers upon,*   *Muhammad ﷺ, / the best of Prophets sent*

2   *And these are a number / of categories of Hadith,*   *Each one with / its own definition*

3   *The first of them / is the ṣaḥīḥ which is that,*   *Whose chain is connected, / having no anomaly or defect*

4   *Narrated by someone who / is precise and has integrity, / from someone like himself,*   *Relied upon in his precision / and transmission*

5   *Ḥasan is that / whose chains are known,*   *But whose narrators are not as / famous as [those of] the ṣaḥīḥ*

6   *All that falls short of ḥasan,*   *Is ḍaʿīf which / has many branches*

7   *And that which is attributed / to the Prophet ﷺ is marfūʿ*   *And that [which is attributed] / to a Successor is maqṭūʿ*

8   *Musnad is that / whose narrators are connected,*   *From its narrator up / to Muṣṭafā ﷺ and is not broken*

9   *That whose chain, / by every narrator hearing,*   *Is connected / to Muṣṭafā ﷺ is muttaṣil*

(١٠) مُسَلْسَلٌ قُلْ مَا عَلَى وَصْفٍ أَتَى   مِثْلُ: أَمَا وَاللهِ أَنْبَانِي الْفَتَى

(١١) كَذَاكَ قَدْ حَدَّثَنِيهِ قَائِمَا   أَوْ بَعْدَ أَنْ حَدَّثَنِي تَبَسَّمَا

(١٢) عَزِيزُ مَرْوِيِّ اثْنَيْنِ أَوْ ثَلَاثَهْ   مَشْهُورُ مَرْوِيٍّ فَوْقَ مَا ثَلَاثَهْ

(١٣) مُعَنْعَنٌ كَعَنْ سَعِيدٍ عَنْ كَرَمْ   وَمُبْهَمٌ مَا فِيهِ رَاوٍ لَمْ يُسَمّْ

(١٤) وَكُلُّ مَا قَلَّتْ رِجَالُهُ عَلَا   وَضِدُّهُ ذَاكَ الَّذِي قَدْ نَزَلَا

(١٥) وَمَا أَضَفْتَهُ إِلَى الْأَصْحَابِ مِنْ   قَوْلٍ وَفِعْلٍ فَهُوَ مَوْقُوفٌ زُكِنْ

(١٦) وَمُرْسَلٌ مِنْهُ الصَّحَابِيُّ سَقَطْ   وَقُلْ غَرِيبٌ مَا رَوَى رَاوٍ فَقَطْ

(١٧) وَكُلُّ مَا لَمْ يَتَّصِلْ بِحَالِ   إِسْنَادُهُ مُنْقَطِعُ الْأَوْصَالِ

(١٨) وَالْمُعْضَلُ السَّاقِطُ مِنْهُ اثْنَانِ   وَمَا أَتَى مُدَلَّسًا نَوْعَانِ

(١٩) الْأَوَّلُ الْإِسْقَاطُ لِلشَّيْخِ وَأَنْ   يَنْقُلَ عَمَّنْ فَوْقَهُ بِعَنْ وَأَنْ

(٢٠) وَالثَّانِ لَا يُسْقِطْهُ لَكِنْ يَصِفْ   أَوْصَافَهُ بِمَا بِهِ لَا يَنْعَرِفْ

10   *Say that musalsal is that* / *which comes with a* / *[specific] description,*   *Such as, "By Allah, the* / *young man informed me"*

11   *Likewise, "He narrated it* / *to me whilst standing,"*   *Or, "After he narrated it* / *to me, he smiled"*

12   *'Azīz is that which is* / *narrated by two or three*   *Mashhūr is narrated* / *by more than three*

13   *Mu'an'an is for example, "from* / *Sa'īd, from Karam"*   *Mubham is that in which a* / *narrator hasn't been named*

14   *Everything that has* / *few narrators is 'ālī,*   *And its opposite is nāzil*

15   *Whatever you attribute* / *to the Companions,*   *By way of statement or action,* / *is known [zukin] as mawqūf*

16   *From the mursal, the* / *Companion has been omitted*   *Say that gharīb is that which* / *only one narrator narrates*

17   *Anything that is disconnected* / *in any form,*   *Its chain has severed* / *[munqaṭi'] ties*

18   *Mu'ḍal contains* / *two breaks [in the chain]*   *Mudallas is of two types:*

19   *First, when the teacher* / *is omitted, yet,*   *He narrates from the one* / *above him using 'an [from]* / *or an [that];*

20   *Second, that he does* / *not omit him, but*   *He describes his qualities* / *in a manner by which* / *he is not known*

(٢١) وَمَا يُخَالِفْ ثِقَةٌ فِيهِ المَلَا   فَالشَّاذُّ وَالمَقْلُوبُ قِسْمَانِ تَلَا

(٢٢) إِبْدَالُ رَاوٍ مَا بِرَاوٍ قِسْمُ   وَقَلْبُ إِسْنَادٍ لِمَتْنٍ قِسْمُ

(٢٣) وَالفَرْدُ مَا قَيَّدْتَهُ بِثِقَةِ   أَوْ قَصْرُ أَوْ جَمْعٍ عَلَى رِوَايَةِ

(٢٤) وَمَا بِعِلَّةٍ غُمُوضٍ أَوْ خَفَا   مُعَلَّلٌ عِنْدَهُمْ قَدْ عُرِفَا

(٢٥) وَذُو اخْتِلَافٍ سَنَدٍ أَوْ مَتْنِ   مُضْطَرِبٌ عِنْدَ أُهَيْلِ الفَنِّ

(٢٦) وَالمُدْرَجَاتُ فِي الحَدِيثِ مَا أَتَتْ   مِنْ بَعْضِ أَلْفَاظِ الرُّوَاةِ اتَّصَلَتْ

(٢٧) وَمَا رَوَى كُلُّ قَرِينٍ عَنْ أَخِهْ   مُدَبَّجٌ فَاعْرِفْهُ حَقًّا وَانْتَخِهْ

(٢٨) مُتَّفِقٌ لَفْظًا وَخَطًّا مُتَّفِقْ   وَضِدُّهُ فِيمَا ذَكَرْنَا المُفْتَرِقْ

(٢٩) مُؤْتَلِفٌ مُتَّفِقُ الخَطِّ فَقَطْ   وَضِدُّهُ مُخْتَلِفٌ فَاخْشَ الغَلَطْ

(٣٠) وَالمُنْكَرُ الفَرْدُ بِهِ رَاوٍ غَدَا   تَعْدِيلُهُ لَا يَحْمِلُ التَّفَرُّدَا

(٣١) مَتْرُوكُهُ مَا وَاحِدٌ بِهِ انْفَرَدْ   وَأَجْمَعُوا لِضَعْفِهِ فَهْوَ كَرَدْ

21   When a reliable narrator   There are two types
contradicts a group, it is shādh   of maqlūb, as follows:

22   One type is substituting   And the other type is
one narrator for another,   juxtaposing a chain
onto the wording

23   Fard is to restrict   Region or particular narrator
to a reliable narrator,

24   That which contains   Is known to them as muʿallal
an obscure or hidden defect,

25   That which contains   Is muḍṭarib according
discrepancies in the   to the experts in this science
chain or the wording,

26   Interpolations in a Hadith   Of some words from
appear in the form,   narrators connectedly

27   That which each contemporary   Is mudabbaj, so know
narrates from his brother,   this is the truth and rejoice!

28   Muttafiq is that which concurs   And the opposite
in pronunciation and writing,   of this is muftariq

29   Mu'talif concurs   And its opposite is mukhtalif,
in writing alone,   so beware of erring!

30   Munkar is narrated   Whose rank does not allow
by a single narrator,   for a solitary narration

31   Matrūk is narrated   Whose weakness in status
by a single narrator,   there is consensus upon, thus
it is like a rejected [tradition]

(٣٢) وَالْكَذِبُ الْمُخْتَلَقِ الْمَصْنُوعِ   عَلَى النَّبِيِّ فَذَلِكَ الْمَوْضُوعُ

(٣٣) وَقَدْ أَتَتْ كَالْجَوْهَرِ الْمَكْنُونِ   سَمَّيْتُهَا مَنْظُومَةَ الْبَيْقُونِي

(٣٤) فَوْقَ الثَّلَاثِينَ بِأَرْبَعٍ أَتَتْ   أَبْيَاتُهَا تَمَّتْ بِخَيْرٍ خُتِمَتْ

32 The concocted and Against the Prophet ﷺ
    manufactured lie, is called mawḍūʿ

33 It has indeed arrived I titled it: The Bayqūnī Poem
    like a hidden pearl,

34 Its categories amount Completed, with goodness
    to thirty-four, they are sealed!

AN EXPLANATION OF THE BAYQŪNĪ POEM
In Hadith Terminology

شرح المنظومة البيقونية في مصطلح الحديث

Sharḥ al-Manẓūma al-Bayqūniyya fī Muṣṭalaḥ al-Ḥadīth

By Imam ʿAbdallah Sirājuddīn al-Ḥusaynī

INTRODUCTION

ALL PRAISE IS DUE TO ALLAH, the Lord of the Worlds, and may prayers and salutations be upon our master Muhammad, the Seal of the Prophets, and upon all of his family and Companions.

To proceed: I have gathered in this book that which is well-known from the sciences of Hadith and their necessary investigations and terminological principles, intending thereby to simplify for the novice the path of reaching understanding, hoping that Allah, the Exalted, inspires me with what is correct and multiplies my reward.

I have tied these investigations and terminological discussions to the didactic poem, *al-Manẓūma al-Bayqūniyya*, because of how easy it is to memorise it, and due to the excellence of its composition and wording.

I have only included in this book the most important principles that the student of Hadith narration or the reader of books on Hadith requires.

It comprises of two main parts: first, an explanation of the science of Hadith; and second, an explanation of some of the terminology used in this science.[1]

---

[1] The author of this commentary, Imam ʿAbdallah Sirājuddīn al-Ḥusaynī ﷺ, is referring here to the first chapter as the first part, and the subsequent chapters as the second part. We have gathered these chapters and re-categorised some of them into larger chapters, while maintaining their original order. Where lacking, we have added chapter titles drawn from the text of the commentary—Pub.

CHAPTER ONE
CLARIFYING THE SCIENCE OF HADITH

HE SCIENCE OF HADITH IS OF TWO KINDS: that which concerns itself with narration [*riwāya*], and that which concerns itself with its comprehension [*dirāya*].

THE SCIENCE OF HADITH NARRATION [*RIWĀYA*]

This science concerns itself with the words, actions, qualities, and tacit approvals of the Prophet ﷺ and the narration thereof, by clarifying their exact formulation and verifying the accuracy of their wordings.

Its subject is the Prophet Muhammad ﷺ, his words, actions, tacit approvals and qualities.

Its benefit is that it prevents one from making mistakes when transmitting the words, actions, tacit approvals and qualities of the Prophet ﷺ.

Its objective is happiness in the two abodes.

Its merit is that it is from the noblest of sciences, as by it we know how to follow the Prophet ﷺ, which Allah ﷻ orders us to do when He says: ⟨*Follow him, so that you may be guided.*⟩[2] And likewise: ⟨*Say: If you love Allah, then follow me and Allah will love you and forgive your sins. Allah is most Forgiving, most Merciful.*⟩[3]

For this reason, the scholars of Hadith have the greatest merit and the most plentiful reward, as has been mentioned in a Hadith narrated by Imam al-Shāfiʿī and Imam al-Bayhaqī, from Ibn Masʿūd ﷺ, in which he said: "The Prophet ﷺ said: 'May Allah illuminate the one who hears my speech, understands it and conveys it. Many bearers of understanding [*fiqh*] [convey it] to someone with greater understanding.'"

---

[2] Qur'an 7:158
[3] Qur'an 3:31

Abū Dāwūd and al-Tirmidhī narrated it with the wording: "May Allah illuminate the one who hears something from me and conveys it just as he heard it. Many of those to whom it is conveyed are more astute than the one who heard it."

Al-Tirmidhī said it is *ḥasan ṣaḥīḥ*.

The notable scholar al-Qasṭallānī said:

> The meaning is that Allah has specified pleasures and joys for this person because he strove to beautify knowledge and revive the Prophetic example [Sunna]. Thus, the Prophet ﷺ has rewarded him by supplicating for a befitting reward for him.

Al-Ṭabarānī narrates in *al-Muʿjam al-Awsaṭ* that Ibn ʿAbbās ﷺ said: "The Prophet ﷺ said: 'O Allah, have mercy upon my caliphs.'[4] We replied: 'Who are your caliphs?' He ﷺ said: 'Those who narrate my traditions and teach them to people.'"[5]

---

[4] Caliph [*khalīfa*] is a successor—Ed.

[5] This has been transmitted [by Shaykh ʿAbd al-Ḥayy al-Kattānī] in *al-Tarātīb al-Idāriyya* (vol. 2, p. 319) in a specific chapter and those who referenced the narration have been mentioned, amongst whom is al-Rāmahurmuzī in *al-Muḥaddith al-Fāṣil*, and Abū al-Asʿad Hibatullah al-Qushayrī and Abū al-Fatḥ al-Ṣābūnī, both in *al-Arbaʿīn*. Likewise, al-Khaṭīb in *Sharaf Aṣḥāb Ahl al-Ḥadīth*, al-Daylamī as well as Ibn Najjār, Niẓām al-Mulk in his *Amālī*, Naṣr al-Maqdisī in *al-Ḥujja* and Abū ʿAlī b. Khunays al-Dīnawarī in his Hadith.

He [al-Kattānī] said: "This was mentioned by one of the *ḥuffāẓ* of the Maghreb, Abū al-Qāsim al-ʿAzfī, as mentioned in [al-Suyūṭī's] *al-Durr al-Munaẓẓam*, so refer to that. Al-Munāwī says: 'This rank is for the people of Hadith, and how great a rank it is, for they are his caliphs in reality.'"

Ḥāfiẓ al-Mundhirī has mentioned it in *al-Targhīb fī Samāʿ al-Ḥadīth wa-Tablīghihi* [from *al-Targhīb wal-Tarhīb*], using an expression that indicates its weakness. Al-Qasṭallānī has likewise cited it in his introduction to his commentary on *Ṣaḥīḥ al-Bukhārī* and wrote: "Undoubtedly, conveying the *sunan* to the Muslims sincerely is one of the offices of the Prophets ﷺ, so whoever establishes this is a caliph of him ﷺ from whom he conveys."

Ḥāfiẓ al-Zurqānī says in his commentary of *al-Mawāhib*: "They (the scholars of Hadith) have been distinguished as being his caliphs due to

For this reason, the predecessors [*salaf*] would call the highly-versed Hadith scholar 'Leader of the Believers' [*Amīr al-Mu'minīn*], because he was a caliph of the Prophet ﷺ, conveying from him.

Abū Dāwūd and Ibn Mājah narrate from 'Abdullah b. 'Amr ؓ that the Prophet ﷺ said: "Knowledge is three things and anything else is [only] meritorious: a decisive verse [of the Qur'an], an established Prophetic practice [Sunna], or a just obligation."

The first to compile
in the science of Hadith narration

The first person to compile Hadith was the prominent Imam and scholar of the Ḥijāz and Sham, Muḥammad b. Muslim b. 'Ubaydillah b. 'Abdullah b. Shihāb al-Zuhrī al-Madanī, which he did at the command of 'Umar b. 'Abd al-'Azīz ؓ. This is based on the narration of Abū Nu'aym by way of Muḥammad b. al-Ḥasan, from Mālik who said: "The first to compile the science [of Hadith] was Ibn Shihāb (al-Zuhrī)."

This is because when the Leader of the Believers, 'Umar b. 'Abd al-'Azīz ؓ, saw the bearers and memorisers of Hadith passing away without leaving behind their likes as successors, and when he saw that innovation and desires had become widespread, he wrote to his appointees in the major centres and to scholars across the world and ordered them to write down the Hadith of the Messenger of Allah ﷺ.

Al-Bukhārī says in his *Ṣaḥīḥ*, [in] 'The Chapter on how Knowledge will be Taken Away:'

> 'Umar b. 'Abd al-'Azīz wrote to Abū Bakr b. Ḥazm and said: "Look for the Hadith of the Messenger ﷺ and record them, for I fear that knowledge may perish and scholars pass away. Only accept the Hadith of the Prophet ﷺ. They [the scholars] should spread knowledge and sit until those that do not know are taught, for knowledge only perishes when it is kept secret."

---

his ﷺ saying: 'O Allah, have mercy upon my caliphs who come after me, who narrate my Hadith and my practice [Sunna] and teach them to people.' Narrated by al-Ṭabarānī."

Abū Nuʿaym relates it in *Tārīkh Aṣbahān* with the wording: "'Umar b. ʿAbd al-ʿAzīz wrote to those far and wide: 'Look for the Hadith of the Messenger 🌸 and gather them.'"

Thereafter came a generation of scholars, each of whom compiled a book, gathering Hadith and organising them by chapters, combined with statements of the Companions and legal verdicts of the Successors.

Imam Mālik authored *al-Muwaṭṭaʾ* in Medina with the purpose of gathering the strong narrations from the people of Ḥijāz. Abū Muḥammad ʿAbd al-Malik b. ʿAbd al-ʿAzīz b. Jurayj authored a work in Mecca, Abū ʿAmr ʿAbd al-Raḥmān al-Awzāʿī authored a work in Shām (the Levant), and Abū Salama Ḥammād b. Dīnār authored a work in Basra.

Thereafter, many people from that era followed suit until some of the foremost scholars opined to single out Hadith of the Prophet 🌸 specifically.

ʿUbaydullah b. Mūsā al-ʿAbsī al-Kūfī compiled a compendium arranged according to the chains of narration [*musnad*], and Musaddad b. Musarhad al-Baṣrī likewise compiled a compendium. Asad b. Mūsā al-Umawī and Nuʿaym b. Ḥammād al-Khuzāʿī each composed a compendium [as well].

The leading scholars then followed their example, such as Imam Aḥmad b. Ḥanbal, Isḥāq b. Rāhūyah, ʿUthmān b. Abī Shayba and others, and few were the scholars who did not compile their Hadith in the form of a *musnad*.

Then came Imam al-Bukhārī who saw these works and who narrated them, but he found them to include both [rigorously] sound [*ṣaḥīḥ*] and fair [*ḥasan*] narrations, while some of them included weak [*ḍaʿīf*] narrations. For this reason, he determined to gather only sound [*ṣaḥīḥ*] narrations.

Imam al-Bukhārī was therefore the first to gather solely sound narrations in a specific collection and Imam Muslim followed suit. May Allah 🌸 reward them both on behalf of the Muslims.[6]

Ḥāfiẓ al-Suyūṭī says in his *Alfiyya*:

---

[6] [Ibn Ḥajar] Introduction to *Fatḥ al-Bārī*; [al-Suyūṭī] *al-Tadrīb*

> *The first to gather Hadith and traditions,*
> *Was Ibn Shihāb at the command of ʿUmar*
>
> *And the first to organise [them] by chapter,*
> *A group from a similar time*
>
> *Like Ibn Jurayj, Hushaym and Mālik,*
> *And Maʿmar and Ibn al-Mubārak*
>
> *And the first to compile [while] confining himself,*
> *To the ṣaḥīḥ, was al-Bukhārī*
>
> *And Muslim after him, and the former [Bukhārī],*
> *Is superior according to the correct position*

THE SCIENCE OF HADITH COMPREHENSION [DIRĀYA]

It is the science by which the reality of the narration [ḥaqīqa al-riwāya] is known, [as well as] its conditions, its types and its rulings, the narrators' states and their conditions, and the categories of what they narrate and that which is related to them.

The reality of the narration is to convey what has occurred of the Sunna and the like, and the attribution of that [narration] through a chain going back to whomever it has been attributed, be this by way of direct narration [taḥdīth],[7] by informing [ikhbār][8] and so on.

The conditions of the narration are the manner in which the narrator receives [taḥammul] the Hadith from amongst the various types of receiving, such as direct audition [samāʿ], or reading it to the teacher [ʿarḍ], or by licensing [ijāza], and the like.

The types are those that are connected [ittiṣāl] or severed [inqiṭāʿ], and so on.

The rulings are that it is either accepted or rejected.

The state of the narrators is either one of uprightness or subject to criticism.

The conditions of the narrators are the same as the conditions of transmitting and receiving.

---

[7] I.e., saying: "so-and-so told us"—Ed.

[8] I.e., saying: "so-and-so informed us"—Ed.

The categories of what is narrated are [found in] the compilations, which include:

- *Jawāmiʿ*. A *jāmiʿ* is a work which compiles Hadith of various topics, such as Hadith pertaining to:

  - ❖ belief
  - ❖ legal rulings
  - ❖ Hadith which soften hearts [*riqāq*]
  - ❖ etiquettes of eating and drinking
  - ❖ travelling, standing and sitting
  - ❖ Qur'anic commentary, history and biography
  - ❖ civil sedition and trials [*fitan*]
  - ❖ virtues and vices

Scholars of Hadith have authored separate works on each of the previously mentioned eight topics.

- *Sunan* [sing. *sunna*]. These are books arranged according to the topics of jurisprudence, such as purification [*ṭahāra*], prayer [*ṣalāt*], alms tax [*zakāt*], fasting [*ṣiyām*], and so on.

- *Masānīd* [sing. *musnad*], which here means a book in which the Hadith have been alphabetically arranged according to the name of the Companion, or arranged chronologically by their entrance into Islam, or by the nobility of their lineage.

- *Maʿājim* [sing. *muʿjam*], which refers to a book in which the Hadith have been arranged according to the names of teachers (from whom they received the Hadith), the date of the teacher's death, alphabetically, the teacher's prominence, or his knowledge and God-consciousness. [In] the majority [of *maʿājim*], however, the names are arranged alphabetically. The three *Maʿājim* of al-Ṭabarānī are of this type.[9]

---

[9] *Al-Muʿjam al-Kabīr, al-Muʿjam al-Ṣaghīr* and *al-Muʿjam al-Awsaṭ*—Tr.

- *Ajzā'* [sing. *juz'*], which refers to a book which gathers the Hadith of one narrator, regardless of whether the narrator is from the generation of the Companions 🕮 or [from the] later [generations]. Examples include the *Juz'* of the Hadith of Abū Bakr al-Ṣiddīq 🕮 and the *Juz'* of the Hadith of Mālik 🕮. The word *juz'* can also be used to refer to a collection of Hadith which focus on a particular topic.

- *Mustakhrajāt*, [sing.] *mustakhraj*, [which] is derived from the word *istikhrāj* and denotes the scholar of Hadith basing his work on one of the collections of Hadith, such as *Ṣaḥīḥ al-Bukhārī*, and referencing the Hadith [therein] with his chains of narration, which are different to those of the author of the book. Their chains of narration then meet at the author's teacher or someone further up the chain.

Shaykh al-Islam Ibn Ḥajar said:

> The precondition is that it does not reach a teacher further up [the chain] in case he lacks a chain of narration which connects him to someone closer, except for a reason, such as elevation ['*uluww*] in the chain [*sanad*] or an important addition.

Examples of this are the *Mustakhraj* on *Ṣaḥīḥ al-Bukhārī* of al-Ismā'īlī and that of al-Barqānī, and similarly the *Mustakhraj* on *Ṣaḥīḥ Muslim* of Abū 'Uwāna al-Isfarāyīnī and others.

- *Mustadrakāt*, [sing.] *mustadrak*, is a book which follows up what the author of another collection omitted, according to the latter's conditions. An example is the *Mustadrak* on the two *Ṣaḥīḥ* collections by al-Ḥākim Abū 'Abdullah al-Naysābūrī.

- *Aṭrāf* [sing. *ṭaraf*], are books which only mention the beginning of a Hadith, pointing to the remainder, and which include the various chains of narrations—either comprehensively or based upon those of certain collections. Examples include the *Aṭrāf* of the two *Ṣaḥīḥ* collections [of al-Bukhārī and Muslim], and the *Aṭrāf* of the [remainder of the] Five Books [namely, the collections of Abū Dāwūd, al-Tirmidhī and al-Nasā'ī], and so on.[10]

The subject matter of this science is the narrator and the narration from the point of view of their acceptance or rejection.

The benefit of the science is that knowledge of which Hadith are accepted and which ones are rejected is attained.

The codification of this science

The first to author a detailed work about this science, with defined foundations and formulated principles, was al-Qāḍī Abū Muḥammad al-Rāmahurmuzī (d. 360 H.) in his book *al-Muḥaddith al-Fāṣil bayn al-Rāwī wal-Wā'ī*, although he was not comprehensive in covering all topics of this science.

Then came al-Ḥākim 'Abdullah b. Muḥammad b. 'Abdullah al-Naysābūrī (d. 450 H.) who authored a work on this topic, but as Ibn Ḥajar said, it was not free of fault.

Then Ḥāfiz Abū Nu'aym Aḥmad b. 'Abdullah al-Aṣbahānī (d. 430 H.) followed suit and worked on the book of al-Ḥākim in a *mustakhraj* form.

Then came Ḥāfiz al-Khaṭīb Abū Bakr al-Baghdādī (d. 463 H.) who authored a work on the principles of Hadith and titled it *al-Kifāya fī 'Ilm al-Riwāya*. He also authored a work on the etiquettes of narration called *al-Jāmi' li-Ādāb al-Shaykh wal-Sāmi'*.

After him came al-Qāḍī 'Iyāḍ (d. 533 H.) who authored a work titled, *al-Ilmā' fī Ḍabṭ al-Riwāya wa-Taqyīd al-Sāmi'*.

And Abū Ḥafṣ 'Umar b. 'Abd al-Majīd al-Mayāniji (d. 580 H.) also authored a *juz'* titled, *Mā Lā Yasa'u al-Muḥadditha Jahluhu*.

---

[10] [Al-Mubārakfūrī] Introduction to *Tuḥfa al-Aḥwadhī*; [al-Kattānī] *al-Risāla al-Mustaṭrafa*; [al-Suyūṭī] *al-Tadrīb*. Whoever wishes to research the different types of works should refer to *al-Risāla al-Mustaṭrafa* and the introduction to *Tuḥfa al-Aḥwadhī*.

Then came the jurist, Ḥāfiẓ Taqī al-Dīn Abū ʿAmr ʿUthmān b. al-Ṣalāḥ ʿAbd al-Raḥmān al-Shahrazūrī, a resident of Damascus (d. 643 H.) who was in charge of teaching Hadith in the Ashrafiyya School. He authored a work popularly known as *Muqaddima Ibn al-Ṣalāḥ*, in which he gathered disparate works which had come before him, adding beneficial points and original contributions to it. For this reason, scholars devoted themselves to it and pursued the methodology he used in didactic poems, abridgements and added notes [*nukat*] to it. Zayn al-ʿIrāqī, Badr al-Zarkashī and Ḥāfiẓ Ibn Ḥajar all added notes [*nukat*] to *Muqaddima Ibn al-Ṣalāḥ*.

Shaykh al-Islam Ḥāfiẓ Muḥyī al-Dīn al-Nawawī (d. 676 H.) abridged *Muqaddima Ibn al-Ṣalāḥ* in a work which he titled, *al-Irshād ilā ʿIlm al-Isnād*, which he further abridged into a different book called *al-Taqrīb wal-Taysīr li-Maʿrifa Sunan al-Bashīr al-Naẓīr* ﷺ. This latter book became the subject of a commentary by Ḥāfiẓ al-Suyūṭī in his book *al-Tadrīb*.

Ḥāfiẓ Zayn al-Dīn Abū al-Faḍl ʿAbd al-Raḥmān al-ʿIrāqī (d. 806 H.) composed a thousand-line poem in which he abridged *Muqaddima Ibn al-Ṣalāḥ* and added to it. He alludes to this in the following verse:

> *I abridged herein the entirety of Ibn al-Ṣalāḥ,*
> *And I added new material to it, as you will see in places*

He also composed a commentary on his poem called *Fatḥ al-Mughīth*, which he completed in 771 H. and which he abridged from a larger commentary he had begun but later turned away from.

Then came Ḥāfiẓ Shihāb al-Dīn Aḥmad b. ʿAlī b. Ḥajar al-ʿAsqalānī (d. 852 H.), and he composed a work called *Nukhba al-Fikar fī Muṣṭalaḥ Ahl al-Athar*, upon which he wrote a commentary titled *Nuzha al-Naẓar fī Tawḍīḥ Nukhba al-Fikar*, which is a comprehensive yet concise commentary. Many commentaries and super-commentaries have been written on this [treatise] by great and eminent scholars.

Then came Ḥāfiẓ Muḥammad b. ʿAbd al-Raḥmān al-Sakhāwī (d. 902 H.) who commented upon the thousand-line didactic poem [*Alfiyya*] of al-ʿIrāqī and called it, *Fatḥ al-Mughīth*, which is the best commentary on al-ʿIrāqī's poem.

Then came Ḥāfiz Jalāl al-Dīn 'Abd al-Raḥmān b. Abū Bakr al-Suyūṭī (d. 911 H.) who wrote a book called *Tadrīb al-Rāwī* in which he commented upon *al-Taqrīb* of Imam al-Nawawī. It is one of the finest and most beneficial works on Hadith terminology.

Ḥāfiz al-Suyūṭī also composed a didactic poem in the sciences of Hadith known as *Alfiyya al-Suyūṭī*. He benefitted others greatly by this work, may Allah reward him well.

Then came the distinguished scholar, 'Umar b. Muḥammad b. Futtūḥ al-Bayqūnī al-Dimashqī al-Shāfiʿī, (d. 1080 H.), who composed a well-known poem on the sciences of Hadith, consisting of 34 lines called *al-Manẓūma al-Bayqūniyya*. There are numerous commentaries and super-commentaries on this, and one of the most important ones is the commentary of the erudite scholar ['Allāma], Ḥāfiz Muḥammad b. 'Abd al-Bāqī b. Yūsuf al-Zurqānī (d. 1122 H.), and 'Allāma 'Aṭiyya al-Ajhūrī (d. 1190 H.) composed a super-commentary [*Ḥāshiya*] on the commentary of al-Zurqānī.

Latterly, the distinguished scholar of Hadith, Shaykh Ṭāhir al-Jazāʾirī al-Dimashqī (d. 1338 H.), authored a work titled *Tawjīh al-Naẓar ilā Uṣūl al-Athar*, which is an excellent and most valuable book.

Likewise, the respected and distinguished scholar, Professor Jamāl al-Dīn al-Qāsimī al-Dimashqī (d. 1332 H.), wrote a book called *Qawāʿid al-Taḥdīth min Funūn Muṣṭalaḥ al-Ḥadīth*, in which he mentioned some noteworthy and beneficial points. May Allah reward them all well.

This represents a summary of well-known works on the science of Hadith terminology. I have omitted many great works, which I decided not to mention out of fear of being too lengthy and tiresome. What I have mentioned here should suffice.

CHAPTER TWO
A CLARIFICATION OF SOME OF THE TERMINOLOGY AGREED UPON IN THE SCIENCE OF HADITH

<table>
<tr><td>

- *Sanad*
- *Isnād*
- *Matn*
- *Mukhrij*

</td><td>

- *Makhraj*
- Hadith *Nabawī*
- *Khabar*
- *Athar*

</td><td>

- *Musnid*
- *Muḥaddith*
- *Ḥāfiẓ*
- Hadith *Qudsī*

</td></tr>
</table>

THE SCHOLARS OF HADITH mention these terms frequently, so it is necessary for the student of this science to be familiar with them.

Sanad (chain): It is the route [*ṭarīq*] that leads to the *matn* (wording)—i.e., the narrators of the Hadith [themselves], who are called that because they connect the Hadith to its source.

Isnād (ascription): It is informing [*ikhbār*] about the route of the *matn*—i.e., citing the narrators of the Hadith.

Matn (wording): It is where the *sanad* ends.

Mukhrij: Grammatically speaking it is the active participle, for they say, "So-and-so referenced [*kharraja*] or extracted [*akhraja*] the Hadith," meaning that they mentioned its narrators.

Mukharrij: With doubling [of the middle letter] or without—it is the one who mentions the narrators of the Hadith, such as al-Bukhārī, Muslim, and so on.

Makhraj (source): Grammatically speaking, it is the noun of place.[11] They say: "The source [*makhraj*] of this Hadith is known, or the source of this Hadith is not known," referring to the narrators of the Hadith. All of the narrators are sources for the Hadith issuing from them.

Hadith *Nabawī*: It is anything attributed to the Prophet ﷺ regarding statements, actions, descriptions or tacit approvals. It is termed Hadith (originated) because it is unlike the Qur'an, which is eternal [*qadīm*].[12] Many scholars of Hadith use the word

---

[11] The noun which denotes where something takes place, such as the *masjid*, which indicates that *sujūd* (prostration) takes place [there].

[12] The scholars of theology say that the speech of Allah is uncreated and has therefore no beginning.

'Hadith' to refer to statements, actions and tacit approvals of the Companions [*Ṣaḥāba*] and the Successors [*Tābiʿīn*], although if it is attributed to the Prophet ﷺ they call it a raised [*marfūʿ*] Hadith, if it is attributed to a Companion they call it a halted [*mawqūf*] Hadith, and if it is attributed to a Successor they call it a Hadith that is cut-off [*maqṭūʿ*], as will be clarified, God willing.

Khabar: [Ibn Ḥajar] says in *Nukhba al-Fikar*: "According to the scholars of this science *khabar* is a synonym for 'Hadith.'"

It is also said that a 'Hadith' is that which has come from the Prophet ﷺ, and a *khabar* is something which has come from someone else. Therefore, it is said that someone who is occupied with history and the like is an *akhbārī*, and someone who is occupied with the Prophetic Sunna is a *muḥaddith*.

Athar: [Imam al-Nawawī] says in *al-Taqrīb*: "The scholars of Hadith call the *marfūʿ* and *mawqūf* traditions *athar*. The jurists of Khorasan refer to the *mawqūf* as *athar*, and to the *marfūʿ* as *khabar*."

Musnid: This is someone who narrates Hadith with his chain of narration, regardless of whether he has knowledge of it or merely narrates it.

Muḥaddith: This is someone who has knowledge of the chains of Hadith, names of the narrators and wordings [*mutūn*]. He has a higher rank than a *musnid*.

Ḥāfiẓ: According to some of the predecessors [*salaf*], it is synonymous with *muḥaddith*. Others, however, qualified it as someone who has memorised numerous Hadith and excelled in knowledge of the various types, both with respect to narration [*riwāya*] and its comprehension [*dirāya*], and who is conversant with the science of defects [*ʿilal*] in Hadith. For this reason, Imam al-Zuhrī said: "It takes forty years of study to become a *ḥāfiẓ*."[13]

'Allāma al-Munāwī mentioned that the people of Hadith have ranks:

> First there is the student [*ṭālib*], and he is a beginner.
> Then there is the *muḥaddith*, he undertakes the bearing
> of Hadith, and is concerned with their narration [*riwāya*]
> and its comprehension [*dirāya*].

---

[13] See the full wording in *Laqṭ al-Durar* [of al-ʿAdawī].

Then the *ḥāfiẓ*, he is someone who has memorised one hundred thousand Hadith, including both the wordings and the chains of narration, and who comprehends what is necessary.

Then the *ḥujja*, he is someone who has memorised three hundred thousand Hadith.

Then the *ḥākim*, he is someone who has knowledge of all of the Hadith, both in their wordings and chains of narration, and of narrator evaluation [*jarḥ wa-taʿdīl*] and their historical contexts.[14]

Some have added the rank of *Amīr al-Muʾminīn*. Ḥāfiẓ al-Suyūṭī says: "A number of people have been given this title, such as Sufyān, Ibn Rāhuwayh, al-Bukhārī, and others."

It is as if the title of *Amīr al-Muʾminīn* is taken from the Hadith narrated by al-Ṭabarānī and others from him ﷺ, in which he said: "O Allah, have mercy upon my caliphs...," as has been mentioned previously.

Hadith *qudsī*: It is a Hadith which the Prophet ﷺ narrates from Allah ﷻ. It is also called Hadith *rabbānī* and Hadith *ilāhī*.

THE DIFFERENCE BETWEEN
A HADITH *QUDSĪ* AND THE QURʾAN

Ibn Ḥajar al-Haytamī says in his commentary on al-Nawawī's Forty Hadith:

Know that three types of speech are attributed to Allah:

1. The first and most noble of them all is the Qurʾan, due it being distinctly different from other types of speech attributed to Allah, and owing to its inimitability [*iʿjāz*] in various ways:

---

[14] It is said in *Laqṭ al-Durar* [of al-ʿAdawī] after the words of al-Munāwī: "Know that these terminologies are for the people of this science, so they are undoubtedly subject to disagreement."

- It is an ever-lasting miracle which withstands the passage of time;
- It is protected from change and alteration;
- It is prohibited for the ritually impure to touch it;
- It is prohibited for a person in a state of major impurity to recite it;
- It is prohibited to paraphrase it;
- It is specified for [reciting during] prayer;
- It is called Qur'an;
- Reciting of each letter carries ten rewards;
- It is prohibited to sell according to Imam Aḥmad, disliked according to us [the Shāfi'īs];
- A passage from it is called an *āya* (verse) or a *sūra* (chapter).

Anything other than the Noble Qur'an, such as the previous scriptures and Divine narrations [Hadith *qudsī*], do not possess any of the previously mentioned qualities.

2. The scriptures of the Prophets ﷺ, which Allah revealed to them, before having been altered and corrupted.

3. The Divine narrations, which have been transmitted by way of singular narrations [*āḥād*]—without the condition of mass-transmission [*tawātur*]—from the Prophet ﷺ, along with his attribution of them to his Lord, are from the speech of Allah and are attributed to Him for the most part. The attribution to Him ﷻ is one of origination [*inshā'*] as He is the first speaker. They may also be attributed to the Prophet ﷺ since he informs us about them, on behalf of Allah, as opposed to the Noble Qur'an, which can only be attributed to Him ﷻ.

It is therefore said about it (the Qur'an), "Allah ﷻ said" and about them (the Divine narrations), "The Messenger of Allah ﷺ said in that which he narrated from his Lord ﷻ."

There is a difference of opinion regarding the remainder of the Sunna—is all of it revelation or not? The verse ❨*And he does not speak from caprice,*❩[15] supports the first position

---

[that it is revelation]. In the same vein, the Prophet ﷺ said: "Indeed, I was given the Book and its like along with it"[16]—which is the Prophetic way [Sunna].

These Divine narrations are not restricted to any method of revelation, but it is conceivable for them to be revealed to the Prophet ﷺ in any number of ways, such as by dreams, or by being suddenly cast into his heart, or by the tongue of the angel [Jibrīl ﷺ].

Formulas used to narrate a Hadith *qudsī*
The erudite scholar Ibn Ḥajar [al-Haytamī] ﷺ says:

This type of narration has two formulas: the first is, "The Messenger of Allah ﷺ said, in that which he narrated from his Lord, the Exalted," which is the expression used by the predecessors [*salaf*], Imam al-Nawawī therefore preferred it in his collection of Forty Hadith and elsewhere.

The second is, "Allah, the Exalted, said, as narrated by the Messenger of Allah ﷺ from Him." The meaning is the same. The wording is that of Ibn Ḥajar al-Haytamī along with some modification of the expression.

---

[16] The wording of the Hadith as narrated by Abū Dāwūd and al-Tirmidhī is from al-Miqdām b. Maʿdikarib who said: "The Prophet ﷺ said: 'Indeed, I was given the Qur'an and its like along with it. There will come a time when a satiated man on his couch will say: "Stick to this Qur'an! Whatever you have found therein to be permissible, declare it permissible, and whatever you found to be forbidden, prohibit it," whereas whatever the Messenger of Allah has prohibited is like what Allah has forbidden...'" Al-Dārimī and Ibn Mājah also narrated it.

The erudite scholar [Mullā ʿAlī] al-Qārī transmits from al-Abhārī that the word *mā* (whatever) in the statement, "Whatever the Messenger of Allah has forbidden," is conjunctive in meaning but disjunctive in utterance, and means: that which the Messenger of Allah ﷺ has forbidden.

What also supports the position that the Prophetic way is from the revelation [*waḥy*] of Allah ﷺ is what Imam Aḥmad [b. Ḥanbal] has narrated in his *Musnad* from Abū Umāma ﷺ, from the Messenger of Allah ﷺ, that he said: "I only say that which I am made to say," and there are numerous other narrations which support this view.

Then Ibn Ḥajar said: "...And its (the Hadith *qudsī's*) attribution to Allah, the Exalted, is of Him originating the words, as He is the speaker of these words in the first place." This is a clear statement that Hadith *qudsī* is the speech of Allah. However, it does not reach the level of inimitability and uniqueness which the Noble Qur'an possesses—in the same way that other scriptures revealed to previous Messengers ﷺ likewise lack the inimitability and elect characteristics of the Noble Qur'an.

Many scholars consider the meaning of the Hadith *qudsī* to be from Allah ﷻ and its wording from the Messenger of Allah ﷺ. Sayyid Sharīf al-Jurjānī says in his *Ta'rīfāt*:

> With respect to its meaning the Hadith *qudsī* is from Allah ﷻ, and with respect to its form [*lafẓ*] it is from the Messenger of Allah ﷺ. Therefore, it is what Allah ﷻ has informed His Prophet ﷺ by inspiration [*ilhām*] or in a dream. Then [the Messenger ﷺ] informed us of this meaning using his ﷺ own expression. The Qur'an is therefore preferred over it, as its [the Qur'an's] wording is also revelation.

The erudite scholar Sa'd al-Taftāzānī says, in his commentary on the Forty Hadith [of al-Nawawī]:

> The difference between the Hadith *qudsī* and the Qur'an is that the wording of the Qur'an is revealed with inimitability, while the Hadith *qudsī* is what Allah ﷻ has informed His Prophet ﷺ by inspiration or in a dream. Then the Prophet ﷺ informed his nation using his own expression based on this meaning. It is therefore neither inimitable nor narrated by mass-transmission [*mutawātir*][17] in the way the Noble Qur'an is.

The erudite scholar Abū al-Baqā' said in the chapter on *al-Qāf* in his *Kulliyāt*:

---

[17] The characteristic of being *mutawātir* is not restricted to the Qur'an, as is apparent from the discussions in the science of Hadith regarding narrations of this level of transmission. It is possible for a Hadith *qudsī* to reach the level of *mutawātir*, but it is not a condition for it—Tr.

The wording and meaning of the Qur'an are from Allah ﷻ, by clear revelation, while the wording of the Hadith *qudsī* is from the Messenger of Allah ﷺ and its meaning is from Allah ﷻ, by way of inspiration or dream.

Abū al-Baqā' then quotes the statement of Ibn Ḥajar and says:

> Some say that the Qur'an is the inimitable utterance that is revealed through the angel Jibrīl ﷺ, while Hadith *qudsī* is not characterised by being inimitable and is not through the medium [of Jibrīl ﷺ].

This means that the Hadith *qudsī* is not inimitable in its nature, nor is it singled out by being through the medium of the angel Jibrīl ﷺ.

The erudite scholar al-Kirmānī[18] says in his commentary on *Ṣaḥīḥ al-Bukhārī*:

> If you were to ask regarding the difference between the Hadith *qudsī* and the Qur'an, I would say that the Qur'an is inimitable in its wording, and it is revealed through the angel Jibrīl ﷺ, whereas this [Hadith *qudsī*] is neither inimitable nor does it come through an intermediary. The like of this is thus called a Hadith that is *qudsī*, or *ilāhī* (divine), or *rabbānī* (lordly).
>
> If you were to say that all Hadith are like this, and how could they not be, since the Messenger ﷺ ⟨*does not speak from caprice,*⟩ [Qur'an 53:3] I would say that the difference is that the Hadith *qudsī* is attributed to Allah ﷻ and is a narration from Him, as opposed to other [Hadith].
>
> The difference [between the Hadith *qudsī* and other Hadith] is that the [Hadith] *qudsī* relates to the transcendent essence [*tanzīhi dhāt*] of Allah ﷻ, and to His mighty and majestic attributes, attributed to the sacred presence [*al-ḥadra al-qudsiyya*] [of Allah], the Exalted and sanctifying.

---

[18] *Sharḥ al-Kirmānī* (vol. 9, p .29), at the beginning of *Kitāb al-Ṣawm*.

The summary from all of these statements is that the scholars are in agreement that the meaning of the Hadith *qudsī* is from Allah ﷻ, and that the difference of opinion is with respect to its wording. Some say that the wording of the Hadith *qudsī* is likewise from Allah ﷻ, whereas others say that the wording is from the Messenger of Allah ﷺ.

THE *BASMALA*, THE *ḤAMDALA*, AND SENDING PRAYERS UPON THE PROPHET ﷺ

The author, may Allah, the Exalted, have mercy upon him, said:

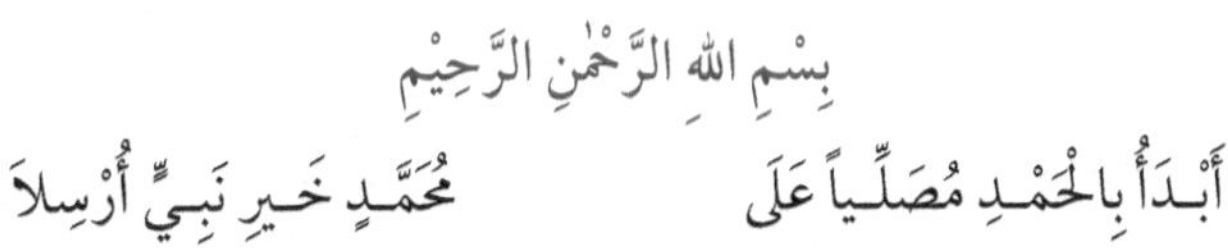

In the name of Allah, most Gracious, most Merciful
I begin with praise, sending prayers upon,
Muhammad ﷺ, the best of Prophets sent

The author begins his didactic poem with *bismillah al-raḥmān al-raḥīm* (in the name of Allah, most Gracious, most Merciful), following the Mighty Book, and emulating the Prophet ﷺ since he began his writings and letters with the *basmala*,[19] as is mentioned concerning his ﷺ letter to Heraclius, and others. And [the author does so] acting upon that which has been narrated from the Prophet ﷺ, that he said: "Every matter of importance that does not begin with *bismillah al-raḥmān al-raḥīm* is defective."[20] The meaning is that it is deficient and lacking in goodness and blessings.

---

[19] The *basmala* refers to *bismillah al-raḥmān al-raḥīm*—Tr.
[20] ʿAbd al-Qādir al-Ruhāwī narrated it in the beginning of his book, *al-Arbaʿīn al-Buldāniyya*, and al-Khaṭīb likewise narrated it from Abū Hurayra ﷺ, raising it to the Prophet ﷺ [*marfūʿan*].

Then he extols with praise of Allah ﷻ, likewise emulating the Mighty Book, as the Opening Chapter [*al-Fātiḥa*] is the Chapter of Praise [*Sūra al-Ḥamd*], and acting upon what is indicated by verses of the Qur'an, that Allah ﷻ begins great matters, such as creating and legislating, with praise.

Allah ﷻ says: ❨*All praise is due to Allah, Who created the heavens and the earth, and made darkness and light.*❩[21] This verse indicates that the matter of creating begins with praise.

Allah ﷻ says: ❨*All praise is due to Allah, Who revealed the Book to His servant and did not allow any crookedness therein.*❩[22] This verse indicates that the matter of legislation and revelation of the Book begins with praise.

The author begins with praise, acting upon what has been mentioned in the Hadith narrated by Abū Dāwūd from Abū Hurayra ﷺ, in which he said: "The Messenger of Allah ﷺ said: 'Every speech with does not begin with praising Allah is amputated.' This is the wording of Abū Dāwūd. Al-Nasā'ī narrates it as does Ibn Ḥibbān in his *Ṣaḥīḥ*, and Ibn Mājah in the 'Chapter of Marriage' with the wording, "*Every matter of importance that does not begin with praise is defective.*"

The erudite scholar al-Sindī says: "This Hadith is considered to be fair [*ḥasan*] by Ibn al-Ṣalāḥ and al-Nawawī."[23] Likewise, al-Suyūṭī indicated that it is *ḥasan*.

---

[21] Qur'an 6:1

[22] Qur'an 18:1

[23] Al-Nawawī says in *al-Adhkār*, after he cites this Hadith and its narrations: "It is a *ḥasan* Hadith. It has been narrated in a connected [*mawṣūl*] chain as we mentioned, and it has also been narrated in a *mursal* form. The connected version has a good [*jayyid*] chain of narration. If a Hadith has been narrated both in a *mawṣūl* and *mursal* form, then the ruling is that it is connected according to the majority of scholars, as it involves an additional reliable narrator [*ziyāda al-thiqa*], which is accepted by the majority.

"The meaning of 'a matter of importance' is a matter that is given due attention and the meaning of 'defective' [lit. cut-off] is deficient and containing few blessings. Amputated [*ajdham*] is [meant] in the same sense, and is with *dhāl* and *jīm*.

"The scholars say that it is recommended for every author, student, teacher or orator to begin with praising Allah, and likewise before every

He then followed the *basmala* and the *ḥamdala* (praising God) with prayers upon the Prophet ﷺ, as it is narrated from him that he ﷺ said: "Every matter of importance that does not begin with praising Allah and sending prayers upon me is defective, incomplete and void of every blessing."[24]

And he acted by what is narrated from Abū Hurayra ؓ who said: "The Messenger of Allah ﷺ said: 'Whoever sends prayers upon me in a book, the angels continue to seek his forgiveness as long as my name remains in that book.'"[25]

---

important matter." (From the chapter on Praising Allah, the Exalted, with Ibn ʿAllān's commentary [*al-Futūḥāt al-Rabbānī*] vol. 3, p. 290)

[24] ʿAbd al-Qādir al-Ruhāwī narrated it in *al-Arbaʿīn* and said that it is unusual [*gharīb*]. Ismāʿīl b. Abū Ziyād is alone in including the part containing "sending prayers," but he is very weak and his narrations and additions are not to be considered. Ibn al-Madīnī, Ibn Mandah and others narrated it with chains that contain weak and unknown narrators. (Al-Munāwī, *Fayḍ al-Qadīr*, vol. 5, p. 14)

The erudite scholar Ibn Ḥajar al-Haytamī narrated it in the commentary on the *Arbaʿīn* (p. 25), saying: "And he (Imām al-Nawawī) sent prayers after praise because of his ﷺ words, 'Every matter of importance that does not begin with praising Allah and sending prayers upon me is defective, incomplete and void of every blessing.' And its chain [*isnād*] is weak, but nevertheless it is under meritorious actions in which one may act upon weak [Hadith]."

[25] [Al-Suyūṭī] says in *Tadrīb al-Rāwī* (p. 292), after mentioning this Hadith: "This Hadith, despite being weak, is good to narrate because of its meaning. One should not be deterred by Ibn al-Jawzī [including it] in *al-Mawḍūʿāt*, as it has chains that preclude the possibility of its fabrication, which necessitate that it ultimately has a basis. Al-Ṭabarānī mentions the Hadith from Abū Hurayra ؓ, as does the father of Shaykh al-Aṣbahānī, and al-Daylamī through another route (from Abū Hurayra ؓ), and al-Ibn ʿAdī from Abū Bakr al-Ṣiddīq ؓ, and al-Aṣbahānī (in *al-Targhīb*) from Ibn ʿAbbās ؓ, and Abū Nuʿaym in *Tārīkh Aṣbahān* from ʿĀʾisha ؓ."

In *Jalāʾ al-Afhām* he [Ibn al-Qayyim] devotes a section to sending prayers upon him ﷺ when writing his name, and cites many Hadith to support this. The erudite scholar Ibn al-Mudābighī mentions in his marginal notes [*ḥāshiya*] on [Ibn Ḥajar] al-Haytamī's commentary on the Forty Hadith, that this Hadith is narrated by al-Dāraquṭnī and others from Abū Hurayra, raising it to the Prophet ﷺ [*marfūʿan*].

For these reasons, Imam al-Shāfi'ī ﷺ said: "I prefer that a person begin an oration or any other matter by praising Allah ﷻ, extolling Him ﷻ and sending prayers upon the Messenger of Allah ﷺ."

By sending prayers upon the Messenger of Allah ﷺ after praising Allah ﷻ, the author presents his gratitude for the Prophet ﷺ after thanking Allah ﷻ with praise.[26] This is because the Prophet ﷺ is the one who guided mankind away from error, by the permission of Allah ﷻ. He rescued them from the darkness of ignorance to the light of truth and wisdom, knowledge and gnosis. Allah ﷻ says: ❲*Indeed you guide to the straight path. The path of Allah to Whom belongs what is within the heavens and on earth...*❳[27]

Allah ﷻ says: ❲*[This is] a book which We have revealed unto you to remove mankind from darkness to light, by the permission of their Lord, to the path of the Mighty and Praiseworthy. Allah is He to Whom belongs what is within the heavens and on earth...*❳[28]

As for prayers [*ṣalāwāt*] in relation to Allah ﷻ, it is narrated by the learned authority of the nation [*hibr al-umma*] and interpreter of the Qur'an [Ibn 'Abbās] that, "Prayers from Allah ﷻ are a mercy, from the servant they are a supplication and from the angels they are a seeking of forgiveness." This is what is well-known amongst later scholars. We shall suffice with this to avoid being lengthy.

This interpretation is challenged by some due to the verse, ❲*Prayers and mercy be upon them from their Lord,*❳[29] as a distinction is made between prayers and mercy, since the conjunction *wāw* denotes something different. My response to this is that prayers are more specific than the general form of mercy; therefore, it is the conjunction of the general concept to the specific. This [linguistic device] has many benefits as confirmed in the books on rhetoric.[30]

---

[26] The erudite scholar al-Zurqānī has indicated this meaning in his commentary on this poem.

[27] Qur'an 42:52

[28] Qur'an 14:1

[29] Qur'an 2:157

[30] See *Sharḥ al-Mawāhib* (vol. 1, p. 11) by the erudite scholar al-Zurqānī, and there are other responses. The meaning of "prayers from Allah" is

CATEGORIES OF HADITH

The author, may Allah, the Exalted, have mercy upon him, said:

وَذِي مِنْ اقْسَامِ الْحَدِيثِ عِدَّه   وَكُلُّ وَاحِدٍ أَتَى وَحَـدَّه

And these are a number of categories of Hadith,
Each one with its own definition

According to the scholars of Hadith, the categories of Hadith differ according to various considerations, such as those which relate to the wording [*matn*] of the Hadith and those which relate to the chain of narration [*sanad*], and those which relate to both.

Some scholars of Hadith divided these types into many categories, some into very few and there were those who struck a balance between the two.

Ḥāfiẓ Ibn al-Ṣalāḥ mentioned sixty-five categories of Hadith, and Imam al-Nawawī in *al-Taqrīb* followed him in this.

The erudite scholar al-Ḥāzimī says:

> This is not the greatest number possible, as Hadith can be classified into innumerable categories, because the statuses of the narrators and their qualities are innumerable, and likewise for the *matn*, the statuses of the wordings and their qualities. Every status or quality other than its subject ought to be singled out and made mention of, therefore making it an independent category.

---

the subject of numerous statements. Careful investigation of it is a lengthy matter, I have been concise in order to avoid being verbose. Whoever wishes to research further should refer to *Tafsīr al-Ālūsī* regarding the verse, ⟨*Indeed Allah and His angels send prayers upon the Prophet*,⟩ and likewise the commentary of al-Zurqānī on *al-Mawāhib*, and other books.

[Out of humility, Imam ʿAbdallah Sirājuddīn does not direct the reader to his own work entirely on the meaning of *ṣalāt*. This book has been translated into English by Abdul Aziz Suraqah and published by Sunni Publications under the title, *Sending Prayers upon the Prophet* ﷺ—Tr.]

In this poem, the author, may Allah, the Exalted, have mercy upon him, has mentioned a number of the most important categories within the science of Hadith which the student of Hadith cannot do without. They amount to thirty-four in number, as the author mentions at the end of the poem:

Its categories amount to thirty-four[31]

He mentions each category separately along with its comprehensive definition.

WAYS OF CATEGORISING WITHIN THE SCIENCE OF HADITH

There are many ways to categorise the sciences of Hadith:[32]

First, from the perspective of whether the Hadith is accepted or rejected.

The accepted [*maqbūl*] Hadith is of two kinds: sound [*ṣaḥīḥ*] and fair [*ḥasan*], and each is either so intrinsically [*li-dhātihi*] or due to supporting narrations [*li-ghayrihi*].

As for rejected [*mardūd*] Hadith, they are weak [*ḍaʿīf*] Hadith and they are of many kinds, some of them have their own name while others do not. This is because if the reason for it being weak relates to a broken chain, it comprises of the *muʿallaq, munqaṭiʿ, muʿḍal, mudallas* and *mursal* (with a difference of opinion about this category), and the *muʿanʿan* and *muʾanʾan* when the condition of having a connected chain is not met in these two.

If the reason for the weakness relates to the integrity [*ʿadāla*] of the narrator, then it comprises of the *mubham* and the narration of someone who is unknown [*majhūl*].

---

[31] This number is based upon the majority of copies in which the author says: "*Its categories amount to...*" He counts the *maqlūb* (inverted) as two categories and the *mudallas* as two categories.

[32] I did not intend by this an in-depth investigation of the categories within the science of Hadith; rather, I merely intended to mention examples of some of the categories.

If the reason for the weakness is the lack of being able to establish the accuracy of the narrator, then it comprises of the *muḍṭarib*; or if the reason for the weakness is contradicting a reliable narrator [*thiqa*], then it is *shādh*; or if it contains a defect that detracts from his reputation [*'illa qādiḥa*], then it is *mu'all*, which will be clarified in due course, God willing, in the appropriate place.

Secondly, Hadith may be classified based upon to whom it is attributed.

If it is attributed to the Prophet ﷺ then it is *marfū'*, and if to a Companion then it is *mawqūf*, or if to a Successor [*Tābi'ī*] then it is *maqṭū'*.

Thirdly, a Hadith may be classified based on whether there is a single narrator or a number of narrators. It may be *gharīb*, *'azīz*, *mashhūr*, *mustafīḍ* or *mutawātir*.

Fourthly, the Hadith may differ due to the qualities of the chain of narration: it may come under the *'ālī* and *nāzil*, *musalsal* and the like.

There are numerous separate categories which we shall mention, God willing.

CHAPTER THREE
ACCEPTED HADITH [MAQBŪL]

THE ACCEPTED [MAQBŪL] HADITH IS OF TWO KINDS: sound [ṣaḥīḥ] and fair [ḥasan], and each is either so intrinsically [li-dhātihi] or due to supporting narrations [li-ghayrihi].

SOUND [ṢAḤĪḤ]

أَوَّلُهَا الصَّحِيحُ وَهْوَ مَا اتَّـصَلْ   إِسْـنَادُهُ وَلَمْ يَشِـذَّ أَوْ يُعَلّ

يَرْوِيـهِ عَدْلٌ ضَابِطٌ عَنْ مِثْلِهِ   مُعْـتَمَدٌ فِي ضَبْـطِهِ وَنَقْلِهِ

The first of them is the ṣaḥīḥ which is that,
Whose chain is connected, having no anomaly or defect

Narrated by someone who is precise and has integrity,
From someone like himself,
Relied upon in his precision and transmission

The ṣaḥīḥ Hadith has a connected chain of narration, its narrators are characterised by integrity ['adl] and accuracy [ḍabṭ], from the beginning to the end of chain, is free of having anomalies [shudhūdh] and likewise free of a defect that detracts from their reputation ['illa qādiḥa].

A Hadith is not judged to be ṣaḥīḥ if it does not fulfil these five conditions:

1. A connected chain [ittiṣāl al-sanad]
2. The integrity of its narrators is confirmed [thubūt al-'adāla]
3. The accuracy of its narrators is confirmed [thubūt al-ḍabṭ]
4. Free of anomalies [salāma min al-shudhūdh]
5. Free of any defect that detracts from the narrators' reputations [salāma min al-'illa al-qādiḥa]

Concerning the restrictions to the definition and what is excluded from it

Ittiṣāl: a connected chain is that chain in which each narrator received the Hadith directly from his teacher [*Shaykh*], from the beginning of the chain until the end.[33] This condition excludes the *munqaṭiʿ*, *muʿḍal*, *muʿallaq*, *mudallas*, and *mursal* (according to the opinion of those who reject it).

ʿAdāla: integrity is that the legally-responsible person [*mukallaf*] is free of flagrant sin [*fisq*] and contravention of social norms [*khawārim al-murūʾa*].[34] This upright person must be a Muslim over the age of puberty [*bāligh*] and of sound mind [*ʿāqil*], free from committing major sins or persistence in minor sins. He must also be free of contraventions of social norms [*murūʾa*]. *Murūʾa* is that a person upholds what is considered to be good, and avoids what is considered to be lowly, protecting oneself from foul things and that which would taint him in the eyes of people.

The narration of a disbeliever is not accepted, nor is that of a child [*ṣabiyy*] according to the more correct view.[35] It is said that the narration of a discerning child [*mumayyaz*] is accepted if he is not known to lie. The narration of an insane person is not accepted [either].[36]

As for the disbeliever, his narrations are not accepted as he is at odds with the very principles of our religion, which could lead him to ruin the essentials of the religion and to corrupt it as much as he is able to.

---

[33] *Ḥāshiya al-Abyārī* (p. 22)

[34] The term in Arabic translates more literally as 'ruining one's virtue,' meaning doing something which would be considered inappropriate —Tr.

[35] *Ḥāshiya al-Abyārī* (p. 84)

[36] That the person be a male or free are not conditions for integrity to be established. Therefore, the narrations of women and slaves are acceptable. There are numerous differences between narrating Hadith and giving testimony, which are explained in detail in the books of legal theory [*uṣūl al-fiqh*]. Many of these have been mentioned in *Ḥāshiya al-Abyārī*.

Allah ﷻ says of the disbelievers: ❪*They will not fail to corrupt you. They only desire your ruin. Rancour has already appeared from their mouths, and what their hearts conceal is far worse.*❫[37] They have already shown this in their hiding the descriptions of the Prophet ﷺ and the signs of his Prophethood that are mentioned in their scriptures.

As for the child, their narrations are not accepted as they could easily mix lies within their speech, since there is no legal injunction prohibiting them from doing so.[38]

The narrations of a flagrant sinner [*fāsiq*] are not accepted. Allah ﷻ says: ❪*O you who believe, if a flagrant sinner comes to you with news, then seek clarification.*❫[39]

Ḥāfiẓ Abū Bakr al-Khaṭīb narrates with his chain of narration from Ibn ʿUmar ﷺ that the Prophet ﷺ said: "Ibn ʿUmar! Your religion, your religion! It is your flesh and blood. Therefore, be careful from whom you take it. Take it from those who are upright, and not from those who deviate," i.e., [who deviate] from sound belief and pious deeds.

Al-Khaṭīb also narrates with a chain from the Leader of the Believers, ʿAlī ﷺ, that he said: "Be careful from whom you take this knowledge, as it is religion."

He also narrates with a chain from Imam Mālik ﷺ who said:

> Do not take knowledge from four, and take from anyone else. Do not take it from a fool who displays his stupidity, even if he narrates more than anyone does. Do not take from a liar who tells lies when talking about people, if this is known to be the case, even if he is not known to lie about the Messenger of Allah ﷺ. Do not take from a person with erroneous opinions who summons people to them. And do not take from a teacher who possesses neither virtue nor worship, since he does not know what he narrates.[40]

---

[37] Qur'an 3:118

[38] As is clarified in the books of *uṣūl al-fiqh*.

[39] Qur'an 49:6

[40] This last kind refers to a pious man who worships without knowledge. They are all mentioned in *Kifāya al-Rāwī* by al-Khaṭīb al-Baghdādī.

The narration of someone who is completely unknown or whose status is unknown is not accepted, since it is stipulated as a precondition that it should be someone whose integrity and accuracy have been established.

That which establishes the integrity of a narrator

Integrity [*'adāla*] is established by being well-known [*shuhra*] amongst the people of knowledge, and widespread praise for someone's integrity, such as for the four Imams,[41] the two Sufyāns[42] and their like. It may also be established by one or two scholars testifying it [*tanṣīṣ*].[43]

Accuracy [*ḍabṭ*] is that a narrator be mindful [*mutayaqqiẓ*] and not heedless, that he commit to memory what he dictates such that he can recall it whenever he wishes when he narrates from his memory—and this is called accuracy of the heart [*ḍabṭ ṣadr*]—and that he safeguards his book from the time he heard the Hadith and corrects it[44] until he narrates from it, and if he narrates from a book he does not lend the book to anyone who may alter it—and this is called *ḍabṭ kitāb*[45]—and that he be knowledgeable of what he is narrating and is aware of what would change the meaning from what was intended if he narrates the meaning [*yarwī bil-ma'nā*] [of the Hadith].[46]

---

[41] The founders of the four schools of law of Islam: Imams Abū Ḥanīfa, al-Shāfi'ī, Mālik and Aḥmad b. Ḥanbal.—Tr.

[42] Sufyān al-Thawrī and Sufyān b. 'Uyayna—Tr.

[43] See *Alfiyya al-'Irāqī* along with its commentaries in the discussion on whose narrations are accepted and whose are rejected.

[44] It was common practice after receiving Hadith in gatherings to compare one's record (written or memorised) with other students in order to correct any errors which may have occurred—Tr.

[45] This applies to a book which is not well-known, nor has been corrected. As for books which are [well-known], such as *Ṣaḥīḥ al-Bukhārī* and *Ṣaḥīḥ Muslim*, and other well-known, corrected books in our time, then there is no such condition that it be protected from the time of hearing to the time of divulging. Rather, the condition is that the copy be corrected based on an authentic original, as is mentioned in *Ḥāshiya al-Abyārī* (p. 23).

[46] It is permissible under certain conditions for a narrator to narrate a Hadith in its meaning and not use the actual words employed when it was narrated to him—Tr.

The narration of someone who is heedless is not accepted, nor of someone who makes frequent errors, due to the lack of accuracy.

Ḍabṭ al-ṣadr may be complete [*tāmm*], which is a level of precision virtually free of error. This level of precision is a condition for a tradition to be intrinsically sound [*ṣaḥīḥ li-dhātihi*] and is what is intended in the previously mentioned definition, as the term used in an absolute sense [*muṭlaq*] refers to complete accuracy [*ḍabṭ tāmm*].

Ḍabṭ al-ṣadr may also be imperfect [*ghayr tāmm*], such that there are errors and it is said about him [the narrator] that sometimes he is accurate and on other occasions he is not. This is a condition for Hadith which are considered sound due to supporting narrations [*ṣaḥīḥ li-ghayrihi*] and narrations which are intrinsically fair [*ḥasan li-dhātihi*].[47]

That which establishes accuracy

A narrator's accuracy [*ḍabṭ*] is established when his narrations concur with [those of] reliable and proficient masters [*al-thiqāt al-mutqinīn*]. If there is an occasional contradiction, then this is overlooked. However, if his narrations frequently contradict those of reliable narrators [*thiqāt*], and rarely accord with them, then his accuracy is considered to be deficient and his narrations cannot be used as proof.[48]

As for anomalies [*shudhūdh*], it is when someone who is reliable contravenes someone who is of a higher rank.

A defect that detracts from the narrator's reputation [*'illa qādiḥa*] is for example describing something as a *mursal* Hadith [*irsāl*] when there is an otherwise connected chain of narration, or a halted tradition [*mawqūf*] when it is a raised [*marfū'*] narration—all of which will be clarified in the section on the defective [*mu'all*] Hadith.

---

[47] [Al-'Adawī] *Ḥāshiya Laqṭ al-Durar* (p. 40); *Ḥāshiya al-Abyārī* (p. 23)
[48] [Al-Suyūṭī] *Al-Tadrīb*

Levels of *ṣaḥīḥ*

The degrees of the *ṣaḥīḥ* Hadith differ due to the qualities of integrity, accuracy and other such qualities upon which *ṣaḥīḥ* Hadith depend. That whose narrators have the highest levels of integrity, accuracy, and the other qualities required for acceptance, is more sound than those below it in level.[49]

Based on this, the scholars of Hadith have categorised the levels of *ṣaḥīḥ* Hadith with regard to soundness and preponderance as follows:

1. The first level is what the two Shaykhs—al-Bukhārī and Muslim—have agreed upon in terms of its narration with its chain [*isnād*]. This is called agreed upon [*muttafaq ʿalayhi*].[50]
2. The second level is what Bukhārī alone narrates.
3. The third level is what Muslim alone narrates.
4. The fourth level is that what is *ṣaḥīḥ* according to the conditions of al-Bukhārī and Muslim [although not mentioned in their collections]. Imam al-Nawawī says:

> The meaning of "according to their conditions" is that the narrators in the chain are mentioned in the collections of al-Bukhārī and Muslim—since they do not mention their conditions in their books or elsewhere.[51]

5. The fifth level is what is *ṣaḥīḥ* according to the conditions of al-Bukhārī.

---

[49] [*Nuzha*] *Sharḥ al-Nukhba* [of Ibn Ḥajar] and elsewhere.

[50] As mentioned by Ḥāfiẓ al-Sakhāwī in *Fatḥ al-Mughīth* (p. 16) where he clarifies that the agreed upon Hadith is that which the two Shaykhs narrated with its chain [*isnād*] and the wording [*matn*] of the Hadith is from the same Companion. He narrates this condition from his teacher Ibn Ḥajar, and then says: "He (Ibn Ḥajar) says: 'In considering the *matn*, which both of them narrate from the same Companion, to be agreed upon, there is an insight into the way of the scholars of Hadith.'"

[51] This is one of the views concerning the meaning of the phrase, "according to their conditions." There are other views as well that the Imams of Hadith held concerning this phrase.

6. The sixth level is what is *ṣaḥīḥ* according to the conditions of Muslim.
7. The seventh level is what is *ṣaḥīḥ* according to other noteworthy scholars, but not according to the conditions of al-Bukhārī or Muslim.[52]

Ḥāfiẓ al-Sakhāwī said:

> Something that is ordinarily lesser in rank can be given preference. For example, Muslim alone may narrate something which has various chains which bring it to the level of mass-transmission [*tawātur*], or which make it well-known to a high degree [*shuhra qawiyya*], and other scholars who stipulated *ṣaḥīḥ* as a condition [in their collections] likewise include this narration. This is stronger than what al-Bukhārī alone narrates, despite the source [*makhraj*] being a single person. This is likewise true for what al-Bukhārī alone narrates compared to what they both agree upon. Furthermore, this is true for any ordinarily lesser category compared to a level higher than it when that (*tawātur* or *shuhra qawiyya* and so on) is joined to it.[53]

The advantage of having these various levels of soundness becomes evident when there is an [apparent] contradiction, where preference needs to be given to one over the other.[54]

---

[52] It should be noted here that it is entirely possible for a Hadith to be *ṣaḥīḥ* but not included in the collections of al-Bukhārī and Muslim. As for those who restrict *ṣaḥīḥ* Hadith to al-Bukhārī and Muslim, this is a modern phenomenon which is not found in the books of the early scholars—Tr.

[53] Al-Sakhāwī, *Fatḥ al-Mughīth* (p. 16)
[What Imam al-Sakhāwī is explaining is that it is theoretically (and practically) possible for a Hadith from a lower category of the seven levels of *ṣaḥīḥ* to be more authentic than a narration from a higher category, if other scholars of Hadith possess different chains which support that which is from an otherwise lower category—Tr.]

[54] Due to the variation in the conditions for acceptance, some narrations are given preference to others whose narrators are of the highest levels of uprightness and accuracy, and other qualities. For this reason, some of the scholars defined [what is] the most sound chain [*aṣaḥḥ al-asānīd*].

Reasons for the superiority
of *Ṣaḥīḥ al-Bukhārī* over *Ṣaḥīḥ Muslim*

The majority of scholars have only given preference to *Ṣaḥīḥ al-Bukhārī* over *Ṣaḥīḥ Muslim* because the conditions upon which soundness is based are more stringent and prevalent in *Ṣaḥīḥ al-Bukhārī* than in *Ṣaḥīḥ Muslim*. These conditions are:

1. A connected chain [*ittiṣāl al-sanad*]
2. The integrity of its narrators is confirmed [*thubūt al-ʿadāla*]
3. The accuracy of its narrators is confirmed [*thubūt al-ḍabṭ*]
4. Free of anomalies [*salāma min al-shudhūdh*]
5. Free of any defect that detracts from the narrators' reputations [*salāma min al-ʿilla al-qādiḥa*]

Preference is given to *Ṣaḥīḥ al-Bukhārī* with regard to the connected chains, because al-Bukhārī stipulated for the *muʿanʿan* Hadith [using 'from'] that there be a confirmed meeting between the narrators, even if only once.[55] Muslim, however, sufficed with the two narrators being contemporaries and the possibility of them having met.

Imam Aḥmad said the most authentic chain is: al-Zuhrī from Sālim, from his father (Ibn ʿUmar) ﷺ. Imam al-Bukhārī said it is: Mālik from Nāfiʿ, from Ibn ʿUmar (which is the Golden Chain). Of a lesser rank is the chain of Burayd b. ʿAbdullah b. Abī Burda from his father, from his grandfather, from his [grandfather's] father Abū Mūsā al-Ashʿarī ﷺ. Of a lesser rank than the previous two is: Suhayl b. Abī Ṣāliḥ from his father, from Abū Hurayra ﷺ.

All of these narrators combine both uprightness and accuracy, except that those mentioned in the first two chains give it precedence over the second chain, and those of the second chain give it precedence over the third. ([Ibn Ḥajar] *Sharḥ al-Nukhba*)

[55] As will be clarified in the discussion on the *muʿanʿan* Hadith, God willing. [See p. 117]

As for the preference shown to him [al-Bukhārī] with respect to integrity and accuracy, Muslim's narrators about whom there is some discussion [*mutakallam fihim*][56] are more in number than those about whom there is some discussion in [*Ṣaḥīḥ*] al-Bukhārī, even though al-Bukhārī did not include much from them. Rather, most of them were his teachers whom al-Bukhārī took from and whose Hadith he had mastered, as opposed to Muslim, the majority of those from whom he alone narrates and about whom there is some discussion were those who had preceded him chronologically. Without doubt, a person knows the Hadith of his own teachers better than the Hadith of those who preceded him.

There are around four hundred and eighty individual narrators in [*Ṣaḥīḥ*] al-Bukhārī, eighty of whom have been spoken of as being weak. As for Muslim, there are six hundred and twenty individual narrators, one hundred and sixty of whom have been spoken of as being weak.[57]

The superiority of *Ṣaḥīḥ al-Bukhārī* with regard to being free of anomalies and defects that detract from the narrators' reputations, there are fewer Hadith that are subject to criticism in *Ṣaḥīḥ al-Bukhārī* than in *Ṣaḥīḥ Muslim*.

Furthermore, al-Bukhārī had greater standing in the sciences than Muslim and was more adept in the craft of Hadith, while Imam Muslim was his student and his primary reference [*khirrīj*].[58] Muslim continued to benefit from him and investigate his traditions. His [al-Bukhārī's] superiority is such that Imam al-Dāraquṭnī said: "Had it not been for al-Bukhārī, Muslim would be neither here nor there."[59]

---

[56] This phrase is generally used by scholars to denote a narrator or a Hadith as weak. However, it should be noted that not every accusation of weakness is accepted. Moreover, each scholar often had his own particular usage of terms. One needs to be familiar with his works and methodology in order to understand his use of a particular expression and what is intended by it—Tr.

[57] [Al-'Adawī] *Laqt al-Durar* (p. 45)

[58] *Khirrīj*, with a *khā'* and a *rā'* with a *shadda* [doubling]; i.e., he frequently referenced Hadith [with their chains] and narrated from al-Bukhārī. (*Laqt al-Durar*)

[59] [Ibn Ḥajar] *Sharḥ al-Nukhba*. The preponderance of al-Bukhārī over Muslim is explained in detail in his introduction to *Fatḥ al-Bārī*.

Types of ṣaḥīḥ

There are two types of ṣaḥīḥ: that which is intrinsically sound [ṣaḥīḥ li-dhātihi] and that which is sound due to supporting narrations [ṣaḥīḥ li-ghayrihi].

As for the intrinsically sound, it is that which comprises of the highest levels of acceptance, and it is that whose definition has been previously discussed.

As for that which is sound due to supporting narrations, it does not comprise of the highest levels of acceptance, such that its accuracy is imperfect [ghayr tāmm al-ḍabṭ]. However, it is narrated by another route which is stronger or equal to it, or by numerous additional routes—at least two—which are lower in rank, and therefore it becomes sound due to supporting narrations [ṣaḥīḥ li-ghayrihi].

That which is sound due to supporting narrations is in reality intrinsically fair [ḥasan li-dhātihi], which is then elevated in rank due to supporting narrations [mutāba'a], which strengthen it to the level of ṣaḥīḥ. Thus, it is known as sound due to supporting narrations [ṣaḥīḥ li-ghayrihi].

An example of this is that which al-Tirmidhī narrates by way of Muḥammad b. 'Amr, from Abū Salama, from Abū Hurayra ﷺ, that the Prophet ﷺ said: "Had it not been that I would cause difficulty for my community, I would have ordered them to use the siwāk (teeth cleaning twig) with every prayer."

Despite being well-known for his truthfulness and his preservation [of knowledge], and although some have even declared him reliable [thiqa] because of this, Muḥammad b. 'Amr was not proficient [mutqin]. Due to his poor memory, some went so far as to say that he was weak. Al-Bukhārī only mentions his narrations alongside other narrations, and Muslim includes him as a supporting narrator [mutāba'a]. Thus, his narration is intrinsically fair [ḥasan li-dhātihi], but due to a supporting narration from another narrator at the level of his teacher's teacher, who was Abū Hurayra ﷺ, it rises to the rank of ṣaḥīḥ.

A group of narrators other than Abū Salama also narrate this Hadith by way of al-A'raj, from Abū Hurayra ﷺ, as found in the narration [that is] in the two Ṣaḥīḥ collections.

Therefore, the Hadith, "Had it not been that I would cause difficulty for my community, I would have ordered them to use the *siwāk* with every prayer," is intrinsically sound [*ṣaḥīḥ li-dhātihi*] based upon the chains in the two *Ṣaḥīḥ* collections, but sound due to supporting narrations [*ṣaḥīḥ li-ghayrihi*] in the chain of al-Tirmidhī by way of Muḥammad b. 'Amr, due to other narrations which come to support the chain of Muḥammad b. 'Amr.

Al-Sakhāwī says: "Another example of this is narrated by al-Tirmidhī by way of Isrā'īl, from 'Āmir b. Shaqīq, from Abū Wā'il, from 'Uthmān b. 'Affān ﷺ, that the Prophet ﷺ 'would run his fingers through his beard.'"

'Āmir alone narrates this Hadith, and al-Bukhārī and Ibn Ḥibbān consider him to be strong but Ibn Ma'īn and Abū Ḥātim consider him to be weak, and al-Bukhārī is of the opinion (in that which al-Tirmidhī mentions in *al-'Ilal*) that this Hadith of his is *ḥasan*. Al-Tirmidhī said it is *ṣaḥīḥ*, as did al-Dāraquṭnī, al-Ḥākim and others. This is due to supporting narrations such as that of Abū Malīḥ al-Raqqī, from al-Walīd b. Zawrān, from Anas ﷺ, which is narrated by Abū Dāwūd and whose chain of narration is *ḥasan*.[60]

Thābit al-Bunānī, from Anas ﷺ, endorses al-Walīd's narration of this Hadith, as is mentioned by al-Ṭabarānī in *al-Mu'jam al-Kabīr*.

Ibn Ḥajar says:

> This narration (the Hadith of 'Uthmān b. 'Affān ﷺ that the Prophet ﷺ "...would run his fingers through his beard") has other supporting narrations, so that, taking everything into consideration, they concluded that the source of this Hadith is *ṣaḥīḥ* even though each individual chain of narration on its own does not reach the level of *ṣaḥīḥ*.[61]

---

[60] This is because Ibn Ḥibbān said that al-Walīd b. Zawrān is *thiqa* (reliable) and no-one believed he was weak, as is mentioned in *Fatḥ al-Mughīth* of al-Sakhāwī.

[61] As mentioned in *Sharḥ al-Sakhāwī 'alā Alfiyya al-'Irāqī* (p. 28).

The ruling on the ṣaḥīḥ Hadith
with regard to it being used as proof

Scholars agree that the ṣaḥīḥ Hadith is a proof [ḥujja] in various legal instances, whether this be in the sphere of worship ['ibādāt], transactions [mu'āmalāt] or elsewhere, and likewise that these narrations must be acted upon.[62]

Ḥāfiẓ Ibn Ḥajar says in *Nukhba al-Fikar*:

> Scholars agree that it is necessary to act upon everything that is declared to be ṣaḥīḥ, even if these narrations are not narrated with their chains by the two Shaykhs [al-Bukhārī and Muslim].

The ṣaḥīḥ Hadith are used as proof in matters of creed if they are definitive [qaṭ'], such that they reach the level of mass-transmission [tawātur], as mentioned in the books of legal theory [uṣūl al-fiqh].

The statements of the scholars regarding the effect that the ṣaḥīḥ Hadith necessitates: being definitive [qaṭ'] or having high probability [al-ẓann al-qawī]

Scholars have differed as to whether the ṣaḥīḥ Hadith necessitates it being definitive [qaṭ'] or having high probability [al-ẓann al-qawī], and have taken one of the following positions:

The first position is that what has been narrated by al-Bukhārī and Muslim, or either one of them, reaches certainty. As for that which has been declared to be ṣaḥīḥ by others, it has a high probability of being ṣaḥīḥ, and this is the position of Ibn al-Ṣalāḥ. To prove this position, he argued that the *umma* has unanimously accepted the two Ṣaḥīḥ collections, and this fact affords certain knowledge after reflection ['ilm yaqīn naẓarī],[63]

---

[62] This phrase means that the narrations must be considered rather than literally acted upon. Due to other circumstances, a ṣaḥīḥ narration may not necessarily be acted upon, depending on the juristic principles of the school in question—Tr.

[63] If a person were to see a mountain before him, he would require no proof to believe that the mountain exists. This type of certainty is called

because of the probability [*ẓann*] that someone who is protected from error will not fall into error, and this *umma* is protected from concurring upon error, based on the Hadith of Ibn 'Umar ﷺ that the Prophet ﷺ said: "Allah will not unite my *umma* upon misguidance, and the hand of Allah is with the group, and whoever deviates does so into the fire."

For this reason, Imam al-Ḥaramayn al-Juwaynī said:

> If a man swore on pains of divorcing his wife that what the two *Ṣaḥīḥ* collections contain, which they consider to be *ṣaḥīḥ*, are the words of the Prophet ﷺ, I would not oblige him to divorce [her], because of the consensus of Muslim scholars regarding their soundness.[64]

The erudite scholar Ibn Kathīr said: "I am with Ibn al-Ṣalāḥ with regard to what he decided upon and guided [others] to."

The author of *al-Tadrīb* also agreed with Ibn al-Ṣalāḥ and added:

> Ibn al-Ṣalāḥ made an exception to what was said to be definitively *ṣaḥīḥ* within the two of them [*Ṣaḥīḥ al-Bukhārī* and *Ṣaḥīḥ Muslim*], excluding those narrations within them which have been spoken of as being weak.[65]

These are Hadith which al-Dāraquṭnī and others criticised, and they are, as Ḥāfiẓ Ibn Ḥajar said:

> ...Two hundred and ten narrations, thirty-two of which are narrated by both al-Bukhārī and Muslim, al-Bukhārī in particular narrating seventy-eight and Muslim narrating one hundred.'[66]

---

unequivocal [*ḍarūrī*]. However, one can also be certain of something based on a number of rational proofs which necessitate the truth of something—this type of certainty requires evidence and only someone who is privy to that evidence will be certain of that conclusion. This is called *'ilm yaqīn naẓarī*, and is alluded to here by the author. The conclusion that is drawn will not be understood by someone who does not understand the proofs which underpin this conclusion—Tr.

[64] [Ibn al-Ṣalāḥ, *Siyāna Ṣaḥīḥ Muslim*]

[65] See footnote 56 [p. 58] for an explanation of the term *mutakallam fīhi*.

[66] [Al-Suyūṭī] *Al-Tadrīb* (p. 72)

Ḥāfiẓ Ibn Ḥajar responded regarding these narrations of al-Bukhārī which were accused of being weak [*mutakallam fīhi*] in his introduction to his commentary [*Fatḥ al-Bārī*] on it [*Ṣaḥīḥ al-Bukhārī*]. Likewise, Imam al-Nawawī responded regarding those specific to Muslim in his commentary on *Ṣaḥīḥ Muslim*.

The second position states that a *ṣaḥīḥ* Hadith reaches a high degree of probability unless it reaches *tawātur*, regardless of whether this is narrated by al-Bukhārī and Muslim, or other than them. Their evidence used to support this is that these narrations are considered to be singular [*āḥād*] if they do not reach the level of *tawātur*. A narration that is *āḥād* reaches high probability.

They said regarding the acceptance of the *umma* of that which is narrated with its chains by al-Bukhārī and Muslim or either one of them, that this acceptance necessitates acting upon what al-Bukhārī and Muslim have rendered *ṣaḥīḥ* without hesitation and investigation, as opposed to anyone else [whose Hadith] must not be acted upon until [these have been] investigated and the conditions of *ṣaḥīḥ* are met. This opinion has been declared sound by al-Nawawī in *al-Taqrīb*, and he cited it therein from the scholars who investigate matters and verify them carefully [*muḥaqqiqīn*] and from the majority.

The third position states that it is definitively *ṣaḥīḥ* if it has been narrated in the two *Ṣaḥīḥ* collections, or if it is well-known [*mashhūr*] with numerous chains which are free of weak narrators and subtle weaknesses, or if it is narrated through a chain consisting of proficient masters of Hadith [*musalsal bil-ḥuffāẓ al-mutqinīn*], such that it is not unusual [*gharīb*] at any point in the chain [*isnād*]. An example of this is the Hadith narrated by Imam Aḥmad, which is also narrated by others from al-Shāfiʿī, and likewise by others from Imam Mālik. This therefore reaches certainty and it is this position which Ḥāfiẓ Ibn Ḥajar has taken.[67]

---

[67] As mentioned in *Sharḥ al-Nukhba*, where he says: "These types which we have mentioned do not reach certainty regarding the veracity of the report except for the scholar of Hadith who is immersed therein, who possesses knowledge of the statuses of narrators, and who is aware of subtle deficiencies. The fact that for someone who is not a scholar of

The rulings for classifying Hadith
as *ṣaḥīḥ*, *ḥasan* and *ḍaʿīf*

Scholars of Hadith have differed regarding the process of classifying Hadith as sound [*ṣaḥīḥ*], fair [*ḥasan*] or weak [*ḍaʿīf*]—is it possible for later generations to do so? Or is it necessary to go back to the documented opinions of the earlier scholars?

Ḥāfiẓ Ibn al-Ṣalāḥ said:

> Whoever from our time (from his time[68] onwards) sees a Hadith with a *ṣaḥīḥ* chain in a collection or a *juzʾ*,[69] which no reliable Hadith master has declared to be *ṣaḥīḥ*, then we cannot classify it as *ṣaḥīḥ* due to weak abilities in these times. Furthermore, if it would be *ṣaḥīḥ*, then the Imams of the early generations would not have neglected it, due to their intense investigation and efforts.[70]

Imam al-Nawawī said: "The most obvious position to me is that it is permissible for someone who is firm [in the science] and whose knowledge is strong to classify Hadith as *ṣaḥīḥ*."

Ḥāfiẓ al-ʿIrāqī said: "This [opinion of Imam al-Nawawī] reflects the practice of the people of Hadith."

A number of Hadith scholars from the later generations have classified Hadith as *ṣaḥīḥ* which were not declared to be *ṣaḥīḥ* by anyone prior to them. As for the contemporaries of Ibn al-Ṣalāḥ, Abū al-Ḥasan b. al-Qaṭṭān (d. 627 H.), the author of *al-Wahm wal-Īhām*, classified a number of Hadith as *ṣaḥīḥ*.

Another example was Ḥāfiẓ Ḍiyāʾ al-Dīn al-Maqdisī (d. 643 H.) who authored a work titled *al-Mukhtāra* in which he gathered only what is *ṣaḥīḥ*, and [in which he] mentioned narrations which had not been declared to be *ṣaḥīḥ* [by anyone] prior to him.

Hadith it does not reach certainty, due to his lacking these skills, does not detract from its reaching certainty for the one who is immersed."

[68] Ibn al-Ṣalāḥ died in the year 643 H.

[69] I.e., with a *ṣaḥīḥ* chain in the view of the person who researches the Hadith.

[70] [Al-Suyūṭī] *Al-Tadrīb* (p. 79)

Ḥāfiẓ Zakī al-Dīn ʿAbd al-ʿAẓīm al-Mundhirī (d. 656 H.) classified narrations as ṣaḥīḥ, as did others after him such as Ḥāfiẓ Sharaf al-Dīn al-Dimyāṭī (d. 705 H.), and others after him such as Shaykh Taqī al-Dīn al-Subkī (752 H.). All of these scholars classified Hadith as ṣaḥīḥ which no-one before them had classified as ṣaḥīḥ.[71]

Since classifying as ṣaḥīḥ is permitted, then it stands to reason that classifying as ḥasan should also be permitted. Al-Mizzī classified the Hadith, "Seeking knowledge is compulsory upon every Muslim," as ḥasan despite many ḥuffāẓ clearly stating that it is weak.

Likewise, classifying Hadith as weak [is also permissible].

As for declaring a Hadith to be fabricated, it is prohibited unless it is clear such as [in the case of] extremely lengthy and ineloquent Hadith which storytellers fabricated, or that which contains something that directly opposes the intellect or scholarly consensus [ijmāʿ].

As for classifying Hadith as mass-transmitted [mutawātir] or widespread [mashhūr], then it is not prohibited if numerous valid chains are found to support this.

One ought to suspend judgement [tawaqquf] when classifying a Hadith as solitary [fard] or unusual [gharīb], and even more so as rare [ʿazīz].[72]

A benefit

If it is said, "The most sound [aṣaḥḥ] in this chapter is such-and-such," as occurs frequently in the *Sunan* of al-Tirmidhī and the *Tārīkh* of al-Bukhārī and others, then [know that] Imam al-Nawawī said in *al-Adhkār*:

> This phrase does not necessarily indicate that the Hadith is ṣaḥīḥ, for they are saying that this is the most sound in this chapter, even if it is weak. Rather, they mean the weightiest of them and the least weak.[73]

---

[71] [Al-Suyūṭī] *Al-Tadrīb* (p. 80)
[72] Ibid. (p. 83)
[73] Ibid. (p. 39)

Fair [Ḥasan]

وَالْحَسَنُ الْمَعْرُوفُ طُرْقاً وَغَدَتْ   رِجَالُهُ لاَ كَالصَّحِيحِ اشْتَهَرَتْ

The ḥasan is that whose chains are known,
But whose narrators are not as famous as [those of] the ṣaḥīḥ

The ḥasan [Hadith] has a chain of narration that is connected through the transmission of upright and accurate narrators, although their accuracy is slightly less than that of the ṣaḥīḥ, which is also free of anomalies and defects that detract from the narrators' reputations [*'illa qādiḥa*].[74]

The conditions of the ḥasan are the same as those of the ṣaḥīḥ, namely:

1. A connected chain [*ittiṣāl al-sanad*]
2. The integrity of its narrators is confirmed [*thubūt al-'adāla*]
3. The accuracy of its narrators is confirmed [*thubūt al-ḍabṭ*]
4. Free of anomalies [*salāma min al-shudhūdh*]
5. Free of any defect that detracts from the narrators' reputations [*salāma min al-'illa al-qādiḥa*]

The condition of a connected *isnād* excludes the *mursal*, *munqaṭi'*, *mu'ḍal*, *mu'allaq*, and the *mu'an'an* of the *mudallis*. The remaining conditions exclude all the other kinds of weak Hadith.

---

[74] This definition is taken from the *Nukhba*, where he [Ibn Ḥajar] defines the intrinsically sound [*ṣaḥīḥ li-dhātihi*] as, "That which is narrated by someone who has integrity and complete accuracy, whose chain is connected, and which contains no defects that detract from the narrators' reputations, or anomalies." Then he said: "If the accuracy is slightly less, then it is intrinsically fair [*ḥasan li-dhātihi*]," to which the author alludes here when he says: "...*whose chains are known, but whose narrators are not as famous as [those of] the ṣaḥīḥ.*"

Therefore, it becomes clear that the difference between the ṣaḥīḥ and the ḥasan is that the ṣaḥīḥ requires complete accuracy, whereas the ḥasan requires accuracy alone.[75]

An example of a ḥasan [Hadith] is the narration of al-Tirmidhī: "Bundār narrated to us, he said: Yaḥyā b. Saʿīd al-Qaṭṭān narrated to us, he said: Bahz b. Ḥakīm narrated to us, he said: my father narrated to me, from my grandfather who said: I said: 'O Messenger of Allah, who is most deserving of complete good treatment?' He ﷺ said: 'Your mother.' Then I said: 'Then whom?' He ﷺ said: 'Your mother.' Then I said: 'Then whom?' He ﷺ said: 'Your mother.' Then I said: 'Then whom?' He ﷺ said: 'Your father, then the closest [in kin] and then the closest [thereafter].'

Al-Tirmidhī said: "It is a ḥasan Hadith. Shuʿba considered Bahz b. Ḥakīm to be weak, although he is reliable according to the people of Hadith."

Types of ḥasan

Ḥasan is of two types: intrinsically fair [ḥasan li-dhātihi], which has been mentioned previously, and fair due to supporting narrations [ḥasan li-ghayrihi], which contains a weakness due to the attribution of the Hadith directly to the Prophet ﷺ even though it is missing a Companion (it is mursal) or [there is] tadlīs,[76] or that some narrators are unknown, or the weakness in memory of an otherwise truthful and trustworthy narrator [ṣadūq al-amīn], or whose chain contains someone who is mastūr,[77] who is neither heedless, nor prone to numerous errors, nor suspected of lying, nor associated with flagrant sin, and whose narrations are supported by a worthy narrator[78] who is in agreement [mutābiʿ] or who corroborates [shāhid].

---

[75] Ḥāshiya al-Abyārī (p. 28)

[76] This term is explained on p. 106-109—Tr.

[77] This is a narrator whose outward state is integrity but whose inward state is unknown, or to use another expression, as some have said, it is he whose integrity has not been confirmed by those qualified to do so, but there are no signs of [any] flagrant sin. Al-Sakhāwī said: "The mastūr is someone about whom neither criticisms [jarḥ] have been established, nor reports of his integrity." ([Al-ʿAdawī] Ḥāshiya Laqt al-Durar, p. 48)

[78] Such that he is of the same rank or a higher one, and not of a lesser or worse one, as he [Ibn Ḥajar] stated specifically in Sharḥ al-Nukhba (p. 92).

It is originally weak due to one of the previously mentioned reasons and it only becomes *hasan* due it being reported through a different chain either by someone who is in agreement [*mutābiʿ*] or who corroborates [*shāhid*].[79] It is therefore said to be fair due to supporting narrations [*hasan li-ghayrihi*].[80]

However, if the weakness of the Hadith is due to the flagrant sin of the narrator or his lying, then even if other narrations are in accordance with it, it still has no bearing on the [rank of the] original weak Hadith, if the other narration is similar to it [i.e., also severely weak], because of the severity of this weakness and it not being restored—although because of the numerous chains it rises and therefore cannot be said to be denounced [*munkar*], or not to have any basis [at all].[81]

An example of this is narrated by al-Tirmidhī, who declared it to be *hasan* by the chain of Shuʿba, from ʿĀṣim b. ʿUbaydullah, from ʿAbdullah b. ʿĀmir b. Rabīʿa, from his father, that [he said:] "A woman from the tribe of Fazāra married for a dowry of a pair of sandals. The Prophet ﷺ then said: 'Are you content with regard to yourself and your wealth for [the dowry of] a pair of sandals?' She said: 'Yes,' so he ﷺ permitted it."Al-Tirmidhī said: "In this chapter [topic][82] (are other narrations) from ʿUmar, Abū Hurayra, ʿĀ'isha and Abū Hadrad ﷺ."

ʿĀṣim is weak due to having a poor memory but al-Tirmidhī says the Hadith is *hasan* due to it being reported through more than one chain.

An example of a weakness due to *tadlīs* is narrated by al-Tirmidhī, who declared it to be *hasan* through the chain of Hushaym, from Zayd b. Abī Ziyād, from ʿAbd al-Raḥmān b. Abī Laylā, from Barā' b. ʿĀzib ﷺ, raising it to the Prophet ﷺ

---

[79] *Mutāba'a* and *shāhid* are types of strengthening narrations and are explained on p. 129-130—Tr.

[80] *Sharḥ al-Nukhba* (p. 92); [Al-ʿAdawī] *Ḥāshiya Laqṭ al-Durar*; *al-Tadrīb*

[81] [It is mentioned by al-Suyūṭī] in *al-Tadrīb* (p. 104): "Shaykh al-Islam (Ibn Ḥajar) says: 'It may be that the chains are so many that they cause it to reach the level of the *mastūr* who had a poor memory [*sayyi' al-ḥifẓ*], if another chain was found which contained a slight weakness [*da'f qarīb muhtamal*]; because of all of this, it is raised to the level of *hasan*.'

[82] A phrase used by al-Tirmidhī to indicate the inclusion of supporting narrations—Tr.

[*marfū'an*]: "It is a duty upon the Muslims to perform *ghusl* (ritual bath) on Friday, and to apply some of his family's perfume. If one does not find some then water is his perfume."

Hushaym is considered to be someone who engaged in *tadlīs*. The reason why al-Tirmidhī declared it to be *ḥasan* is because Abū Yaḥyā al-Taymī reported the same Hadith, as found in [*Sunan*] *al-Tirmidhī*, and the same wording is also reported by Abū Saʿīd and others.[83]

Degrees of *ḥasan*

The varying degrees of *ḥasan* are like those of the *ṣaḥīḥ*. Ḥāfiẓ al-Dhahabī said:

> The highest *ḥasan* chains are Bahz b. Ḥakīm, from his father, from his grandfather, and ʿAmr b. Shuʿayb, from his father, from his grandfather, and Ibn Isḥāq, from al-Taymī, and the likes of that which are said to be *ṣaḥīḥ*, which is the lowest level of *ṣaḥīḥ*.
>
> Thereafter comes that which there is disagreement about as to whether it is *ḥasan* or *ḍaʿīf* (weak), such as the Hadith of al-Ḥārith b. ʿAbdullāh, ʿĀṣim b. Ḍamra, and Ḥajjāj b. Arṭā, and the like.[84]

The ruling on the *ḥasan*

According to all of the jurists and most of the Hadith scholars, both types of *ḥasan* are like the *ṣaḥīḥ* with regard to being used as proof and being acted upon, even though below it in strength.

For this reason, a group of scholars, including al-Ḥākim and Ibn Ḥibbān, regarded the *ḥasan* as a type of *ṣaḥīḥ*. However, those who do so do not deny the fact that it is of a lower rank in strength, given that they prefer the *ṣaḥīḥ* over it when there is an apparent contradiction.[85]

---

[83] See all of the preceding in *al-Tadrīb* [of al-Suyūṭī] (p. 104).

[84] Ibid. (p. 91)

[85] *Ḥāshiya al-Abyārī*. Then he [al-Abyārī] said: "Whenever the difference is linguistic, whoever said it was *ṣaḥīḥ* meant in it being used as proof and being acted upon, and whoever included it from the *ṣaḥīḥ* meant that the level was lower in strength."

A principle

A chain of narration may be sound [*ṣaḥīḥ*] or fair [*ḥasan*] due to its narrators being reliable, but overall the Hadith may be neither *ṣaḥīḥ* nor *ḥasan* due to an irregularity in the wording, or a subtle weakness it may contain.

Bearing this in mind, when a Hadith scholar says, "This Hadith has a sound chain [*ṣaḥīḥ al-isnād*] or a fair chain [*ḥasan al-isnād*]," as mentioned in the *Mustadrak* of al-Ḥākim and elsewhere, then this does not mean that the wording is *ṣaḥīḥ* or *ḥasan*, because of what we have mentioned.

However, when a Hadith scholar says, "This Hadith is *ṣaḥīḥ* (or *ḥasan*)," without restricting it to the wording or the chain, then this denotes that the Hadith is sound in both chain and wording. Therefore, the statement of the Hadith scholar, "This Hadith has a *ṣaḥīḥ* or *ḥasan* chain" is less than them saying, "This Hadith is *ṣaḥīḥ* (or *ḥasan*)."

However, if a reliable *ḥāfiẓ* confines himself to saying 'ṣaḥīḥ chain' or 'ḥasan chain,' but does not mention a subtle weakness in the wording, nor criticises it, then the apparent understanding is that the wording is *ṣaḥīḥ* or *ḥasan*, because the lack of a subtle weakness or criticism is the default.[86]

A benefit

In *Sunan al-Tirmidhī* and elsewhere, there occurs the combining of *ḥasan* and *ṣaḥīḥ* in a single Hadith. This appears to be problematic, since *ḥasan* is that which falls short of being *ṣaḥīḥ*, so how then can one affirm and deny something at the same time? The best answer [to this] is given by Ibn Ḥajar in *Sharḥ al-Nukhba*, the summary of which is that the Hadith which is called *ḥasan ṣaḥīḥ* may either have multiple chains, or a single chain.

If there are multiple chains, then the term *ḥasan ṣaḥīḥ* refers to both of its chains [if there are only two], or all [of them]; some are *ṣaḥīḥ* and the others are *ḥasan*. Based on this, the term *ḥasan ṣaḥīḥ* is above that which is *ṣaḥīḥ* with a single chain, due to the

---

[86] [Al-Suyūṭī] *Al-Tadrīb* (p. 92). Ibn Ḥajar said: "I have no doubt that a scholar does not deviate from saying *ṣaḥīḥ* to saying 'ṣaḥīḥ chain' except for a specific reason."

numerous chains of the first[87] and the single chain of the latter. The most one can say of this is that he omitted the conjunctive particle 'and' [*wāw*], and should have said that it is "*ḥasan* and *ṣaḥīḥ*."

If the Hadith does not have multiple chains, then the difference of opinion amongst the Imams of Hadith is based upon the status of the narrators, meaning that it is *ḥasan* [or] *ṣaḥīḥ*.

This is because some of the Imams of Hadith said about a certain narrator, "He is truthful [*ṣadūq*],"[88] while others said, "He is reliable [*thiqa*]," and no preference was given by an independent jurist [*mujtahid*] to either position, or it could be that he preferred one over the other but wishes to indicate the possible doubt in the narrator, so he says *ḥasan ṣaḥīḥ*. It is as if he is saying, "It is *ḥasan* according to some, *ṣaḥīḥ* according to others." The most that one can say is that there is an omitted particle 'or' [*aw*], meaning that it is '*ḥasan* or *ṣaḥīḥ*.'

Based upon this interpretation, then that which has been called *ḥasan ṣaḥīḥ* is lower in rank than that which is called *ṣaḥīḥ*, given that affirming *ṣaḥīḥ* is stronger than merely tentatively attributing it.[89]

TERMS FOR THE ACCEPTED HADITH

- *Jayyid*
- *Qawī*
- *Ṣāliḥ*
- *Maʿrūf*
- *Maḥfūẓ*
- *Mujawwad*
- *Thābit*
- *Mushabbah*

These above mentioned terms are used by the scholars of Hadith to describe an accepted report, except that each one has a particular significance and a specific consideration.

---

[87] Since multiple chains strengthen a Hadith.

[88] This is the classification of a narrator who is accepted but who is below the rank of reliable [*thiqa*]—Tr.

[89] [Ibn Ḥajar] *Sharḥ al-Nukhba* (p. 50); [Al-ʿAdawī] *Ḥāshiya Laqṭ al-Durar*; [Al-Suyūṭī] *al-Tadrīb*

Jayyid (good) is equivalent to *ṣaḥīḥ*, as indicated by the words of Imam al-Tirmidhī in *Kitāb al-Ṭibb* in his *Sunan*, where he says: "This Hadith is *jayyid ḥasan*." Likewise in the words of Imam Aḥmad ﷺ, "The best [*ajwad*] of chains is al-Zuhrī, from Sālim, from his father." From this we know that *jayyid* refers to soundness [*ṣiḥḥa*].

Those of them endowed with insight chose to use the term *jayyid* instead of the term *ṣaḥīḥ* for a reason. It is as if, according to them, the Hadith is raised from the level of intrinsically fair [*ḥasan li-dhātihi*], and they are unsure whether it reaches the level of *ṣaḥīḥ*. Therefore, the term indicates a lower rank than *ṣaḥīḥ*, and this is likewise the case for the term *qawī* (strong).[90]

As for *ṣāliḥ* (valid), it includes both the *ṣaḥīḥ* and *ḥasan*, due to both being valid as proof [*iḥtijāj*]. It is also used for a weak [*ḍaʿīf*] Hadith that can be used to strengthen another Hadith.[91]

As for *maʿrūf* (affirmed), it is the opposite of *munkar* (denounced), and *maḥfūẓ* (preserved) is the opposite of *shādh* (anomalous), as will become clear, God willing.

As for *mujawwad* (articulate) and *thābit* (affirmed), they include both the *ṣaḥīḥ* and *ḥasan*.

As for *mushabbah* (likened), it is used for the *ḥasan*, and that which is similar to it, and is used in relation to the *ḥasan* in the same way *jayyid* is used for the *ṣaḥīḥ*.[92]

These terms have been gathered in the poem of Ḥāfiẓ al-Suyūṭī in the following lines:

> *To denote acceptance,*
> *They use jayyid and thābit,*
> *Ṣāliḥ and mujawwad*
>
> *These [terms] are between ṣaḥīḥ and ḥasan,*
> *And they regard mushabbah as close to ḥasan*
>
> *Is thābit specific to ṣaḥīḥ, or does it include ḥasan?*
> *A difference [of opinion herein] is affirmed*

---

[90] [Al-Suyūṭī] *Al-Tadrīb* (p. 104)

[91] It is used to describe a Hadith which is weak but not extremely so. It is not valid to use by itself as a proof, but it can be used to strengthen other narrations [*mutābaʿa* and *shawāhid*].

[92] *Al-Tadrīb* (p. 105); *Ḥāshiya al-Abyārī*

CHAPTER FOUR
REJECTED HADITH [*MARDŪD*]

S FOR REJECTED [*MARDŪD*] HADITH, they are weak [*ḍaʿīf*] Hadith and they are of many kinds, some of them have their own name while others do not.

WEAK [*ḌAʿĪF*]

وَكُلُّ مَا عَنْ رُتْبَةِ الْحُسْنِ قَصُرْ   فَهْوَ الضَّعِيفُ وَهْوَ أَقْسَاماً كَثُرْ

All that falls short of ḥasan,
Is ḍaʿīf which has many branches

Ḍaʿīf is that which lacks the conditions stipulated for acceptance for fair [*ḥasan*] and sound [*ṣaḥīḥ*] [Hadith], which are:

1. A connected chain [*ittiṣāl al-sanad*]
2. The integrity of its narrators is confirmed [*thubūt al-ʿadāla*]
3. The accuracy of its narrators is confirmed [*thubūt al-ḍabṭ*]
4. Free of anomalies [*salāma min al-shudhūdh*]
5. Free of any defect that detracts from the narrators' reputations [*salāma min al-ʿilla al-qādiḥa*]

[It also] lacks supporting narrations where required. This is in the case of the *mastūr* and the like of it as previously mentioned.[93]

Types of *ḍaʿīf*

There are many types of *ḍaʿīf* Hadith, some of which have specific terms while others do not. Scholars of Hadith have taken many positions regarding these different types. Ḥāfiẓ Ibn al-Ṣalāḥ

---

[93] See footnote 77 [p. 67]—Tr.

has categorised them according to their lacking one or more of the conditions for acceptance. According to him, the number of types amount to forty-two.

Some have even reached sixty-three types, and some have said there are one hundred and twenty-nine according to logical categorisations or eighty-one according to their theoretical occurrence, even if some may not exist in reality.

Ḥāfiẓ al-'Irāqī has explained this at length, but all of that, as Ḥāfiẓ Ibn Ḥajar said, is tiresome and devoid of any benefit.[94]

Perhaps we could mention a brief summary of the types of ḍaʿīf narrations and explain the reasons for the variations in a simple way appropriate for a beginner, so we say thus:

When the Hadith lacks the condition of having a connected chain—and if this occurs at the beginning of the chain, even if all the way to the end [i.e., the entire chain], then it is suspended [*muʿallaq*]. If it occurs at the end of the chain, it is initially disconnected [*mursal*]—there being a difference of opinion regarding its validity as proof. If the break is the middle of the chain, if there is only one missing narrator, it is severed [*munqaṭiʿ*]. If there are two breaks, one after another [i.e., consecutively], it is problematic [*muʿḍal*]. The *muʿanʿan* whose chain has not been decisively judged to be connected is also included in this category.

When the condition of the narrator's integrity is lacking—and if the reason for this is that the narrator himself is or his status as a narrator are unknown, one says about the Hadith that it is weak because the narrator himself is or his status as a narrator are unknown [*al-jahl bi-ʿayn al-rāwī aw bi-ḥālihi*]. If the narrator is called by an unspecified name then it is called 'unclear' [*mubham*]. If the lack of the integrity is due to his flagrant sin [*fisq*] or lying [*kadhib*], then it is included under the term 'abandoned' [*matrūk*]. If this includes contradicting [narrators] then it is denounced [*munkar*], based upon the view of those who made contradiction a condition.

---

[94] *Al-Tadrīb* [of al-Suyūṭī] and elsewhere.

When the condition of accuracy [ḍabṭ] is lacking—and if this is due to the heedlessness [ghafla] of the narrator, or frequent forgetfulness, or frequent errors when narrating, then it is also included within the term *matrūk*. If there is irreconcilable confusion in his narrations then it is inconsistent [muḍṭarib].

When there is a subtle but debilitating defect ['illa] in the Hadith, then it is 'defective' [mu'allal].

When there are anomalies [shudhūdh]—i.e., contradictions between reliable narrators—then it is *shādh*.

There are types of weak Hadith which have a specific term and those which do not have a specific term, but of which only the cause of their weakness is mentioned.

The ruling on acting upon weak Hadith

The scholars have differed regarding acting upon weak Hadith and are of three schools:

The first school says that they are not permissible to act upon at all, and such is the opinion of Qāḍī Abū Bakr b. al-'Arabī, and Ibn Sayyid al-Nās cited this position from Yaḥyā b. Ma'īn.

The second school says that they are to be acted upon universally, and this is attributed to Abū Dāwūd and Imam Aḥmad [b. Ḥanbal].

The third school says that they are acted upon in the case of meritorious acts, in admonitions and exhortations, and stories and the like, which have no bearing on rulings of creed ['aqā'id] and law [aḥkām]. This is the relied upon position according to the verifying Imams [al-a'imma al-muḥaqqiqīn].

Al-Maymūnī narrates from Imam Aḥmad that he said: "It is permissible to exercise a degree of laxity [tasāhul] regarding Hadith related to softening hearts [riqāq], until something comes along which establishes a ruling."[95]

---

[95] [Al-Kifāya fī 'Ilm al-Riwāya, Khaṭīb al-Baghdādī]

Al-Bayhaqī narrates in *al-Madkhal* from Ibn Mahdī that he said:

> When we narrate from the Prophet ﷺ regarding the permissible and the impermissible and rulings, we are strict regarding the chains of narrations and critiquing narrators. However, where we narrate regarding virtuous acts, rewards and punishments, we are less strict with the chains of narrations and more forgiving with respect to the narrators.

This has also been narrated from Ibn al-Mubārak.

Ibn 'Abd al-Barr said: "Hadith regarding meritorious acts [*faḍā'il*] do not require that which is [required when] used to establish proofs."[96]

Imam al-Nawawī says in *al-Adhkār*:

> The scholars of Hadith and jurisprudence have said that it is permissible and recommended to act upon weak Hadith regarding meritorious behaviour and [its] encouragement [*targhīb*] as long as they are not fabricated. As for legal rulings, such as what is permissible and impermissible, sales and purchases, marriage and divorce, and the like, then only *ṣaḥīḥ* or *ḥasan* Hadith are acted upon, except if one is exercising caution therein; for example, if there were a weak Hadith regarding the disliked nature of a certain type of transaction or marriage, then it is recommended to refrain from it, although it is not compulsory.

---

[96] Imam al-Nawawī has mentioned in *al-Taqrīb* the acceptability of [using] weak Hadith in [support of] meritorious actions, as has al-'Irāqī in his commentary on the *Alfiyya*, Ibn Ḥajar al-'Asqalānī in *Sharḥ al-Nukhba*, Shaykh Zakariyyā al-Anṣārī in his commentary on *Alfiyya al-'Irāqī*, Ḥāfiẓ al-Suyūṭī in *al-Tadrīb* and elsewhere, and Ibn Ḥajar [al-Haytamī] al-Makkī in his commentary on *al-Arba'īn*. The erudite scholar al-Laknawī has a treatise titled *al-Ajwiba al-Fāḍila* which contains an extremely detailed research into this matter.

Conditions for acting upon weak Hadith
according to the verifying scholars

Ḥāfiẓ Ibn Ḥajar explained that acting upon weak Hadith has conditions:

1. The first is that it regards practical meritorious matters and the like, as has been mentioned.
2. The weakness must not be severe. This therefore excludes narrations unique to liars, those suspected of lying, or who are prone to serious errors.
3. It falls under something which is [already] acted upon.
4. One does not believe when acting upon it that it is reliably established, rather one does so out of caution.[97]

The ruling on narrating weak Hadith
without clarifying its weakness

It is permissible according to the scholars of Hadith and others to exercise a degree of laxity regarding chains of narration and to narrate them, except for fabrications, and to act upon them without clarifying their weakness, in matters other than the attributes of God, and legal rulings such as the permissible and the impermissible, and the like. This is fine in matters such as stories, meritorious acts, admonitions and exhortations, and other matters which are not related to rulings of creed and law.[98]

---

[97] Shams al-Dīn al-Sakhāwī said in *al-Qawl al-Badī' fī al-Ṣalāti 'alā al-Ḥabīb al-Shafī'* 🕮: "I heard our Shaykh, Ibn Ḥajar al-'Asqalānī, often say: 'There are three conditions for acting upon a weak narration:

First, which is universally accepted, that it is not extremely weak, such as one that is narrated only by a liar, someone who is suspected of lying or someone who is prone to serious errors;

Second, that it comes under a general principle. This therefore excludes invented things which have no basis;

Third, that one does not believe by acting upon it that it is definitively established, so that one avoids attributing to the Prophet 🕮 something that he did not say [i.e., may not have said].'

The last two conditions are narrated from Ibn 'Abd al-Salām and Ibn Daqīq al-'Īd. Al-'Alā'ī mentioned that there is complete agreement regarding the first condition." ([Al-Laknawī] *Al-Ajwiba al-Fāḍila*, p. 43)

[98] [Al-Suyūṭī] *Al-Tadrīb*, p. 192

The manner of narrating weak Hadith

If you wish to narrate a weak Hadith without a chain of narration, do not say, "The Prophet ﷺ said such-and-such," nor anything similar which implies it is a confirmed statement of the Prophet ﷺ. Rather, one should say, "Such-and-such has been narrated from him," or "Such-and-such has reached us from him," or "Such-and-such comes to us from him," or "Such-and-such has been narrated from him," and the like of such phrases that indicate a weakness [*ṣīgha al-tamrīḍ*],[99] such as, "some of them narrate."

Similarly, the same manner should be used for the Hadith about which there is doubt regarding its soundness or weakness.

As for a sound [*ṣaḥīḥ*] Hadith, it should be narrated in a way that indicates decisively that it is sound, and it is inappropriate to do so in a way that indicates some weakness, just as it is inappropriate to narrate a weak Hadith in a way that indicates decisively it is sound [*ṣīgha al-jazm*].[100]

---

[99] This is a technique used in both the sciences of Hadith and jurisprudence to indicate that something is weak. It is often a verb in the passive voice, such as 'it was said,' as opposed to 'he said,' which is the active voice—Tr.

[100] [Al-Nawawī] *Al-Taqrīb* and its commentary [*al-Tadrīb* by al-Suyūṭī].

CHAPTER FIVE

THE CATEGORIES OF HADITH WITH REGARD TO THOSE TO WHOM THEY ARE ATTRIBUTED

There are three categories: *marfū‘*, *maqtū‘* and *mawqūf*.

RAISED [*MARFŪ‘*]

وَمَا أُضِيفَ لِلنَّبِي الْـمَرْفُوعُ

And that which is attributed to the Prophet ﷺ is marfū‘

The *marfū‘*[101] Hadith is that which a Companion [*Ṣaḥābī*], Successor [*Tābi‘ī*] or someone after them has attributed to the Prophet ﷺ, regardless of whether this is a statement, action, tacit approval or description, and whether explicit [*taṣrīḥan*] or implicit [*ḥukman*], and whether the chain is connected or not.

By restricting attribution to the Prophet ﷺ, it excludes the halted [*mawqūf*] Hadith which is attributed to a Companion, and likewise excludes the cut-off [*maqtū‘*] Hadith which is attributed to a Successor or someone thereafter.

Examples

A *marfū‘* Hadith pertaining to statements is to attribute a statement transmitted in the wording [*matn*] of a Hadith to the Prophet ﷺ, such as a narrator saying, "the Prophet ﷺ said," or "he ﷺ narrated to us," or "he ﷺ informed us," and the like.

A *marfū‘* Hadith pertaining to actions is to attribute an action transmitted in the Hadith to the Prophet ﷺ, such as the statement of our liege lord ‘Alī ؓ, "We were at a funeral in the Baqī‘ al-Gharqad [cemetery] and the Prophet ﷺ came to us and sat, and we sat around him, and in his hand was a staff with which he struck the ground..."

---

[101] It is called 'raised' [*marfū‘*] because it has been raised by being attributed to the Prophet ﷺ. ([Al-‘Adawī] *Laqṭ al-Durar*)

A *marfū'* Hadith pertaining to a description is the statement of 'Alī ﷺ, "The Prophet ﷺ was neither overly tall, nor was he very short, and he was of middle stature among people…"

A *marfū'* Hadith pertaining to a tacit approval is the narration of him ﷺ approving something which was done before him, such as someone eating a lizard in front of him, and his approving it [by not reprimanding it].

Types of *marfū'*

Marfū' can either be explicit, which is when the Hadith is attributed to the Prophet ﷺ clearly, such as a statement or an action, as has been mentioned, or it can be implicit [and have the same status] and there are many types. For example, when a Companion says, "We were commanded to," or "We were forbidden to," or "It was made compulsory upon us," or "It was made impermissible for us." All of these are types of *marfū'*—knowing that the agent in all of these was the Prophet ﷺ.[102]

CUT-OFF [*MAQṬŪ'*]

وَمَا لِتَابِعٍ هُوَ الْـمَقْطُوعُ

And that [which is attributed] to a Successor is maqṭū'

The *maqṭū'* is that statement or action which is attributed to a Successor [*Tābi'ī*] or anyone thereafter, whether he is a junior or senior Successor, and whether the chain is connected or not.[103]

---

[102] The remaining types will be mentioned in the discussion of the *mawqūf*, God willing. [See p. 82-89]

[103] The scholars of Hadith have only included the *mawqūf*, which is attributed to a Companion, and the *maqṭū'*, which is attributed to a Successor, in the science of Hadith, because in certain instances they may both have the status of a *marfū'* Hadith attributed to the Prophet ﷺ, as al-Sakhāwī drew attention to in *Fatḥ al-Mughīth* (p. 52).

Based on the condition of being attributed to a Successor, it excludes anything which is attributed to the Prophet ﷺ or a Companion.

A Successor is defined as a Muslim who met a Companion and died upon the religion of Islam, regardless of whether his meeting with the Companion was for a long or short period.

A Successor is of two types: junior and senior. A junior Successor is someone who narrates the majority of his Hadith from other Successors, with only a small number of narrations from Companions, such as Abū Ḥāzim Salama b. Dīnār and Yaḥyā b. Saʿīd al-Anṣārī. As for senior Successors, they are those who narrate most of their Hadith from Companions and a small number from other Successors, such as Saʿīd b. al-Musayyib, Qays b. Abī Ḥāzim and ʿUbaydullah b. ʿAdī b. al-Khiyār and the like.

The *maqṭūʿ* may be called halted [*mawqūf*] if it is qualified, such as one saying, "*Mawqūf* to ʿAṭāʾ," or "So-and-so narrated it as *mawqūf*[104] to Mujāhid," or "Maʿmar narrated it as *mawqūf* to Hammām," as it appears in the books of Hadith. However, when the term *mawqūf* is used without qualification, it denotes that statement or action which is attributed to a Companion.

Ḥāfiẓ al-Suyūṭī says:

> *What is attributed to a Successor is maqṭūʿ,*
> *And mawqūf is understood [as such] if it is qualified*

An example of the *maqṭūʿ* is the statement of Mujāhid, who is one of the Successors, "Neither the shy person nor the arrogant one will attain knowledge."[105]

Likewise, the statement of Mālik, who is from the followers of the Successors [*tābiʿ al-Tābiʿīn*], when he would bid farewell, "Fear Allah and spread this knowledge and teach it. Do not conceal it."

The ruling on the *maqṭūʿ*

The *maqṭūʿ* is not a substantial proof [*ḥujja*] when there is no evidence that it has the ruling of being raised [*marfūʿ*]. If however

---

[104] The actual term used here is the past tense verb *waqafa* from which the term *mawqūf* is derived.—Tr.

[105] Since both archetypes refrain from asking questions—Tr.

there is a contextual indication [*qarīna*] that it is from the Prophet ﷺ, then it has the ruling of being so [*lahu ḥukm al-marfū'*]. Likewise, if there is evidence that it is *mawqūf* from a Companion, it has the ruling of being so [*lahu ḥukm al-mawqūf*].

Those Hadith which are *maqṭū'*, but have the ruling of *marfū'*, include statements of Successors regarding reasons for revelation of Qur'anic verses, and likewise their statements about those things that the intellect cannot deduce, which they can only have taken from the Prophet ﷺ. These have all the ruling of being raised after being initially disconnected [*marfū' mursal*].[106]

As for the statement of a Successor, "From the *sunna* is such-and-such," al-Nawawī has verified in the introduction to his commentary on *Ṣaḥīḥ Muslim* that it is connected after being halted [*mawqūf muttaṣil*]. And he also transmitted from some of the Shāfi'īs the verdict that it has the ruling of *marfū' mursal*. Al-'Irāqī verified that it is *mawqūf*, and brings forth as proof that the Successors frequently used the word '*sunna*' to mean the *sunna* of the Righteous Caliphs [*al-khulafā' al-rāshidūn*].

When a Successor says, "We were commanded to do such-and-such," and the like, is this considered to be *mawqūf* or *marfū' mursal*? Imam al-Ghazālī mentioned two possibilities, without giving preference to either of the two.

Shaykh Zakariyyā al-Anṣārī said: "It is understood from some of what al-Ghazālī mentioned thereafter, that the preferred opinion is that it is *marfū' mursal*."[107]

HALTED [*MAWQŪF*]

وَمَا أَضَفْتَهُ إِلَى الأَصْحَابِ مِنْ   قَولٍ وَفِعْلٍ فَهْوَ مَوْقُوفٌ زُكِنْ

Whatever you attribute to the Companions,
By way of statement or action, is known [zukin] as mawqūf

---

[106] [Al-Suyūṭī] *Al-Tadrīb* (p. 112); *Ḥāshiya al-Abyārī*
[107] *Fatḥ al-Bāqī* (p. 138)

Mawqūf is a Hadith which is attributed to the Companions ﷺ [*Ṣaḥāba*], be it a statement, an action or a tacit approval, and whether the chain of narration is connected to them or severed [*munqaṭiʿ*]. By being limited to what is attributed to the Companions, it excludes the *marfūʿ* (raised) and *maqṭūʿ* (cut-off). Some of the jurists called the *mawqūf* an *athar*, and the *marfūʿ* a *khabar*.

Imam al-Nawawī says: "According to the scholars of Hadith, all of these are called *athar*, meaning that the term *athar* is used for both the *marfūʿ* and the *mawqūf*."[108]

A Companion [*Ṣaḥābī*] is defined as someone who met the Prophet ﷺ while believing in him, and died upon Islam. What is meant by 'meeting' includes sitting and walking with him ﷺ, or one party going to the other, even if no words were exchanged. It also includes one seeing the other.[109]

The condition of meeting whilst being a believer in the Prophet ﷺ excludes those who met him whilst they disbelieved in him.

An example of a *mawqūf* Hadith are the words of our liege lord ʿUmar ﷺ, "Become learned before being becoming a leader."

Types of *mawqūf*

There are two types of *mawqūf* Hadith with regard to its ruling:

1. *Mawqūf* which has the ruling of *marfūʿ*;
2. *Mawqūf* which does not have the ruling of *marfūʿ*.

The first type has several different forms:

---

[108] What supports this usage is the name given by Imam Abū Jaʿfar Muḥammad b. Jarīr al-Ṭabarī to his book *Tahdhīb al-Āthār*, which includes *marfūʿ* traditions as its primary focus and *mawqūf* traditions secondarily. Similarly, the book *Maʿānī al-Āthār* by Imam al-Ṭaḥāwī includes both *marfūʿ* and *mawqūf* narrations.
([Al-Ṣanʿānī] *Tawḍīḥ al-Afkār*, vol. 1, p. 262)
[109] The word 'meeting' is more general than merely seeing, for there were some Companions who met the Prophet ﷺ but never saw him physically since they were blind, such as Ibn Umm Maktūm and others.

First, when a Companion says, "We were ordered," or "We were prohibited," or "It was made compulsory upon us," or "It was made permissible for us," and other similar wordings which give a ruling using the passive voice. All of the previously mentioned [wordings] are considered to be raised [*marfūʿ*] because the one who ordered and prohibited and made something compulsory is the Prophet ﷺ.

An example of this is the words of Umm ʿAṭiyya ؆ who said: "We were prohibited from attending funerals but it was not enforced on us."[110]

Similarly, the statement of Anas ؆, "Bilāl was ordered to double [the phrases] in the call to prayer [*adhān*], but to tighten [them to one] in the pre-prayer call [*iqāma*]."

Second, when a Companion says, "During the lifetime of the Prophet ﷺ whilst he was amongst us, we used to do such-and-such," or "We used to say such-and-such," or "They would do such-and-such," or "They would say such-and-such," or "We would not see a problem with doing such-and-such," or "They would not see a problem doing such-and-such."

An example of this is the saying of Jābir ؆, "We would practice coitus interruptus [during sexual intercourse] in the age of the Prophet ﷺ," as is the saying of Ibn ʿUmar, "We would express preference for different people in the time of the Prophet ﷺ, saying, 'Abū Bakr [is superior], then ʿUmar, then ʿUthmān,' and he would not rebuke us for that."

Another example of this is what al-Bayhaqī narrates from al-Mughīra b. Shuʿba ؆, [who said:] "The Companions of the Messenger of Allah ﷺ would knock on his door with their fingernails."[111]

Third, when a Companion says, "Such-and-such is of the Sunna," or "You have hit on the Sunna," or "The Sunna is such-and-such."

An example of this is narrated by Abū Dāwūd, from ʿAlī ؆ who said: "It is of the Sunna to place one's hand over the other beneath the navel during the prayer."

---

[110] I.e., "the prohibition was not made incumbent upon us as were other prohibitions."

[111] [Al-Nawawī] *Al-Taqrīb*

Similarly, that which is narrated by al-Ḥakim with his chain of narration from Ibn ʿUmar 🙵 that he said: "It is of the Sunna that when you enter the mosque you do so with your right foot first, and when you leave, you do so with the left foot first."[112]

By this, they meant the Sunna of the Prophet 🙵, the evidence for which is what al-Bukhārī narrates from Sālim, from Ibn ʿUmar 🙵 that he said: "If you intend the Sunna, then pray in the intense heat."

Ibn Shihāb said [of this]: "I then said to Sālim: 'Did the Messenger of Allah 🙵 do it?' He said: 'In saying this, did they mean anything other than the Sunna of the Prophet 🙵?'"

Fourth, when a Companion speaks of matters that have been transmitted [*naqliyya*][113] or performs an act in which there is no scope to exercise opinion or rational judgement, or he judges an action to be one of obedience to Allah 🙵 and His Messenger 🙵, or one of disobedience.

An example of speech is the saying of ʿAmr b. ʿAbasa 🙵, "On the Day of Rising, the worldly life [*dunyā*] will be brought forth, and a distinction will be made between what was performed for the sake of Allah, the Exalted, and what was performed for other than His sake will be thrown into the Fire of *Jahannam*."[114]

---

[112] [Ibn Ḥajar] *Fatḥ al-Bārī* (vol. 1, p. 437)

[113] And [on the condition] that this Companion did not take from Judaeo-Christian traditions [*Isrāʾīliyyāt*], as Ibn Ḥajar stipulated: "...That he did not take it from the books of *Banī Isrāʾīl* of old, or from them directly by word of mouth." This excludes those who were known to do this, such as ʿAbdullah b. Salām, and ʿAbdullah b. ʿAmr b. al-ʿĀṣ, because it happened that in the Battle of Yarmūk he obtained many of the books of the People of the Book, and he would relate what was contained within them about hidden things until some of his companions would say to him, "Narrate to us from the Prophet 🙵, and do not relate to us from these scriptures."

Things such as this, transmitted matters that someone informs about, are not considered to be raised [to the Prophet 🙵] because of their strongly equivocal nature. See the commentary of al-Sakhāwī (p. 51), and *Laqṭ al-Durar* [of al-ʿAdawī] (p. 94).

[ʿAbdullah b. ʿAmr b. al-ʿĀṣ had a collection of Hadith which he called *al-Ṣaḥīfa*, but that is considered to have been entirely from the Prophet 🙵—Ed.]

[114] Al-Mundhirī, *al-Targhīb wal-Tarhīb*

An example of an action is the prayer of ʿAlī ☺ in the solar eclipse prayer with more than two bowings in each unit of the prayer.

An example of a ruling is that which is narrated by al-Tirmidhī from ʿAmmār ☺ who said: "Whoever fasts on the Day of Uncertainty[115] has disobeyed Abū al-Qāsim[116] ☺."

Fifth, the statements of Companions regarding the reasons for verses of the Qurʾan being revealed, such as the statement of Ibn ʿAbbās ☺ who said: "When the people of Yemen would perform the *hajj*, they would travel without adequate provisions, saying that they were people of reliance on God [*mutawakkilūn*]. When they entered Mecca, they asked the people and Allah, Mighty and Majestic is He, revealed the verse, ❴*Take provisions, and the best of provisions is God-consciousness* [*taqwā*].❵"[117]
(Narrated by al-Bukhārī).

Similarly, statements of Companions regarding exegesis of Qurʾanic verses and their meanings, in a way that is not related to linguistics, and in which there is no scope for opinion or the exercise of intellect, such as commentary on a hidden matter of the worldly or other-worldly life, or of Heaven and Hell, or specifying a particular reward or punishment, and so on,[118] such as the words of Abū Hurayra ☺ regarding the verse, ❴*It burns the skins of men,*❵[119] he said: "On the Day of Rising, Hellfire will face them and the fire will scorch them until it leaves no flesh on the bone."

As for a Companion commenting on a linguistic meaning, or clarifying a ruling of a verse, then there is the possibility for him to do this from [his own] opinion, so this does not have the ruling of being raised [*marfūʿ*].

---

[115] This refers to the day after the 29th of Shaʿbān when not certain that it is the first day of Ramaḍān and it is prohibited—Tr.

[116] The Prophet Muhammad's ☺ surname of relationship [*kunya*]—Tr.

[117] Qurʾan 2:197

[118] *Sharḥ al-Sakhāwī* (p. 48)

[119] Qurʾan 74:29

Sixth, when a Successor [*Tābi'ī*] or anyone after them says, when mentioning a Companion, "he raises it [*yarfa'uhu*]," or "he raises the Hadith," or "he attributes it [*yanmīhi*]," or "he reaches by means of it [*yablughu bi*]," or "he narrates it," or "he narrated it," or "by narration," then all of these have the ruling of *marfū'*.

Ḥāfiẓ al-'Irāqī says:

Their saying, "he raises it," or "he reaches by means of it,"
Or "narrating it," or "he attributes it," then it is marfū' so take note

An example of this is narrated by al-Bukhārī from Ibn 'Abbās ﷺ, [who said:] "Healing is found in three things: drinking honey, cupping and cauterising with fire," raising the Hadith.

Likewise, Mālik narrates in *al-Muwaṭṭaʾ* from Abū Ḥāzim, from Sahl b. Sa'd that he said: "People were ordered that a man should put his right hand on his left forearm in the prayer." Abū Ḥāzim says: "I only know that he attributes [*yanmī*] this." Mālik said: "He raises this."

Related to this is when it is said when mentioning a Companion, "He said: 'He said...'" The subject of the second verb in "he said" is the Prophet ﷺ, as al-'Irāqī mentioned, and the example he gave of this is that which al-Khaṭīb narrated with his chain of narration from Abū Hurayra ﷺ who said: "He ﷺ said: "The angels send prayers upon anyone as long as he remains in his place of prayer.'"

As for when a Companion says of the Prophet ﷺ, "He raises it," it takes the ruling of him saying, "From Allah ﷻ," and the Hadith is considered to be *ilāhī*,[120] the examples of which are many.

Of this type there is that which has been narrated from Abū Hurayra ﷺ that he said: "The Messenger of Allah ﷺ said, raising it: 'My believing servant has the best standing in My sight. He praises Me whilst I withdraw his soul from between his two sides.'" This is a Hadith *qudsī*. Likewise, the statement of a Companion, "From the Prophet ﷺ, he narrates it," means that the Prophet ﷺ narrates it from His Lord ﷻ.

---

[120] Al-Sakhāwī, *Fatḥ al-Mughīth* (p. 49); [Al-Suyūṭī] *al-Tadrīb* (p. 115); [al-Ṣan'ānī] *Tawḍīḥ al-Afkār* (vol. 1, p. 257); Ḥāshiya al-Abyārī

If it is asked what is the reason for a Successor to deviate from the words of the Companion, "I heard the Messenger of Allah ﷺ say such-and-such," or "The Messenger of Allah ﷺ said such-and-such," or the like, to saying, "he raised it," or "he attributed it," or any like the preceding?

There are various reasons for this:

First, when the reason for it was to lighten and make easier and preferring to summarise the expression.

Secondly, that the one who said, "He raised it," or the like, doubted on it being reliably traced back to the Prophet ﷺ. If he were to say, "The Messenger of Allah ﷺ said," it would indicate his certainty about its attribution to the Prophet ﷺ. However, since he had some doubt, he ascribed the attribution to someone else by saying, "He raised it to the Prophet ﷺ," or something similar.

Thirdly, it could have been done out of scrupulousness, in the sense of knowing that there is a difference of opinion regarding the Hadith that has been narrated in meaning [ma'nā].

Fourthly, that the one who said, "He raised it," was certain that the Companion attributed it to the Prophet ﷺ but he was in doubt with regard to what form of narration he had heard—whether it was, "The Messenger of Allah ﷺ said," or "The Prophet ﷺ said," or the like, such as "I heard the Prophet ﷺ say," or "The Prophet ﷺ narrated to me." The narrator therefore did not want to change the word 'Prophet' to 'Messenger' and the like, or the words "I heard" to "He narrated to me," and so on.[121]

The second type is that which does not have the ruling of being raised [marfū'], and it is anything other than what has the rank of marfū'.

With regard to the ruling of the halted [mawqūf] Hadith, then it is not a decisive proof when it does not have the ruling of being marfū'.[122]

---

[121] Al-Qasṭallānī, introduction to *Minhāj al-Ibtihāj*;
[al-Ṣan'ānī] *Tawḍīḥ al-Afkār; Sharḥ al-Sakhāwī*

[122] *Ḥāshiya al-Abyārī*; [al-Qāsimī] *Qawā'id al-Ḥadīth*. In any case, this is the ruling of the *mawqūf* in general terms. Details regarding the opinions of the imams on this matter are found in the books of legal theory, and it is not the place to discuss them here.

A rule: If there is a contradiction in a Hadith being [classified as] *marfū'* or *mawqūf*, such that a reliable [*thiqa*] narrator narrates a Hadith as *marfū'* and another reliable narrator narrates it as *mawqūf*, then it is considered to be *marfū'* as he affirms its being *marfū'*, whereas the other either negates it or is silent regarding it, and the one who affirms is given precedence over both of them.

SUPPORTED [*MUSNAD*]

Musnad is that whose narrators are connected,
From its narrator up to Muṣṭafā ﷺ, and is not broken

The *musnad* is a Hadith whose chain of narration is connected up to the Prophet ﷺ with a connection that is obvious.

A connected chain excludes the *munqaṭi'*, *mu'ḍal*, *mudallas* and so on. It being raised to the Prophet ﷺ excludes the *mawqūf* and *maqṭū'*.

The definition for the *musnad* given by the author is the relied upon position according to the majority of scholars of Hadith. Al-Ḥākim took this position, and [Ibn Ḥajar] the author of *Nukhba al-Fikar* was unequivocal about it.

Ibn 'Abd al-Barr defined it as that which is narrated from the Prophet ﷺ, whether the chain is connected [*muttaṣil*] or severed [*munqaṭi'*], making it synonymous with *marfū'*.

Al-Khaṭīb defined it as being connected to the end of the chain, including the *marfū'*, the *mawqūf* and the *maqṭū'*.

The *musnad* Hadith may be *ṣaḥīḥ*, *ḥasan* or *ḍa'īf*.

Connected [*Muttaṣil*] which is also called *Mawṣūl*

وَمَا بِسَمْعِ كُلِّ رَاوٍ يَتَّصِلْ   إِسْنَادُهُ لِلْمُصْطَفَى فَالْمُتَّصِلْ

That whose chain, by every narrator hearing,
Is connected to Muṣṭafā ﷺ is muttaṣil

The *muttaṣil* Hadith is that in whose chain of narration each narrator heard it directly from the one above him, from the beginning until the end of the chain, regardless whether it is raised [*marfū'*] or halted [*mawqūf*].[123]

The condition of having a connected chain excludes the following categories: *munqaṭi'*, *mu'ḍal*, *mursal*, *mu'allaq*, and the *mu'an'an* of a *mudallis* before his direct hearing has been established.[124]

The stipulation of it being connected by [each narrator] having heard it directly excludes a connected chain transmitted by licensing [*ijāza*], such as someone saying, "So-and-so licensed me; he said: 'so-and-so licensed me.'" This would not be considered to be connected.[125]

The *muttaṣil* Hadith includes the *marfū'* and *mawqūf*. A *marfū'* is, for example, such as: Mālik from Nāfi', from Ibn 'Umar ؓ, from the Prophet ﷺ. *Mawqūf* is, for example, Mālik from Nāfi', from Ibn 'Umar ؓ.

Therefore, the *musnad* Hadith—with regard to the one to whom the statement is attributed—is more specific than the *muttaṣil*, so every *musnad* Hadith is *muttaṣil*, but not vice versa.

The ruling for the *muttaṣil* Hadith is the same as for the *musnad* Hadith: it may be *ṣaḥīḥ*, *ḥasan* or *ḍa'īf*.

---

[123] What the author says: "[that it reaches to] Muṣṭafā ﷺ," this not a condition, as al-Zurqānī has pointed out.

[124] The meaning of these categories will be clarified in chapter seven [p. 103-118]—Tr.

[125] This is according to Ibn al-Ṣalāḥ and others, as opposed to Ibn Jamā'a. ([Al-Suyūṭī] *Al-Tadrīb*; *Ḥāshiya al-Abyārī*)

CONCATENATED [*MUSALSAL*]

مُسَلْسَلٌ قُلْ مَا عَلَى وَصْفٍ أَتَى   مِثْلُ أَمَا وَاللهَّ أَنْبَانِي الْفَتَى

كَـذَاكَ قَدْ حَدَّثَنِيهِ قَائِـمـاً   أَوْ بَـعْدَ أَنْ حَدَّثَنِي تَبَسَّما

Say that musalsal is that which comes with a [specific] description,
Such as, "By Allah, the young man informed me"

Likewise, "He narrated it to me whilst standing,"
Or, "After he narrated it to me, he smiled"

The *musalsal* Hadith is that in which the narrators in the chain narrated it one-by-one in a particular state or with a particular quality, regardless of whether this quality relates to the narrators or the chain itself, or whether the common quality within the chain relates to the method of narration or a particular time or place when narrating it, or whether the states of the narrators or their qualities may relate to a statement, an action or both.[126]

Therefore, we know then that the *musalsal* is a quality of the chain and is of various types:

1. **A wording of the narrators.** For example, in the narration of al-Tirmidhī from Mu'ādh b. Jabal ﷺ, that the Prophet ﷺ said to him: "Mu'ādh! Indeed I love you, so say after every prayer: 'O Allah! Assist me in Your remembrance, in Your gratitude and in worshipping You in the best way.'" The common factor when narrating this Hadith is that every narrator would say, "And I love you, so say after every prayer..."

2. **A common action of the narrators.** For example, in the narration of Muslim from Abū Hurayra ﷺ who said: "Abū al-Qāsim ﷺ clasped his hands with mine and said: 'Allah created the earth on a Saturday...'" The common trait here is that every narrator would clasp hands with the one from whom he received it.

---

[126] This is the definition of Ḥāfiẓ al-ʿIrāqī, and we have chosen this one because it is comprehensive.

Similar to this type are those whose common trait is a handshake, or taking by the hand, or putting hand on head, and so on. The author alludes to this when he says:

Likewise, "He narrated it to me whilst standing,"

3.   **A statement and an action together**. For example, the narration of al-Ḥākim from Anas ﷺ who said: "The Prophet ﷺ said: 'A servant will not experience the sweetness of faith until he believes in destiny—that of it which is good and that of it which is evil, that of it which is sweet and that which is bitter,' and the Messenger of Allah ﷺ grasped his beard and said: 'I believe in destiny—that of it which is good and that of it which is evil, that of it which is sweet and that which is bitter.'"

The common trait here is that every narrator grasped his beard and said, "I believe in destiny..."

4.   **A common spoken trait amongst the narrators**. For example, in the narration of al-Tirmidhī from ʿAbdullah b. Salām ﷺ who said: "We, a number of Companions of the Messenger of Allah ﷺ, sat and we discussed some matters, and we said: 'Had we known which act was the most beloved to Allah, we would do it,' so Allah revealed the verse, ❨*What is contained within the heavens and the earth praises Allah. And He is Mighty and Wise. O You who believe, why do you say that which you do not do?*❩"[127] Ibn al-Salām said: "The Prophet ﷺ then recited this verse to us." The common trait then became that each narrator would say, "And so-and-so then recited this verse to us."[128]

5.   **A common practical attribute of the narrators**. For example, the *musalsal* Hadith of the jurists, which is the Hadith of Ibn ʿUmar ﷺ who said (raising it to the Prophet ﷺ): "The buyer and seller have a choice..."

---

[127] Qur'an 61:1-2

[128] Abū Salama, the narrator of this Hadith from Ibn Salām, said: "So ʿAbdullah b. Salām ﷺ read this verse to us," then the one who narrated from Abū Salama, who was Yaḥyā, said: "So Abū Salama ﷺ read this verse to us," and so on until the end of the chain.

The common trait of this Hadith is that it was narrated by jurists. Likewise, there are Hadith narrated by masters [of Hadith], Qur'an reciters, scribes, and so on.

6.   **A common feature of the chain and the method of narration.** This is when the Hadith is narrated in the same manner, such as each narrator saying, "I heard so-and-so," or "he narrated to us," or "he informed us," or "I saw so-and-so saying: 'I saw so-and-so doing,'" and so on. The author indicates this type when he says:

Such as, "By Allah, the young man informed me"

7.   **A narration on the same occasion.** An example of this is what al-Daylamī narrated from Ibn ʿAbbās ※ that he said: "I witnessed the Prophet ※ on the day of ʿĪd al-Fiṭr or ʿĪd al-Aḍḥā. When he finished the prayer, he turned to face us, saying: 'People! You have attained great good. Whoever wants to leave should leave and whoever wants to remain to hear the sermon should stay.'"[129] The common trait was that each narrator narrated it on the day of ʿĪd, saying, "So-and-so narrated to me on the day of ʿĪd..."

8.   **A narration at the same place.** For example, al-Daylamī narrates from Ibn ʿAbbās ※ that he said: "I heard the Prophet ※ say: 'The *multazam*[130] is a place where prayers are answered. A servant does not supplicate there with a prayer except that it is answered.'" Ibn ʿAbbās ※ said: "By Allah, I never supplicated to Allah there since I heard that Hadith, except that my supplication was answered." The common trait here is that each narrator says, "I never supplicated to Allah there at all since I heard that Hadith, except that my supplication was answered."[131]

---

[129] Al-Suyūṭī said of this Hadith: "The context seems irregular, and in the chain of narration there is someone who is suspect."

[130] A side of the Kaʿba which pilgrims cling on to and from which it derives its name, since the verb *iltazama* means to hold on to something—Tr.

[131] The erudite scholar al-Abyārī has clarified how this Hadith is considered to be *musalsal* of place, by saying: "Having prayers answered,

The different kinds of *musalsal* are unlimited, as Ḥāfiẓ Ibn al-Ṣalāḥ said. It is possible for the common trait to be present in the majority of the chain of narration but absent in other parts.

The ruling on the *musalsal* Hadith

Ḥāfiẓ al-ʿIrāqī said: "Rarely is a *musalsal* Hadith free of some kind of weakness, meaning the quality common [to the narration] throughout the Hadith, not the wording of the Hadith itself." This means that the wording of the Hadith could well be sound, but the quality common [to the narration] within the chain could be doubtful, such as the *musalsal* Hadith on clasping hands, for its wording is sound as it appears in *Ṣaḥīḥ Muslim* as has been mentioned,[132] but the presence of this shared feature is doubtful.[133]

Ḥāfiẓ al-Suyūṭī says [in his poem]:

> *Rarely is the tasalsul free of a weakness,*
> *It could well be disconnected*

[Al-Suyūṭī says] in *al-Tadrīb*: "Shaykh al-Islam Ibn Ḥajar says: 'Amongst the most sound of *musalsal* Hadith on the face of this earth is the one whose common trait is the reciting of *Sūra al-Ṣaff*.'"

I say: so too the Hadith of the masters of Hadith [*ḥuffāẓ*] and jurists. Furthermore, he mentions in *Sharḥ al-Nukhba* that the Hadith of the *ḥuffāẓ*, if it is not unusual in having a single narrator at some point in its chain [*gharīb*], reaches certain knowledge.

A benefit of the *musalsal* Hadith is that it indicates the narrators' extra degree of precision, and of following the Prophet ﷺ in word and deed such as grasping the beard and clasping hands.

---

even though it is a quality of Allah ﷻ, is related to the place of narration, as the meaning is that the answering of prayers occurs at the *multazam*, but not in its absolute sense [i.e., in other places as well]."

[132] [See p. 91, nr. 2]

[133] Al-Sakhāwī, *Fatḥ al-Mughīth* (p. 353)

CHAPTER SIX
THE CATEGORIES OF HADITH
WITH REGARD TO THEIR PATHS

CCORDING TO THE SCHOLARS OF HADITH TERMINOLOGY, the Hadith are categorised with regard to their paths into *āḥād* and *mutawātir*. The *āḥād* then divides into *gharīb*, *ʿazīz* and *mashhūr*, and *mustafīḍ* according to some views.

UNUSUAL [*GHARĪB*]

وَقُلْ غَرِيبٌ مَا رَوَى رَاوٍ فَقَطْ

Say that gharīb is that which only one narrator narrates

A *gharīb* Hadith is that which one narrator alone narrates, which no-one else does, or he alone narrates something additional in the wording or the chain, whether this addition is absolute or with the condition that it is from a scholar whose Hadith are agreed upon because he is reliable and upright, such as Imam al-Zuhrī and Qatāda, and their likes.[134]

It is called *gharīb* as its narrators are alone in narrating it from others, like someone who has become stranded, alone and away from his homeland.

There are several types of *gharīb* Hadith:

1. *Gharīb* in both its chain and wording, which is what only one person narrates, either all of it or some of it.

An example of something that is *gharīb* both in its chain [*isnād*] and its wording [*matn*] is the Hadith regarding the sale and gifting of clientage [*walāʾ*]. It is not sound except by way of ʿAbdullah b. Dīnār from Ibn ʿUmar ﷺ.[135]

---

[134] Al-Sakhāwī, *Fatḥ al-Mughīth*; [al-Qāsimī] *Qawāʿid al-Taḥdīth*
[135] Al-Sakhāwī, *Sharḥ Alfiyya al-ʿIrāqī*; al-Anṣārī, *Sharḥ Alfiyya al-ʿIrāqī*

An example of a Hadith which is *gharīb* in some of its wording is the Hadith of *zakāt al-Fiṭr*, "The Prophet ﷺ made obligatory the ʿĪd charity of Ramaḍān—a *ṣāʿ* of dates or of barley—upon the slave and the free person, male and female, young and old ['of the Muslims.']" Out of all of the narrators of this Hadith, Mālik alone narrated it with the addition "of the Muslims" at the end.

An example that is *gharīb* in part of its chain is the Hadith of Umm Zarʿ in the narration of al-Ṭabarānī. The preponderant version is the narration of ʿĪsā b. Yūnus and others from Hishām b. ʿUrwa, from his brother ʿAbdullah, from their father, from ʿĀʾisha ﷺ, as narrated by al-Bukhārī and Muslim. Al-Ṭabarānī narrated it from the Hadith of al-Darāwardī, from Hishām, from his father, without mentioning his brother [ʿAbdullah].

> 2.   *Gharīb* in its chain alone. This is when the Hadith is known from a number of Companions narrating it, and some narrators alone do so from a different Companion. From this perspective it is *gharīb*, despite its wording not being *gharīb*.[136]

An example of this is the Hadith of ʿAbd al-Majīd b. ʿAbd al-ʿAzīz b. Abī Rawwād from Mālik, from Zayd b. Aslam, from ʿAṭāʾ b. Yasār, from Abū Saʿīd al-Khudrī ﷺ, from the Prophet ﷺ who said: "Actions are by intention."

Al-Khalīlī Abū Yaʿlā al-Qāḍī said: "ʿAbd al-Majīd made an error, as it is not protected from corruption [*ghayr maḥfūẓ*] from Zayd b. Aslam."[137]

Abū al-Fath al-Yaʿmurī said: "The entire chain is *gharīb* but the wording is sound." Ibn al-Ṣalāḥ said: "Of this type are *gharīb* narrations of teachers in chains of Hadith whose wordings are sound. Al-Tirmidhī calls this type, '*gharīb* by this path.'"

---

[136] See the three commentaries on *Alfiyya al-ʿIrāqī*
[by al-Sakhāwī, Zakariyyā al-Anṣārī and al-Suyūṭī]
[137] The narrations of Zayd b. Aslam are accepted when there is a contradiction between his narration and that of ʿAbd al-Majīd—Tr.

The ruling on the *gharīb*

The unusual [*gharīb*] Hadith could be *ṣaḥīḥ* by the narrator, who is alone in what he narrates, being reliable [*thiqa*], and fulfils the conditions of being sound [*ṣaḥīḥ*], such as [being narrated by] individuals whose narrations are included in the two *Ṣaḥīḥ* collections [al-Bukhārī and Muslim].

It could also be fair [*ḥasan*], and there are many of this type in the *Sunan* of al-Tirmidhī.

It could also be weak [*ḍaʿīf*], and this is the norm with *gharīb* narrations. For this reason, Imam Aḥmad ﷺ said: "Do not record these *gharīb* Hadith, as they are denounced [*manākīr*] and most of them are from weak narrators."

The Greatest Imam, Abū Ḥanīfa ﷺ, said: "Whoever seeks them (i.e., *gharīb* Hadith) is considered a liar."[138]

Mālik said: "The worst of knowledge is that which is *gharīb*, and the best of knowledge is the most obvious which people narrate."

ʿAbd al-Razzāq said: "We used to view the *gharīb* Hadith as something good, but it was actually something bad."

RARE [ʿAZĪZ]

عَزِيـزٌ مَرْوِي اثْـنَيْنِ أَوْ ثَلاَثَهْ

ʿAzīz is that which is narrated by two or three

The *ʿazīz* Hadith is that which only two or three have narrated, even if thereafter a hundred people narrate it. This is opinion of Ibn Mandah. Ibn al-Ṣalāḥ concurred, as did Imam al-Nawawī in *al-Taqrīb*, when he said: "If two or three narrators alone narrate the Hadith, it is called rare [*ʿazīz*]."[139] The author has also taken this position.

---

[138] *Sharḥ al-Sakhāwī* (p. 345) and elsewhere.

[139] In *Laqṭ al-Durar*, the author [al-ʿAdawī] says: "Based on this, the *ʿazīz* and *mashhūr* share in one quality and differ in another [*ʿumūm wa-khuṣūṣ min wajh*]."

Ḥāfiẓ al-Sakhāwī has transmitted from the scholars of Hadith from whom he received it that the ʿazīz is that in which the number of narrators at any given level [ṭabaqa] is only two,[140] meaning that in the remaining levels, there are no fewer than two narrators. Rather there are two or more.[141]

An example of the ʿazīz is that which the two Shaykhs (Al-Bukhārī and Muslim) narrated from the Hadith of Anas ﷺ, and al-Bukhārī from the Hadith of Abū Hurayra ﷺ, that the Prophet ﷺ said: "None of you truly believes until I become more beloved to him than his own father, his child..."

Qatāda and ʿAbd al-ʿAzīz b. Ṣuhayb narrated it from Anas ﷺ, and Shuʿba and Saʿīd narrated it from Qatāda, and Ismāʿīl b. ʿUlayya and ʿAbd al-Wārith narrated it from ʿAbd al-ʿAzīz, and a large group narrated it from each of them.

The ʿazīz [Hadith] may be ṣaḥīḥ, ḥasan or ḍaʿīf.

WELL-KNOWN [MASHHŪR]

مَشْـهُورُ مَرْوِي فَوقَ مَا ثَلاَثَهْ

Mashhūr is narrated by more than three

[This term is used in the science of logic [manṭiq] to describe the relationship between two things, where each has a shared quality with the other but is distinct in another aspect—Tr.]

[140] Al-Sakhāwī, *Fatḥ al-Mughīth* (p. 344)

[141] Shaykh ʿAlī al-Qārī said: "Some have specified the *mashhūr* as having [a minimum of] three narrators and the ʿazīz as having two." The author of *Nukhba al-Fikar*, Ibn Ḥajar, also chose this opinion where he defined the ʿazīz as, "...that which is narrated is not narrated by fewer than two from two."

Ḥāfiẓ al-Sakhāwī said: "Our teacher (Ibn Ḥajar) said that the meaning of the definition of ʿazīz is that it is not narrated by fewer than two, and if it comes from more than two in some parts of the chain then it does not change anything. This is because the lowest number is considered, rather than the highest number." (*Fatḥ al-Mughīth*, p. 344)

Mashhūr is that which is narrated by a group [*jamāʿa*]—three or more[142]—from a group, such that in each level of the chain, there are no fewer than three people narrating it.[143]

The words of the author, "*Mashhūr is narrated by more than three,*" actually mean three or more, in the same manner as is said about the verse, ⟨*If the women are more than two,*⟩[144] [meaning two or more].

An example of the *mashhūr* Hadith is that which is narrated by Anas ﷺ that, "The Prophet ﷺ supplicated with the *qunūt* for a month after bowing [in prayer], supplicating against *Riʿl* and *Dhakwān*."[145]

The two Shaykhs (al-Bukhārī and Muslim) narrated the Hadith with its *isnād* from Sulaymān al-Taymī, from Abū Mijlaz, from Anas ﷺ—and someone other than Abū Mijlaz narrated it from Anas ﷺ, and someone other than Sulaymān narrated it from Abū Mijlaz, and a group narrated it from Sulaymān.

The ruling on the *mashhūr*: it could be *ṣaḥīḥ*, *ḥasan* or *ḍaʿīf*.

Reminder

The previously mentioned definition and example of *mashhūr* is according to the people of Hadith. The word *mashhūr* may also be used for a Hadith that has become widespread amongst the common people, even though it may not be *mashhūr* according to the definition of the scholars of Hadith. [Based on the usage of the laity], it could include a Hadith which only has one chain of narration, or more, or even a Hadith which has no chain whatsoever[146] [and by extension, no basis]. Many books have been written on [such] Hadith which are well-known.[147]

---

[142] The Arabic term here denotes three or more, as grammatically a plural is three or more, since Arabic has a dual form—Tr.

[143] This is the meaning of the words of al-Nawawī and al-ʿIrāqī in defining of the *mashhūr*, that it is narrated by a group. [Ibn Ḥajar] defined it in *Sharḥ al-Nukhba* as, "That which has various paths which are more than two in number."

[144] Qurʾan 4:11

[145] The name of two tribes who murdered a convoy of seventy Muslims who were passing by these two sub-clans of Banū Sulaym—Tr.

[146] *Sharḥ al-Sakhāwī* (p. 345)

[147] Amongst the most famous examples include *al-Maqāṣid al-Ḥasana* by al-Sakhāwī and *Kashf al-Khafāʾ* by al-ʿAjlūnī—Tr.

ABUNDANT [*MUSTAFĪḌ*]

The *mustafīḍ* is identical to the *mashhūr* according to the view of a group of jurists and scholars of legal theory, and some scholars of Hadith. It is so-termed because of its prevalence.

Some however differentiated between the *mustafīḍ* and *mashhūr*, considering the *mustafīḍ* to be that which has the exact same number of narrators at the beginning, at the end and in between. As for the *mashhūr*, it is more general and includes that which has an equal number of narrators throughout, and that which does not.[148]

MASS-TRANSMITTED [*MUTAWĀTIR*]

The *mutawātir* Hadith is that which a group narrates from a group[149] such that it reaches a limit that conventional experience shows collusion upon a lie to be impossible, on the condition that it relates to something physical, such as seeing or hearing something.[150]

The condition of a group narrating from another group excludes the unusual [*gharīb*] and the rare [*ʿazīz*]. The condition of it negating the possibility of being a lie upon which they have colluded excludes the *mashhūr*.

Ḥāfiẓ al-Suyūṭī says:

> *When a substantial number of people,*
> *Necessitates the impossibility,*
> *Of them colluding upon a lie*
>
> *Is thus mutawātir,*
> *Some specified the number ten,*
> *And this position is superior in my view*

---

[148] *Sharḥ al-Sakhāwī* (p. 345); [al-ʿAdawī] *Laqṭ al-Durar* (p. 30)

[149] Without stipulating a set number, as opposed to those who restrict it to a specific number. Those who specify a number differ on the actual number, as mentioned in *Alfiyya al-Suyūṭī*.

[150] Al-Sakhāwī, *Sharḥ Alfiyya al-ʿIrāqī*; al-Anṣārī, *Sharḥ Alfiyya al-ʿIrāqī*

There are four conditions for *mutawātir* to be established:

1. A significant number of narrators;
2. The virtual[151] impossibility of their colluding upon a lie;
3. That this significant number be present from the beginning to the end of the chain;
4. The matter conveyed is something physical, whether direct seeing or audition.

There are many examples of *mutawātir* Hadith, which include, "Whoever lies against me deliberately should prepare his seat in Hellfire."[152]

Imam al-Nawawī says in his introduction to *Sharḥ Ṣaḥīḥ Muslim*: "[This Hadith] comes from two hundred Companions."

Ḥāfiẓ al-Sakhāwī transmitted from his teacher Ibn Ḥajar that among the Hadith considered to be *mutawātir* are the Hadith of intercession, and the Pool,[153] for the numbers of those who narrate them are more than forty. Likewise the Hadith about seeing Allah ﷻ in the Afterlife, and others.[154]

---

[151] The word used is conventionally [*al-ʿāda*] impossible, as opposed to rationally [*ʿaqlan*] impossible, since it is conceived to be possible for this to occur but the remoteness of this possibility renders it impossible in practice—Tr.

[152] Some have understood this to apply to lying in general, such as the Hadith, "Whoever narrates from me something which is considered to be a lie, then he becomes one of the liars," and the like. Ḥāfiẓ al-Sakhāwī has enumerated the names of the Companions who narrate this Hadith, as found in the two *Ṣaḥīḥ* collections and elsewhere.

[153] The *Ḥawḍ* is a large fountain forming part of the landscape on the Day of Judgement. Each Prophet will have their own—Tr.

[154] Ḥāfiẓ al-Suyūṭī has authored a collection titled *al-Azhār al-Mutanāthira fī al-Akhbār al-Mutawātira*, in which he narrates many *mutawātir* Hadith with their various chains of narration.

Types of *mutawātir*

There are two types of *mutawātir* Hadith: in form [*lafẓī*] and in meaning [*ma'nawī*].

The first is that whose narrators agree on its wording, or that which carries the ruling of having the same wording, and which has the same meaning, such as the Hadith, "Whoever deliberately lies against me should prepare his seat in Hellfire," and so on.

That which is narrated in meaning contains a difference in the wording and meaning, which ultimately returns to one general meaning [*ma'nā kullī*].[155] This type informs us of different occurrences although all contain a common theme and this common theme is the *mutawātir* aspect. For example, the Hadith about raising one's hands in supplication has been mentioned in a hundred narrations, albeit in different situations. Each specific situation is not *mutawātir*, but rather the shared aspect—which is the raising of one's hands in supplication—is the *mutawātir* aspect when all narrations are considered.[156]

The ruling on the *mutawātir*

[Ibn Ḥajar], the author of *Sharḥ al-Nukhba* said:

> The relied upon position is that the *mutawātir* report establishes unequivocal knowledge [*al-'ilm al-ḍarūrī*], which a person is obliged to affirm with certainty, such that he cannot deny the truth of it to himself. It is also said that the *mutawātir* only establishes certainty after reflection [*al-'ilm al-naẓarī*], although this opinion is not considered.[157]

---

[155] [Al-Suyūṭī] *Al-Tadrīb* (p. 374); *Ḥāshiya al-Abyārī* (p. 20)

[156] *Al-Tadrīb*; *Ḥāshiya al-Abyārī*. An example of this is if man narrated from Ḥātim that he gave a camel, and someone else narrated that he gave a horse, and someone else narrated it was a gold dinar, and so on. The shared theme which is *mutawātir* in the various narrations is the giving, as the act of giving is present in all cases.

[157] Ibn Ḥajar mentioned various evidences to prove that *mutawātir* establishes unequivocal certainty [*al-'ilm al-yaqīnī al-ḍarūrī*], so refer to them if you wish. In any case, the discussion of *mutawātir* belongs in the discussions of legal theory [*uṣūl al-fiqh*]. You will find the details regarding the conditions and rulings there.

THE CATEGORIES OF HADITH WITH REGARD TO THE CHAIN OF NARRATION BEING CONNECTED OR DISCONNECTED

HADITH DIFFERS REGARDING WHETHER THE CHAIN OF NARRATION is connected or disconnected. The connected chain is that in which each narrator of the chain, from the beginning of the chain to the end, received the Hadith from his teacher. As for the disconnected chain, it has various categories:

- *Munqaṭiʿ*
- *Muʿḍal*
- *Mursal*
- *Muʿallaq*
- *Muʿanʿan* from someone who is *mudallis*
- Likewise, *muʿanʿan* before direct audition has been established

SEVERED [MUNQAṬIʿ]

وَكُلُّ مَا لَمْ يَتَّصِلْ بِحَالِ   إِسْـنَادُهُ مُنْـقَطِعُ الأَوْصَالِ

Anything that is disconnected in any form,
Its chain has severed [munqaṭiʿ] ties

The *munqaṭiʿ* Hadith is that which is missing one narrator before the Companion in one place, or in various places such that the break in the chain does not exceed one. This break cannot be at the beginning of the chain.

The condition of there being only one break excludes the *muʿḍal*, and the condition of it being before the Companion excludes the *mursal*, and the condition of the break not being in the beginning of the chain excludes the *muʿallaq*.

This is the well-known definition, and this definition was chosen by Ḥāfiẓ al-ʿIrāqī and Ḥāfiẓ Ibn Ḥajar.

Ibn ʿAbd al-Barr, al-Khaṭīb al-Baghdādī and groups of jurists defined it as, "A Hadith which contains any kind of break in the chain, regardless of whether the missing narrator is at the beginning, middle or end, and regardless of whether there is one missing narrator or more."

The author has chosen the latter definition, as he says:

> Anything that is disconnected in any form,
> Its chain has severed [munqaṭiʿ] ties

According to this definition, the *munqaṭiʿ* includes the *mursal*, *muʿḍal* and *muʿallaq*.

The break in the chain could be apparent [*ẓāhir*], and this is when a narrator narrates from someone about whom it is known that he was not his contemporary.[158]

The break could also be hidden [*khafī*], such that someone narrates from his contemporary without meeting him, or he met him but did not take any Hadith from him, or he heard certain Hadith from him but not that particular Hadith. These latter types are only known to the people of deep insight regarding the science of narrators.

An example of a *munqaṭiʿ* Hadith is that which is narrated by ʿAbd al-Razzāq, from al-Thawrī, from Abū Isḥāq, from Zayd b. Yuthayʿ, from Ḥudhayfa ﷺ, who raised it (to the Prophet ﷺ), "If you appoint Abū Bakr to be leader, he is strong and trustworthy, and for Allah's sake he is not distracted by criticism..."

Ibn al-Ṣalāḥ said:

> There are two separate breaks in the chain: the first of them is because ʿAbd al-Razzāq did not hear it from al-Thawrī; rather, he only narrated it from al-Nuʿmān b. Abī Shayba al-Janadī, from al-Thawrī. Secondly, al-Thawrī did not hear it from Abū Isḥāq; rather, he only narrated it from Sharīk, from Abū Isḥāq.

---

[158] They lived at different times which makes it impossible for the claimant to have heard from him directly, therefore there must be (at least) one narrator who is missing—Tr.

The ruling on the *munqaṭiʿ*

The *munqaṭiʿ* Hadith is rejected [*mardūd*], meaning it is weak and cannot be used as evidence for a ruling, given that the missing person in the chain is unknown.

It has already been mentioned that among the conditions for accepting a Hadith is that the uprightness and accuracy of a narrator are reliably established. If the *munqaṭiʿ* Hadith is narrated by a separate, connected route, which clarifies that the narrator who has been omitted is reliable, then it is accepted.

A benefit

That the narrators met is established through a chain which explicitly mentions the narrator saying that he heard so-and-so say, or that so-and-so narrated to him, even if just once. That the narrators did not meet is known by the narrator himself saying so, or by the decisive statement by a highly conversant Imam of Hadith, as explained [by Ibn Ḥajar] in *Sharḥ al-Nukhba*.

PROBLEMATIC [MUʿḌAL]

وَالْمُعْـضَلُ السَّـاقِطُ مِنْهُ اثْنَانِ

Muʿḍal contains two breaks [in the chain]

The *muʿḍal* Hadith is that in which there are two or more missing narrators, except at the beginning of the chain, and these breaks are consecutive. This last condition of being consecutive excludes the Hadith which is severed [*munqaṭiʿ*] in two (non-consecutive) places.

An example of the *muʿḍal* is the statement of Imam Mālik in *al-Muwaṭṭa'*, "It reached me from Abū Hurayra ﷺ that the Messenger of Allah ﷺ said: 'A slave [*mamlūk*] should have normal food and clothing, and he is not responsible for work other than what he is capable of.'" Imam Mālik narrates this in a connected form, outside of the *Muwaṭṭa'*, from Muḥammad b. ʿAjlān, from his father, from Abū Hurayra ﷺ. Therefore, we know that [the first narration] contains two missing narrators after the Companion.

The ruling on the *mu'ḍal*

The *mu'ḍal* is worse than the *munqaṭi'* because the narrators omitted from the chain are unknown. This is only if the *munqaṭi'* contains only one break in the chain. If there are two breaks in the chain then it is equally as bad as the *mu'ḍal*.

MISLEADING [MUDALLAS]

وَمَـا أَتَـى مُدَلَّـساً نَوْعَانِ

الأَوَّلُ الإِسْـقَاطُ لِلشَّيْـخِ وَأَنْ   يَنْقُلَ عَمَّنْ فوقَـهُ بِـعَنْ وَأَنْ

وَالثَّانِي لاَ يُسْقِطُهُ لَكِـنْ يَصِفْ   أَوْصَافَهُ بِمَـا بِـهِ لاَ يَنْعَرِفْ

Mudallas is of two types:

First, when the teacher is omitted, yet,
He narrates from the one above him using 'an [from] or an [that];

Second, when he does not omit him, but,
He describes his qualities in a manner by which he is not known

The *mudallas* is the Hadith in which the narrator has attempted to hide a flaw in the chain using one of a number of ways.

Types of *tadlīs*

There are two types of *tadlīs* [misleading]: that which relates to the chain [*tadlīs al-isnād*], and that which relates to the teachers [*tadlīs al-shuyūkh*].

First, *tadlīs al-isnād* is that:

1. A narrator narrates from someone he met that which he did not hear from him directly, or;

2. He narrates from a contemporary whom he did not meet while giving the impression that he did hear it from him, by saying "from [*'an*] so-and-so," or saying "so-and-so said," or saying "that [*anna*] so-and-so did such-and-such," or "that so-and-so said such-and-such," and other such expressions that give the impression that the chain is connected, but do not necessarily require this [to be the case].

As for someone narrating from someone else who was not a contemporary, while using a phrase that indicates the chain is connected, then it is not considered to be *tadlīs* according to the correct and well-known opinion. Rather, it is severed [*munqaṭi'*] and called *irsāl ẓāhir* (apparent initial disconnection).

If he declares that he heard it directly, but he did not hear from his teacher, and he did not read the Hadith to him, then this is considered an explicit lie, and he becomes seriously flawed [*majrūḥ*][159] and his narrations are rejected [*mardūd al-riwāya*].

The author alludes to this type of *tadlīs* when he says:

> *First, when the teacher is omitted, yet,*
> *He narrates from him using 'an or an*

The ruling on *tadlīs al-isnād*

This type of *tadlīs* is highly disliked and most scholars consider it to be blameworthy, to the extent that some reject the narrations of anyone who was known to do this even if he clarifies [elsewhere] that he heard from the narrator directly, as al-Nawawī said. Then later he [al-Nawawī] explained that there are some details to the sound position regarding this:

If the *mudallis*[160] uses an ambiguous expression which does not clarify that the Hadith is connected, such as someone saying, "from [*'an*] so-and-so," then it is not accepted and it is given the ruling of being severed [*munqaṭi'*].

---

[159] A term used in *jarḥ wa-ta'dīl* (narrator evaluation) which indicates that his narrations cannot be accepted—Tr.

[160] Someone who engaged in *tadlīs* as described here—Tr.

If, however, he makes clear that it is connected [*muttaṣil*], by saying in some narrations [from the same person], "so-and-so narrated to me," or "I heard so-and-so," or "he narrated to us," or "he informed us," or the like, then it is accepted and can be used as proof as long as he is a reliable [*thiqa*] narrator, because the narration which contains an expression denoting a connected chain indicates that the narrations which contain ambiguous expressions (such as "from so-and-so" and the like) are also connected. This is understood from the words of al-Suyūṭī:

> *If they declare unequivocally that it is connected,*
> *Then the chosen [position] is that it is accepted,*
> *The majority have declared it ṣaḥīḥ*

Therefore it becomes clear that a Hadith from a *mudallis* that is found in the two Ṣaḥīḥ collections or another Ṣaḥīḥ collection with an ambiguous expression, such as 'from' [*'an*], has another narration in which he declares unequivocally that he heard it directly. The narration which contains the ambiguous expression that is interpretable to imply connection is considered to be connected based upon the narration in which direct hearing is expressed clearly. The compiler of the Ṣaḥīḥ collection did not include the narration with the unambiguous expression, as it did not meet his conditions [for other reasons]. Ḥāfiẓ al-Suyūṭī says:

> *That which occurs in the two Ṣaḥīḥ collections,*
> *With the phrase 'from,' is worthy of being regarded as sound*

An example of this is where al-Bukhārī says: "Musaddad narrated to us, saying: 'Yaḥyā narrated to us from Shu'ba, from Qatāda, from Anas ﷺ,' and 'from Ḥusayn al-Mu'allim who said: "Qatāda narrated to us from Anas ﷺ, from the Prophet ﷺ that he said: 'None of you truly believes until he loves for his brother what he loves for himself.'"'" Thus both Shu'ba and Ḥusayn al-Mu'allim narrated from Qatāda, from Anas ﷺ. Qatāda would narrate with *tadlīs*, and the narration in [Ṣaḥīḥ] al-Bukhārī does not explicitly state that he heard it directly from Anas ﷺ. However, he is regarded as having heard it directly because Imam Aḥmad and al-Nasā'ī declared unequivocally that Qatāda had heard this Hadith from Anas ﷺ.

The ruling on *tadlīs al-shuyūkh*

The second type is *tadlīs al-shuyūkh* which is when a narrator calls his teacher by a name, *kunya*,[161] title, tribal or geographical affiliation, or description by which he is not commonly known.

An example of this is Abū Bakr b. Mujāhid al-Muqrī' saying: "'Abdullah b. Abī 'Abdillah told us," by which he intended 'Abdullah b. Abī Dāwūd al-Sijistānī, the author of the *Sunan*.

The ruling regarding this type of *tadlīs* is that it is disliked amongst the scholars of Hadith, since using a name of a teacher by which he is not recognised could lead to him to being considered unknown. A researcher could search for this narrator and not recognise him and it could lead to the teacher [the one from whom the *mudallis* narrates] being disregarded.

The extent to which this type is disliked depends upon the reason the narrator did it. The worst type is when the teacher is weak, and the narrator tries to cover this fact so that he is not viewed as someone who narrates from weak teachers, as did one of those who engaged in *tadlīs* regarding Muḥammad b. al-Sā'ib al-Kalbī, who was weak, such that he used the name 'Ḥammād.'[162] There is no doubt that this is prohibited as it involves deception and treachery.

The reason could be that the teacher is younger in age than the narrator, or slightly older, or significantly older but he died at an old age such that younger students also took Hadith from this teacher.[163]

Another reason could be that it was done to give the impression that the narrator had a large number of teachers, such that he narrates from one teacher in a particular place with a description, and then uses another description on another occasion, all in order to give the impression that the teacher is different in each instance.

---

[161] Such as Abū so-and-so, or Ibn so-and-so, and so on—Tr.

[162] *Sharḥ al-Sakhāwī* (p. 79)

[163] I.e., the narrator who engaged in *tadlīs* did not want to be known to have taken Hadith from those younger than him, or a contemporary, or to have younger students share his teacher—Tr.

INITIALLY DISCONNECTED [*MURSAL*]

وَمُرْسَلٌ مِنْهُ الصَّحَابِيُّ سَقَطْ

From the mursal, the Companion has been omitted

Mursal is a Hadith in which a Successor [*Tābiʿī*] raises a statement, action or tacit approval to the Messenger of Allah ﷺ, regardless of whether he is a junior or senior *Tābiʿī*, on the condition that he didn't hear it directly from the Prophet ﷺ.

A junior Successor is someone whose narrations are primarily from people other than the Companions ﷺ, and a senior Successor is someone whose narrations are primarily from the Companions themselves, as has already been mentioned.

The stipulation that the Successor didn't hear from the Prophet ﷺ directly that which he raised to him ﷺ excludes those who met and heard from the Prophet ﷺ whilst being a disbeliever, and then became Muslim after the passing away of the Prophet ﷺ, and then narrated what they had heard from him ﷺ. This is the case with al-Tanūkhī, the messenger of Heraclius. Despite him being a Successor, his narrations have the ruling of being connected [*muttaṣil*] not *mursal*.

Al-Zarkashī says: "Based on this, the riddle is often posed that a Successor says: 'The Prophet ﷺ said such-and-such yet the narration is supported [*musnad*] and not *mursal*.'"[164]

The *mursal* likewise excludes the narrations of someone who heard from the Prophet ﷺ whilst being a disbeliever, then became Muslim *before* his ﷺ passing away but did not meet him, and then narrated what he heard from him ﷺ.[165]

As for the author's definition of the *mursal* as a Hadith whose chain of narrations makes no mention of a Companion, then there are some critical views on that, because if it were known that the only person missing from the chain of narration was a

---

[164] *Ḥāshiya al-Abyārī*
[165] *Ḥāshiya al-Ajhūrī; Ḥāshiya al-Abyārī*

Companion, then the *mursal* would be universally accepted, and none of the Imams would reject this since a Companion is upright regardless of whether his name is known or not.

For example, Imam al-Shāfiʿī ﷺ said: "Malik informed us from Zayd b. Aslam, from Saʿīd b. al-Musayyib, that the Messenger of Allah ﷺ forbade the sale of meat in exchange for animals."

Mālik narrates in *al-Muwaṭṭaʾ* from ʿAṭāʾ b. Yasār that the Messenger of Allah ﷺ said: "When a servant [of Allah] becomes ill, Allah dispatches two angels and says: 'Find out what he says to his visitors.' If, when they come to him, he praises and exalts Allah, they [his praise and exaltations] are raised to Allah—and He knows best—so He says: 'My servant has the right on Me that if should I take his life, I will admit him into Heaven, and if I cure him, I will exchange his flesh for better flesh and his blood for better blood and I will forgive his wrongdoing.'"

The ruling on the *mursal*

The scholars differed regarding the ruling of the *mursal*, but there are three verdicts which are the most well-known:

The first verdict is that they are absolutely permissible to use, and this is the verdict of Imam Abū Ḥanīfa, Mālik and Aḥmad [b. Ḥanbal], based on the well-known opinion of the latter two, of their followers among the jurists, the scholars of Hadith and legal theory [*uṣūl al-fiqh*]. Their proofs are:

1. The Prophet ﷺ praised the Successors and bore witness to their virtue when he said: "The best generation is my generation, then those who follow them, then those who follow them," as found in the two *Ṣaḥīḥ* collections.

2. The Successor who omitted the name of the Companion either has integrity or not. If not, then his narrations are not to be used as proof because of his lack of integrity, not because the name of the Companion is missing. If he has integrity, it is not conceivable for him to remove the name of the narrator between himself and the Prophet ﷺ unless he

had integrity [in doing so], without any doubt about his integrity. If not, then his actions are deceptive and this impairs his own integrity.[166]

The second verdict is that it is a weak Hadith and cannot be used as proof. This has been cited in *al-Taqrīb* from the majority of scholars of Hadith, as well as many of the jurists and scholars of legal theory. Likewise, Imam Muslim mentioned this position in the introduction to his *Ṣaḥīḥ*, where he says: "In our view and that of the people of Hadith, the *mursal* Hadith is not proof."

They only considered this Hadith to be weak due to circumstances of the missing person being unknown, as he could be a Companion or a Successor. If the latter, it is possible that he may be weak and it is possible that he may be reliable. If the latter, it may be that he heard it from a Companion or from another Successor. Based on the latter, the previous possibility (that the Successor be either reliable or weak) still remains, therefore the number of narrators [Successors from other Successors] could be as much as what is rationally possible without ending, or by detailed investigation [*istiqrā'*] which would lead to six or seven, and this is the greatest number that has been found regarding narrations of Successors from other Successors.

---

[166] If someone asked, what would cause a reliable [*thiqa*] narrator to omit mentioning another reliable narrator, then there are various reasons:

First, he may have heard the Hadith from a number of reliable narrators and thus it was *ṣaḥīḥ* according to him. He therefore omits the narrator relying on it being sound from his teachers, as has been established authentically from Ibrāhīm al-Nakhaʿī that he said: "What I have narrated to you from (using the formula *ʿan*) Ibn Masʿūd ﷺ, I have heard it from more than one person. What I have narrated to you giving a name [of the narrator from Ibn Masʿūd], then it is from whoever I mentioned by name."

Second, he may have forgotten who narrated [the Hadith] to him, but he remembered the wording and therefore narrated it in this way (i.e., omitting the Companion). This is because the norm in his narrating is that he only does so from reliable narrators.

Third, it may be that he did not intend to narrate it but as a reminder, or when issuing a *fatwa*, so he mentions the wording of the Hadith as this is the purpose in this situation, and not the chain of narration. ([Al-Ṣanʿānī] *Tawḍīḥ al-Afkār*, vol. 1, p. 299, cited from Ibn Ḥajar)

The third verdict is that there is some detail, and this is the position of al-Shāfiʿī: a *mursal* Hadith may be used as proof if there is a supporting narration which is narrated in fully connected manner [*musnad*], or by another *mursal* narration, or if it was acted upon by some of the Companions, or the majority of scholars.[167]

The *mursal* of a Companion and its ruling

Everything that has preceded with regard to the *mursal* and the subsequent differences of opinion about its ruling all relate to the *mursal* narration of a Successor. As for the *mursal* of a Companion, it is that which a Companion narrates from the Prophet ﷺ, be it an action or a statement, but then it transpires that he didn't hear from him ﷺ directly, or he was not present due to his youth.

An example of this is the statement of ʿĀʾisha ﷺ, "The first revelation to come to the Prophet ﷺ was true vision experienced during sleep..."[168]

Likewise, the narration of Anas and Ibn ʿAbbās ﷺ regarding the Hadith of the splitting of the moon; neither of them witnessed this. However, the narrations of Ibn Masʿūd, Ḥudhayfa and Jubayr b. Muṭʿim ﷺ [concerning that] are all connected.[169]

Similarly, when a Companion narrates something from the Prophet ﷺ without witnessing it himself due to accepting Islam [at a] later [stage]. For example, he may have accepted Islam towards the end of the life of the Prophet ﷺ, but then narrates an event that occurred at the beginning of prophecy.

The majority consider the *mursal* of a Companion to be connected and sound, and that they can be used as proof,[170] since most of their narrations are from other Companions, all of whom

---

[167] As mentioned by al-Nawawī in the introduction to his commentary on *Ṣaḥīḥ Muslim*. The full conditions of al-Shāfiʿī ﷺ for accepting a *mursal* Hadith can be found in his book *al-Risāla*.

[168] [Al-Nawawī's] Commentary to the introduction of *Ṣaḥīḥ Muslim* (p. 30)

[Revelation began during the Prophet's ﷺ marriage to Lady Khadīja ﷺ and therefore was not witnessed by Lady ʿĀʾisha ﷺ—Tr.]

[169] [Ibn Ḥajar] *Fatḥ al-Bārī* (vol. 7, p. 139)

[170] There are many examples of this in the two *Ṣaḥīḥ* collections.

have integrity. That they are not named does not harm their status as narrators.

As for their narrations from people other than the Companions, then this is rare. If they narrated them, they clarified it. Furthermore, the majority of the Companions' narrations from Successors are not raised to the Prophet ﷺ [*marfū'*], but are rather Judaeo-Christian traditions [*Isrā'īliyyāt*], or stories, or attributions being halted at Companions [*mawqūfāt*].[171]

A principle

If there is a contradiction between a connected narration and a *mursal* narration, the position of the majority of the scholars of Hadith, jurists and legal theorists is to prefer the connected [*muttaṣil*] narration to the *mursal* narration, regardless of whether there are many narrators or just one, because the connected narration is considered to be an addition,[172] which is accepted from an accurate, reliable narrator.

An example of this is the Hadith, "There is no marriage without a guardian." Isrā'īl and a number of others narrate this from Abū Isḥāq al-Sabī'ī, from Abū Burda, from Abū Mūsā ﷺ, from the Prophet ﷺ. It is also narrated by al-Thawrī and Shu'ba, from Abū Isḥāq, from Abū Burda, from the Prophet ﷺ in a *mursal* form, as it excludes the mention of Abū Mūsā ﷺ.

Al-Bukhārī was asked about this Hadith and judged in favour of those who viewed it as connected, saying: "The addition from a reliable narrator is accepted."

A benefit

It is mentioned [by Ibn Ḥajar] in *Sharḥ al-Nukhba*[173] that the majority of Hadith scholars differentiated between the initially disconnected [*mursal*] and severed [*munqaṭi'*]. They called that which a Successor attributed to the Prophet ﷺ *mursal*, and that which has a missing narrator before a Companion *munqaṭi'*, in the manner described in the respective chapters.

---

[171] *Sharḥ al-Sakhāwī* (p. 62); [Al-Suyūṭī] *al-Tadrīb* (p. 126)
[172] There is a separate chapter in the books of Hadith regarding additions to Hadith that come from reliable narrators [*ziyāda al-thiqa*]—Tr.
[173] [Ibn Ḥajar] *Sharḥ al-Nukhba*; [Al-'Adawī] *Ḥāshiya Laqṭ al-Durar* (p. 38)

This differentiation is related to the usage of the terms *mursal* and *munqaṭi'* when expressed as nouns. As for when they are used as verbs derived from *irsāl* and *inqiṭā'*, then the verb of *irsāl* is used to denote both the *mursal* and *munqaṭi'*. So they say, "So-and-so narrated the Hadith by *irsāl* [*arsala al-ḥadīth fulān*]," regardless of whether the Hadith is *mursal* or *munqaṭi'*. However, they do not say, "*qaṭa'a fulān*," since one may mistakenly think the Hadith is cut-off [*maqṭū'*] whilst the intention is that it is *munqaṭi'*.

SUSPENDED [*MU'ALLAQ*]

A *mu'allaq* Hadith has a chain of narration which omits one or more narrators consecutively from the beginning of the chain, even if that be the entire chain. It is attributed to whoever is omitted in the chain above the narrator.

An example of where only one narrator is omitted is where al-Bukhārī says: "Malik narrated from al-Zuhrī, from Abū Salama, from Abū Hurayra ﷺ, from the Prophet ﷺ: 'Do not distinguish in terms of merit amongst the Prophets...,'" because someone is [omitted] between al-Bukhārī and Mālik.

An example in which all the narrators are omitted except for the Companion is when al-Bukhārī says: "...And 'Ā'isha ﷺ said: 'The Prophet ﷺ would remember Allah in every state.'"

An example in which all the narrators are omitted except for the Companion is when al-Bukhārī says: "...And the delegation of 'Abd al-Qays said to the Prophet ﷺ: 'Command us with several actions which if we do them, by these we would enter Paradise...'"

The *mu'allaq* includes the *marfū'*, as previously mentioned, as well as the *mawqūf* and *maqṭū'*.

This is like what is said by al-Bukhārī, [that] "'Ā'isha ﷺ said: 'The women of the Anṣār are blessed women: their modesty did not prevent them from seeking understanding of the religion.'"

Similarly, what is said by al-Bukhārī, [that] "Mujāhid said: 'Neither the shy nor the arrogant will learn knowledge.'"

The ruling on the *mu'allaq*

The ruling on the *mu'allaq* Hadith is that it is weak due to our lack of knowledge of the status of the narrator or narrators omitted from the chain [*isnād*]. An exception to this are the *mu'allaq* Hadith contained in collections in which soundness (being *ṣaḥīḥ*) is held to, such as *Ṣaḥīḥ al-Bukhārī* and *Ṣaḥīḥ Muslim*. This occurs more commonly in *Ṣaḥīḥ al-Bukhārī*, and such Hadith in the two of them have special rulings.

Al-Nawawī said:

> [Those Hadith in *Ṣaḥīḥ al-Bukhārī*] which use a phrase that indicates decisiveness [*ṣīgha al-jazm*], such as "So-and-so said," or "did," or "ordered," or "narrated," or "mentioned," then it has the ruling of being authentically from the one to whom it (i.e., that Hadith) is attributed. However, those which do not use such decisive expressions, such as "it is narrated," or "it is mentioned," or "it is cited," or "it is said," or "it was narrated from," or "it was mentioned," or "it was cited from so-and-so,"[174] then it does not have the ruling of being authentically transmitted from the one to whom it is attributed.

This means that it could either be weak or sound, and those which may be weak are not seriously weak, because of him [al-Bukhārī] including them in a book characterised by being *Ṣaḥīḥ*.

This is the summary ruling for the *mu'allaq* Hadith found in the two *Ṣaḥīḥ* books. As for the details, they are clarified in the larger works on the topic.[175]

---

[174] The former expressions are given in the active voice, whereas the latter are expressed in the passive voice, which is an indication of weakness—Tr.

[175] See the introduction [of Ibn Ḥajar] to *Fatḥ al-Bārī* and [of al-Nawawī] to *Sharḥ Ṣaḥīḥ Muslim*.

Transmitted Using 'From' [Mu'an'an]

$$\text{مُعَنْعَنٌ كَعَنْ سَعِيدٍ عَنْ كَرَمْ}$$

Mu'an'an is for example, "from Sa'īd, from Karam"

The *mu'an'an* is a Hadith in whose chain of narration there is mention of "from ['an][176] so-and-so, from so-and-so," without clarifying if the Hadith was transmitted by direct narration [taḥdīth], informing [ikhbār] or direct audition [samā']. *Mu'an'an* describes the chain of narration.

Their saying, "a *mu'an'an* Hadith" means its chain is *mu'an'an*.

The ruling on the *mu'an'an*

The scholars have differed regarding the ruling on the *mu'an'an*—is it considered to be connected [muttaṣil] or severed [munqaṭi']? The majority of Hadith scholars, jurists and scholars of legal theory hold the view that it is considered to be connected if two conditions are met:

1.   The narrator was not a *mudallis*[177]
2.   Confirmation that the narrator who narrates in a *mu'an'an* form met the one from whom he narrates, in accordance with the school of al-Bukhārī and his teacher, 'Alī b. al-Madīnī, and others.[178] Or, if it is established that both narrators lived during the same era with the possibility that they met, even if there is no confirmation [thereof], and even if it is not reliably

---

[176] With an *'ayn* as opposed to a *hamza*—Tr.

[177] See the chapter on the *mudallas* [p. 106-109] to understand this condition—Tr.

[178] Al-Sakhāwī said: "Those who stated clearly that the meeting of two narrators must be confirmed include 'Alī al-Madīnī and al-Bukhārī, both of whom made it a condition for a Hadith to be *ṣaḥīḥ*, despite those who claim that al-Bukhārī only restricted himself to this condition in his *Ṣaḥīḥ*. Similarly, al-Nawawī also attributed the condition of a meeting to the verifying scholars [muḥaqqiqīn]. Rather, the words of al-Shāfi'ī imply this, as our teacher [Ibn Ḥajar] says. Likewise, this is implied in the commentary of *al-Risāla* by al-Ṣayrafī." (*Fatḥ al-Mughīth*, p. 66)

established that they met or spoke to each other, and this is according to Imam Muslim.[179] Based on this, the *mu'an'an* Hadith which are found in the two *Ṣaḥīḥ* collections have the ruling of being connected, since they meet the conditions of each author [al-Bukhārī and Muslim]. They have been declared as being narrated directly, or that they were heard, in numerous chains of narrations which are found in other *Mustakhraj*[180] collections related to the two *Ṣaḥīḥ* collections.

Transmitted using 'that' [Mu'an'an]

The author, may Allah have mercy upon him, does not mention this category of Hadith nor its ruling.

It is a Hadith whose chain of narration contains the phrase "So-and-so narrated to us that [*anna*] so-and-so."

The majority of scholars held the opinion that the ruling on narration "from [*'an*] so-and-so," or "that [*an*] so-and-so [said],"[181] is the same. The point is not the words but rather whether there was a meeting between the narrators, or whether they were contemporaries with the possibility that they met, and that the chain be free of *tadlīs* (misleading). Ḥāfiẓ al-'Irāqī said:

> *I say: The correct position is that whoever understands:*
> *That which he narrated with the preceding condition,*
>
> *Is judged to be connected, whether it was narrated,*
> *With 'he said,' or 'from,' or 'that,' since all are equal*

---

[179] Al-Sakhāwī said in his *Sharḥ*: "Muslim agrees with the body [*jamā'a*] [of people of knowledge] that when it is known that it is impossible for the Successor to have met that Companion, one judges this to be disconnected. Thus, his being content with their being contemporaries is only in the case where it is possible that they met." (p. 68)

[180] *Mustakhraj* is a collection in which the author relates the same Hadith contained in another collection of Hadith, but brings different chains of narration to support those found in the original—Tr.

[181] *Mu'an'an*—i.e., "from [*'an*] so-and-so from so-and-so," is with *'ayn*, whereas *mu'an'an*—i.e., "he narrated *that* [*an*] so-and-so...," is with *hamza* —Ed.

CHAPTER EIGHT
UNCLEAR, UNKNOWN, ANOMALOUS AND INVERTED

UNCLEAR [MUBHAM]

وَمُبْهَمٌ مَا فِيهِ رَاوٍ لَمْ يُسَمّ

Mubham is that in which a narrator hasn't been named

The *mubham* is the Hadith in whose chain of narration or wording [*matn*] there is a man or a woman who are not named, rather they are referred to by a general term.

The *mubham* Hadith is therefore of two types:

First, the *mubham* element is in the Hadith's chain of narration such that some of the narrators are not named, but are only referred to by a general term.

An example of this is that which Abū Dāwūd narrated by way of Ḥajjāj b. Furāfiṣa, from a man, from Abū Salama, from Abū Hurayra ﷺ, from the Prophet ﷺ that he said: "The believer is simple and generous..." The unnamed man in the chain is Yaḥyā b. Abū Kathīr, as is clarified by another narration in [*Sunan*] Abū Dāwūd.

Second, the *mubham* element is in the wording of the Hadith, such that the Companion, or someone after him, says, "A man asked the Prophet ﷺ..." and so on.

An example of this is narrated by the two Shaykhs [al-Bukhārī and Muslim] from the Hadith of ʿĀ'isha ﷺ that, "A woman[182] asked the Prophet ﷺ about bathing following menses, so he told her how to take a bath, saying: 'Take a piece of cloth scented with musk and purify yourself with it.' She said: 'How do I clean myself with it?' He ﷺ said: '*Subḥān Allah!* Purify yourself with it!' I then pulled her close and said to her: 'Wipe off any traces of blood with it.'"

---

[182] The woman was Asmā bint Shakal ﷺ as mentioned in the narration of Muslim and others.

Types of *mubham*

There are many types of *mubham* Hadith, some of which are more unclear than others. For example, they may mention: a man, a woman, a son, daughter, father, brother, sister, brother's son, sister's son, paternal uncle or aunt, maternal uncle or aunt, and the like.

The ruling on the *mubham*

As has been mentioned, there are two types:

The first is that in which the *mubham* element is in the wording of the Hadith, and the second is when it occurs in the chain of narration. There is no disagreement regarding the first type and it being valid to use as proof, as long as the conditions for its acceptance are met and are present therein.

As for the second type, if the *mubham* person was one of the Companions ﷺ, for example that a reliable Successor says, "from a man from amongst the Companions," or the like, then it is accepted according to the majority, given that all the Companions had integrity [*'udūl*] ﷺ. If, however, the unnamed individual is not a Companion, for example a Successor or someone after him, then the Hadith cannot be used as proof due to the uncertainty regarding his status. Since his name is not known, then how can his integrity be known? As has been mentioned already, among the conditions for accepting a Hadith is the establishment of the narrator's integrity [*'adāla*] and accuracy [*dabt*].[183] If this uncertainty is removed, and the person becomes known due to another narration, and it transpires that he is reliable, then the Hadith becomes acceptable to use as proof, as was the case in the previously mentioned Hadith, "The believer is simple and generous."

For that reason, scholars have sought to ascertain which narrators are unnamed in chains of narration, and they have compiled many books on the topic.

---

[183] See the conditions for *ṣaḥīḥ* and *ḥasan* Hadith [p. 50-54].

UNKNOWN [*MAJĀHĪL*]

There are three types of *majāhīl* [sing. *majhūl*]:

1. *majhūl al-ʿayn*: an unknown person
2. *majhūl al-ḥāl ẓāhiran wa-bāṭinan*: someone whose state, both inwardly and outwardly, is unknown
3. *majhūl al-ḥāl bāṭinan lā ẓāhiran*: someone whose inward state is unknown, but [his] outward [is] not [unknown]

The first type is someone from whom only one person narrates while naming him specifically. The ruling is that his narrations are rejected according to the majority of scholars.[184]

A minimum number of two people with integrity must narrate from an individual in order to remove the status of being *majhūl al-ʿayn*. [Al-Nawawī] says in *al-Taqrīb*: "If two people with integrity narrate from an individual and name him, he is no longer *majhūl al-ʿayn*." However, the mere fact that two people with integrity narrate from him does not establish his integrity, but rather by someone declaring him to have integrity.

The second type is someone whose state, inwardly and outwardly, is unknown; that is to say, his integrity, or lack thereof of, and that he is known from whom two narrators with integrity who narrate from him. Such a person's narrations are not accepted according to the majority of scholars.[185]

The third type is someone whose inward state is not known—and he is also known as *mastūr*, who outwardly has integrity but whose inward state remains unclear.[186] There is a difference of opinion regarding this person amongst the people of knowledge: some accept him and others reject him, the full details of which are explained in the books of legal theory.[187]

---

[184] See the commentaries on *Alfiyya al-ʿIrāqī* [by al-Sakhāwī, Zakariyyā al-Anṣārī and al-Suyūṭī] which all contain comprehensive details.

[185] [Al-Nawawī] *Al-Taqrīb* and its commentary [*al-Tadrīb* by al-Suyūṭī]; [Zakariyyā al-Anṣārī] *Fatḥ al-Bāqī*

[186] The meaning of 'inward integrity' [*al-ʿadāla al-bāṭina*] is that which his state is in reality—this goes back to those who evaluate narrators—while 'outward integrity' [*al-ʿadāla al-ẓāhira*] refers to what is known from one's outward state. (*Ḥāshiya al-Qārī*, p. 154)

[187] *Ḥāshiya al-Qārī* (p. 155)

ANOMALOUS [*SHĀDH*] AND ITS OPPOSITE: PRESERVED [*MAḤFŪẒ*]

وَمَا يُخَالِفْ ثِقَةٌ بِهِ الْـمَلاَ فَالشَّاذُّ

When a reliable narrator contradicts a group, it is shādh

A *shādh* Hadith is when a reliable person narrates a Hadith which contradicts those of a higher rank—whether in its wording or in its chain, and whether this is due to the latter [narrator's] greater accuracy or because there are a greater number.[188]

The preponderant narration, which is that of a larger group or a more reliable narrator, is called *maḥfūẓ*; the subordinate narration, of the contradictory reliable narrator, is called *shādh*.

An example of a Hadith which is *shādh* due to a defect is that which is narrated by al-Tirmidhī, al-Nasāʾī and Ibn Mājah by way of Ibn ʿUyayna, from ʿAmr b. Dīnār, from ʿAwsaja (the freedman of Ibn ʿAbbās), from Ibn ʿAbbās 🙵, that a man passed away in the time of the Messenger of Allah 🙵 and left no inheritor except a freedman, so the Prophet 🙵 paid the inheritance to him.

Ibn Jurayj and others supported [*tābaʿa*] the narration of Ibn ʿUyayna, but Ḥammād b. Zayd differed from them, for he narrated it from ʿAmr b. Dīnār, from ʿAwsaja, but did not mention Ibn ʿAbbās 🙵, rather he narrated it in a *mursal* form.

Based on this, it becomes clear that Ḥammād was alone in narrating it in a *mursal* form. He contradicted the narrations of Ibn ʿUyayna, Ibn Jurayj and others, all of whose narrations are connected [as opposed to being *mursal*]. Therefore, the narration of Ḥammād is *shādh* and the narration of Ibn ʿUyayna is *maḥfūẓ*, despite both Ḥammād and Ibn ʿUyayna being reliable.

---

[188] This is the definition which the majority of scholars have settled upon, as well as al-Shāfiʿī. The definition of the [poem's] author, "*When a reliable narrator contradicts a group,*" includes contradicting someone who is more reliable. The narrations of a group of narrators are given preference because they are collectively more accurate and precise than one narrator alone. Similarly, a more reliable individual is given preference over someone who is reliable [as well].

An example of a Hadith which is *shādh* because of an addition in the wording of the Hadith is narrated by Muslim from Nubaysha al-Hudhalī who said: "The Prophet ﷺ said: 'The days of *tashrīq* [at the end of *hajj*] are days of eating and drinking.'"

This Hadith has been narrated in this way in all of its various chains. However, Mūsā b. ʿUlayy—the diminutive [of ʿAlī]—Ibn Rabāḥ narrated it from his father, from ʿUqba b. ʿĀmir ﷺ, with the addition, "the Day of ʿArafa." The narration of Mūsā is therefore *shādh* as he contradicts numerous other narrators due to his addition.[189]

Another Hadith from this category is the Hadith about the delegation of ʿAbd al-Qays, that the Prophet ﷺ commanded them to do four things and forbade them to do four things. He ordered them to believe in Allah alone. He ﷺ said: "Do you know what belief in Allah alone means?" They said: "Allah and His Messenger know best." He ﷺ said: "Bearing witness that there is no god but Allah and that Muhammad is His Messenger, establishing the prayer, paying *zakāt*, fasting the month of Ramadan, and paying a fifth from the spoils of war..."

Ḥāfiẓ Ibn Ḥajar and ʿAllāma al-ʿAynī both mention in their commentaries that both al-Bukhārī and Muslim narrated this Hadith with its chain [*isnād*], as well as those who compiled collections based on theirs [*mustakhraj*], as well as al-Nasāʾī and Ibn Khuzayma, but none of them mentioned *hajj*. Both of them said that the narration of al-Bayhaqī in *al-Sunan al-Kubra* which mentions the words, "and to perform the pilgrimage in the House," but without mention of a number, is *shādh*.[190]

---

[189] This is mentioned in all the commentaries on *Alfiyya al-ʿIrāqī*, al-Qasṭallānī's introduction [to *Minhāj al-Ibtihāj*], and elsewhere. Al-Sakhāwī says in his commentary: "Despite this, Ibn Khuzayma, Ibn Ḥibbān and al-Ḥākim declared the narration of Mūsā to be *ṣaḥīḥ*, saying that it is *ṣaḥīḥ* according to the conditions of Muslim. Al-Tirmidhī said: 'The Hadith is *ḥasan ṣaḥīḥ*, and it is as if this is because the additional wording is from a reliable narrator and does not contradict [the other narration] since it could be interpreted to apply to those present at ʿArafa.'" Al-Qasṭallānī also mentions this in his introduction.

[190] Ibn Ḥajar then mentions that which comes in a narration in the *Musnad* of Imam Aḥmad [b. Ḥanbal], in which the word '*hajj*' is mentioned. He responded to the opinion that if it is to be reckoned with,

What is preserved [*maḥfūẓ*] is that which is narrated by a more reliable group or person, which contradicts the narration of someone who is [himself] reliable, but with an addition or an omission, in either the wording of the Hadith, or the chain of narration.

The ruling on the *shādh* Hadith is that it is rejected and cannot be used as proof, rather what suffices as proof is its contrary, namely that which is *maḥfūẓ*.

INVERTED [*MAQLŪB*]

وَالْمَقْلُوبُ قِسْمَانِ تَلاَ

إِبْـدَالُ رَاوٍ مَـا بِـرَاوٍ قِـسْمُ   وَقَلْبُ إِسْنَادٍ لِتْـنٍ قِـسْمُ

There are two types of maqlūb, as follows:

One type is substituting one narrator for another,
And the other type is juxtaposing a chain onto the wording

The *maqlūb* Hadith is when a narrator has been substituted for another narrator who is his contemporary. Or, it may be when a chain of narration has been taken from one Hadith and appended to another Hadith. It may also be when an original, well-known wording [of a Hadith], has been substituted for one which is not well-known—regardless of whether this was intentional or due to forgetfulness. Therefore, there are two types of *maqlūb*: those in which the change occurs in the chain of the Hadith, and [those in which it occurs] in the wording [of the Hadith]. When the change occurs in the chain, there are, again, two types:

The first type is when the name of the narrator has been reversed, such as a narrator called Kaʿb b. Murra, for example, being called Murra b. Kaʿb, regardless of whether this is intentional or not.

---

the mention of 'hajj' is *maḥfūẓ*, not *shādh*. (*Fatḥ al-Bārī*, vol. 1, p. 124; [al-ʿAynī] *ʿUmda al-Qārī*, vol. 1, p. 362)

The second type is when a Hadith is well-known to be narrated by a certain narrator, or well-known to have been transmitted through a particular chain, and this has been substituted for something similar from a contemporary narrator, whether this change is intentional or not.

An example of it being intentional, as mentioned by al-ʿIrāqī, is that which is narrated by Ḥammād b. ʿAmr al-Naṣībī from al-Aʿmash, from Abū Ṣāliḥ, from Abū Hurayra ﷺ, raising it to the Prophet ﷺ [marfūʿan], "If you meet the idolaters in the streets, do not initiate the greetings of peace and force them to the narrowest part of it."

A part of the chain of this Hadith is maqlūb. Ḥammād b. ʿAmr al-Naṣībī—an abandoned narrator [matrūk]—changed it to being from al-Aʿmash, making him the sole narrator, whereas it is well-known to be narrated from Suhayl b. Abī Ṣāliḥ, from his father, from Abū Hurayra ﷺ, as found in [Ṣaḥīḥ] Muslim. It has not been narrated by al-Aʿmash.

This is why the scholars of Hadith dislike pursuing the gharīb Hadith, as they are rarely sound.

An example of maqlūb in the chain due to forgetfulness[191] is that which is narrated by Jarīr b. Ḥāzim from Thābit al-Bunānī, from Anas ﷺ who said: "The Prophet ﷺ said: 'When the call for prayer [iqāma] is given, do not stand until you see me.'"

In this Hadith, the chain was mistakenly changed to Jarīr b. Ḥāzim, whereas the well-known version is from Yaḥyā b. Abī Kathīr, from ʿAbdullah b. Abī Qatāda, from his father, from the Prophet ﷺ, as found in [Ṣaḥīḥ] Muslim and [Sunan] al-Nasāʾī.

An example of where the entire chain was changed intentionally is when the people of Baghdād tested Imam al-Bukhārī, may Allah have mercy upon him, by changing one hundred Hadith, and he narrated them with their correct chains of narration.[192]

---

[191] Ḥāshiya al-Abyārī

[192] This was when he entered Baghdad, and the people of Hadith had heard about him. They gathered together and intentionally interchanged the chains and wordings of one hundred Hadith, giving the wording of one Hadith with the chain of another. They gave them to ten scholars of Hadith, to each scholar ten Hadith, and told them to put them before al-Bukhārī when they attended the assembly.

Secondly, the change may occur in the wording, such that [the narrator] puts a word or several words in a place different from that of well-known narrations, whether intentionally or due to forgetfulness.

An example of this is the Hadith of Abū Hurayra ﷺ as found in [*Ṣaḥīḥ*] Muslim, which is the Hadith about the seven whom Allah will grant the shade of His throne on the Day of Rising, and contains [the following], "...a man who gives voluntary charity and hides his act such that his *right* hand does not know what his *left* hand gives."

In this version, one of the narrators mistakenly changed a part of the Hadith. It should in fact be, "...such that his *left* hand does not know what his *right* hand gives," as found in the two *Ṣaḥīḥ* collections.

The ruling on the *maqlūb*

If the change occurs due to forgetfulness, there is no blame since this was the result of an unintentional mistake. However, if this occurs frequently, it renders the narrator weak due to his inaccuracy.

When the gathering had settled, one of the ten men hastened to ask al-Bukhārī about one of the Hadith [that had been narrated to him]. Al-Bukhārī replied: "I don't know it." So they asked him about another Hadith, to which he replied that he did not know it. The man continued in this fashion until he had asked him about ten Hadith. Then, a second person hurried to ask him about his ten, and so on until they had completed all of the hundred inverted [*maqlūb*] Hadith, with al-Bukhārī replying each time: "I don't know it."

Then he turned to the first man and said: "As for the first Hadith you narrated, then the correct chain is such-and-such and the correct wording is such-and-such. As for the second Hadith you narrated, it is thus...," until he completed all ten in this fashion, matching the correct wordings of the Hadith to their chains and the correct chains to their wordings. Thus, people bore witness to his memory and they humbled themselves before his merit. May Allah benefit us by him, *āmīn*!

If the change was made intentionally, then the ruling differs according to the reason behind it: if it was done to confuse the narrator [*ighrāb*], as mentioned previously, this is not permitted and is forbidden. If, however, it is done as a test, then many scholars of Hadith did this, for example the scholars of Baghdad to al-Bukhārī. This event has been used as a proof that it is permissible to do for the purpose of testing.

However, Ḥāfiẓ Ibn Ḥajar said: "A condition of it being permissible is that it is not done continuously, rather it should stop when the need ceases to exist." Al-ʿIrāqī said: "Regarding the permissibility of such an act, there are some views, since if this is done by the people of Hadith, it does not remain a Hadith."[193]

Ḥaramī rebuked Shuʿba when he made Hadith *maqlūb* [in order to test] Abān b. Abī ʿAyyāsh and said: "What a dreadful thing he [Shuʿba] did!"

There are numerous reasons for someone intentionally making a Hadith *maqlūb*, the most important of which we shall mention:

A narrator may desire to make himself the sole narrator of an otherwise well-known Hadith, to give people the impression that he is the only narrator through this chain, and therefore changes the Hadith. This act is called 'theft' by the scholars of Hadith and someone guilty of doing so is called a 'thief.'

A narrator may wish to examine the state of a Hadith scholar and determine whether he is a master [*ḥāfiẓ*] of Hadith or not, and whether or not he is aware of the effect of making the Hadith *maqlūb*. If it transpires that he is proficient and cognisant and a master of Hadith, then he proceeds to narrate Hadith from him. If, however, it transpires that he is heedless and ignorant, he disregards him. Examples of this type are what occurred with the people of Baghdad and al-Bukhārī, and with the students of Muḥammad b. ʿAjlān.[194]

---

[193] Al-Ajhūrī said that this means that it is not permissible for this Hadith with a disordered chain to become an independent Hadith.

[194] Ibn Ḥajar related this from Saʿīd al-Qaṭṭān who said: "I entered Kufa where Muḥammad b. ʿAjlān was to be found. Malīḥ b. al-Jarrāḥ, the student of Hadith, was also there, and Wakīʿ, Ḥafṣ b. Ghiyāth and Yūsuf b. Khālid al-Samtī.

It may be a mistake by the narrator and [due to] his forgetfulness, as we saw previously in some of the examples.

The ruling of the *maqlūb* Hadith is that it must be referred back to its original, affirmed [*thābit*] version, and this affirmed version is the one to be acted upon.

"We would all go to Muḥammad b. ʿAjlān. Yūsuf al-Samtī said: 'Shall we invert [*naqlib*] his Hadith in order to test his proficiency?' They did so, attributing that which was from Saʿīd to his [Muḥammad b. ʿAjlān's] father, and that which was from his father to Saʿīd.

"Yaḥyā said: 'I said to them: "I don't see this as being permitted."' Then they went to him [Muḥammad b. ʿAjlān] and gave him a volume [of Hadith]. He perused it and upon reaching the end of the book, the Shaykh realised [what happened] and said: 'Repeat it,' and he repeated [the Hadith] to him. He [Muḥammad b. ʿAjlān] then said: 'That which is from my father is [in reality] from Saʿīd, and that which is from Saʿīd is [in reality] from my father.' He then turned to Yūsuf and said: 'If you were intending to disgrace me and find fault with me, then may Allah strip you of Islam,' and to Ḥafṣ he said: 'May Allah test you regarding your hands,' and he said to Malīḥ: 'May Allah bring about no benefit through your knowledge.'

"Yaḥyā said: 'Malīḥ died and no-one had benefitted from his knowledge. Ḥafṣ was given the tribulation of paralysis in his hands and in his religion by being made a judge. By the time Yūsuf died, he had been accused of heresy.'"

Ḥāfiẓ al-Sakhāwī transmitted this story in his commentary (p. 17), from the book *al-Muḥaddith al-Fāṣil* by al-Rāmahurmuzī.

CHAPTER NINE
INVESTIGATION [*I'TIBĀR*] AND ITS OUTCOMES

I'TIBĀR IS TO RESEARCH THE CHAINS of a Hadith using *jawāmi'* [sing. *jāmi'*], *masānīd* [sing. *musnad*] and *ajzā'* [sing. *juz'*][195] in order to establish whether a Hadith has supporting narrations [*shāhid* or *mutābi'*] or whether it is solitarily narrated [*fard*].

SUPPORTIVE [*MUTĀBA'A*]

A *mutābi'* is person who narrates a Hadith in which he supports another narration from his teacher or his teacher's teacher, or someone further up the chain of the narration, up to the end of the chain, and regardless of whether this Hadith shares with it in wording or meaning.

If the supporting Hadith comes from the teacher of the narrator, it is considered to be complete [*tāmm*], and if it is from someone above him [meaning later on in the chain], it is deficient [*nāqiṣa* or *qāṣira*].

This is called *mutāba' 'alayhi*, the narrator is called the *mutābi'* and the narration is called *mutāba'a*.

An example of *mutāba'a* is narrated by al-Tirmidhī from Muḥammad b. 'Amr, from Abū Salama, from Abū Hurayra ﷺ, raising it to the Prophet ﷺ [*marfū'an*], "Had I not feared that I should cause difficulty for my people, I would have ordered them to use the tooth-stick with every prayer."

This narration of Muḥammad b. 'Amr is also narrated by a number of others. They however narrate this Hadith from al-A'raj, from Abū Hurayra ﷺ, as reported in the two *Ṣaḥīḥ* collections, and the wording is the same.

---

[195] See p. 31-33 in the chapter on *dirāya* for information on the types of Hadith collections—Tr.

Corroboration [*Shāhid*]

This is a Hadith narrated by an individual that is in accordance with the narration of another individual with regard to its meaning, or both the wording and meaning although from a different Companion.[196]

An example of *shāhid* is that which is narrated by al-Tirmidhī by way of Hushaym, from Yazīd b. Abū Ziyād, from ʿAbd al-Raḥmān b. Abī Laylā, from al-Barrāʾ b. ʿĀzib ⬧, raising it to the Prophet ⬧ [*marfūʿan*], "It is a right upon the Muslims that they should perform the ritual bath on Friday."

Abū Yaḥyā al-Taymī supports the narration of Hushaym in this Hadith, narrating it [as a *Tābiʿī*] from Yazīd, from ʿAbd al-Raḥmān b. Abī Laylā, from al-Barrāʾ b. ʿĀzib ⬧, raising it to the Prophet ⬧ [*marfūʿan*].

It has a *shāhid* narration from Abū Saʿīd ⬧ in the two *Ṣaḥīḥ* collections that the Prophet ⬧ said: "The ritual bath on Friday is compulsory for every mature person."

Solitary [*Fard*]

أَوْ جَمْعٍ او قَصْرٍ عَلَـى رِوَايَةٍ   وَالْـفَرْدُ مَا قَيَّـدْتَهُ بِـثِقَـةٍ

Fard is to restrict to a reliable narrator,
Region or a particular narrator

There are two types of *fard*:[197] *muṭlaq* and *muqayyad*.

---

[196] [Ibn Ḥajar] says in *Sharḥ al-Nukhba*, after defining the *tābiʿ* and *shāhid* similarly to how we have above: "Some specified the *mutābaʿa* to relate to the wording, regardless of whether it is from the same Companion or not, and the *shāhid* to relate to the meaning, likewise (regardless of whether it is from the same Companion or not.

...(He said:) The term *mutābaʿa* can be used for the *shāhid* and vice versa. The matter is simple in that each one has the effect of strengthening [another narration]." (p. 57)

[197] *Fard* (solitary) is not to be confused with *farḍ* (obligatory)—Ed.

Fard muṭlaq is a Hadith which is narrated by just one narrator out of all the narrators, whether he is reliable or otherwise.[198]

As Ibn al-Ṣalāḥ mentioned, the ruling on the *fard muṭlaq* is that if the narrator who alone narrates it is someone who does not contradict other narrators, and is completely accurate [*ḍabṭ tāmm*], then his solitary narration is *ṣaḥīḥ* and is acceptable to use as proof.

An example of this is the Hadith which prohibits the sale and gifting of clientage [*walā'*]. The eminent Successor [*Tābi'ī*] 'Abdullah b. Dīnār alone narrates this from Ibn 'Umar ﷺ.

If a narrator is close to having complete accuracy, then his solitary narrations are *ḥasan* and acceptable. An example of this is the Hadith of Isrā'īl from Yūsuf b. Abī Burda, from his father from 'Ā'isha ﷺ who said: "The Prophet ﷺ would say: '[I seek] Your forgiveness' on exiting out of the bathroom." Al-Tirmidhī said: "It is *ḥasan gharīb* (fair but unusual)—we do not know this Hadith except from Isrā'īl, from Yūsuf b. Abī Burda."

If a narrator is far from being completely accurate, then his narrations are weak and rejected. An example of this is the Hadith of Abū Zukayr from Hishām b. 'Urwa, from his father, from 'Ā'isha ﷺ, raising it to the Prophet ﷺ [*marfū'an*], "Eat fresh dates with dried dates, for if the son of Adam does so, the Devil becomes angry." Al-Nasā'ī said: "Abū Zukayr alone narrated this Hadith, and he does not reach the level required to have his solitary narrations accepted. On the contrary the people declare him a weak narrator."

If he is a reliable narrator who contradicts someone who is of a higher rank, then his narration is also anomalous [*shādh*] and rejected.[199]

Fard muqayyad, which is also called *fard nisbī*, is a Hadith which is solitarily narrated with regard to a particular quality, and is of various types:

---

[198] See *Fatḥ al-Mughīth* of al-Sakhāwī and the introduction of al-Qasṭallānī [to *Minhāj al-Ibtihāj*].

[199] *Ḥāshiya al-Abyārī* (p. 54). He mentions a beneficial point from Ibn Daqīq al-'Īd, "If it is said that so-and-so alone narrates this Hadith from so-and-so, it is possible that it is *fard muṭlaq*, or it may be that he alone narrated it from this individual specifically, but that it is also narrated from someone else."

First, that which is specific to a reliable narrator, such as their saying, "No reliable person narrates it except so-and-so," such as the Hadith, "On the [Day of 'Īd] al-Aḍḥā and al-Fiṭr, he ﷺ would recite [Sūra] Qāf and ﴾Aqtarabat al-sā'a (The Hour has come near)﴿[200] [Sūra al-Qamar]." No other reliable narrator except Ḍamra b. Sa'īd al-Māzinī narrates this Hadith. He alone narrated it from 'Ubaydullah b. 'Abdullah, from Abū Wāqid al-Laythī, from the Prophet ﷺ, as narrated by Muslim and the authors of the Sunan.[201]

Other narrators who are not reliable narrate it, such as Ibn Lahī'a who is weak according to the majority of scholars due to his confusion after his books were burnt, for he narrated it from Khālid b. Yazīd, from al-Zuhrī, from 'Urwa, from 'Ā'isha ﵂.

Second, that which is restricted to a specific region, for example Mecca, Medina or Basra, such as their saying, "No-one except the people of Basra narrate this Hadith," or "The people of Egypt alone narrated this," meaning a number of them.

An example of this is narrated by Abū Dāwūd[202] from Abū Dāwūd al-Ṭayālisī, from Hammām, from Qatāda, from Abū Naḍra, from Abū Sa'īd al-Khudrī ﵂ who said: "The Prophet ﷺ ordered us to recite the Opening Chapter [al-Fātiḥa] of the Book and whatever is easy."

Al-Ḥākim says: "Only the people of Basra make mention of the order in it, from the beginning to the end of the chain [isnād] and no-one narrates it with this wording except them."

And if someone says, "The people of such-and-such a place alone narrate this Hadith," and they intend figuratively just one individual from this land, just as they attribute the action of one person to a tribe [by referring to the tribe as a whole], then it is considered to be *fard muṭlaq*, such as the previously mentioned Hadith, "Eat fresh dates with dried dates" as we have previously seen.

---

[200] Qur'an 54:1
[201] Al-Tirmidhī, al-Nasā'ī, Abū Dāwūd and Ibn Mājah.
[202] The author of the *Sunan*—Ed.

Al-Ḥākim says: "This [Hadith] is from the *fard* narrations of the Basrans, distinct from [those of] the Medinans," since Abū Zukayr alone narrated it from Hishām b. ʿUrwa. Al-Ḥākim said it was a *fard* narration of the Basrans when he in fact intended one specific Basran.

Third, it may be restricted to a particular narrator from another particular narrator, such as their saying, "So-and-so alone narrated it from so-and-so," or: "No-one narrated it from so-and-so, except so-and-so."

An example is that which the authors of the *Sunan* narrated by way of Sufyān b. ʿUyayna, from Wāʾil b. Dāwūd, from his son Bakr b. Wāʾil, from al-Zuhrī, from Anas 🙏, that the Prophet 🙏 gave a wedding meal for [his 🙏 marriage to] Ṣafiyya with a gruel of parched barley [*sawīq*] and dates.

Ibn Ṭāhir said: "It is *gharīb*. No-one else narrated it from Bakr except his father Wāʾil, and no-one narrated it from Wāʾil except Ibn ʿUyayna." Therefore, al-Tirmidhī said it was *hasan gharīb*.

However, the narration of Wāʾil from his son does not necessarily mean that it is *fard muṭlaq*, as al-Dāraquṭnī mentions in his work *al-ʿIlal* that Muḥammad b. al-Ṣalt al-Tawwazī narrated it from Ibn ʿUyayna, from Ziyād b. Saʿd, from al-Zuhrī.

The author refers to these three types in the line:

Fard is to restrict to a reliable narrator,
Region or particular narrator

The ruling on *fard muqayyad*

As for the first type, the one restricted to reliable narrators, its ruling is similar to that of the *fard muṭlaq*. One must examine whether the sole narrator is reliable and establish whether his solitary narrations can serve as proof, that is to say whether he has a high degree of accuracy [*ḍabṭ tāmm*], or if he is close to this or not.

As for the second and third types, the ruling on them is that one must investigate whether the route reaches a level of high precision and accuracy, and if so then it is sound [*ṣaḥīḥ*]. If it is close then it is fair [*hasan*], but if it is far from this then it is weak [*ḍaʿīf*].

Thus, in any type of *fard muqayyad*, the fact of it being narrated by one person does not necessitate it to be ruled *daʿīf*.[203]

A benefit

The term *fard* (solitary) is rarely used to mean *fard nisbī* (particular); rather, the more common term for this is *gharīb* (unusual). [Ibn Ḥajar] says in *Sharḥ al-Nukhba*:

> This is because *gharīb* and *fard* are synonyms both linguistically and in their technical usage, except that the people who use technical terms alternate between them, even though one is more common than the other: *fard* is more commonly used to mean *fard muṭlaq* and *gharīb* is more commonly used to mean *fard nisbī*.
>
> This is in relation their uses as nouns. When used in a derived verbal form, they make no distinction. They then refer to both *fard muṭlaq* and *nisbī*, [such as when] saying, "*tafarrada bihi fulān*," or "*aghraba bihi fulān*."

---

[203] [Al-Suyūṭī] *Al-Tadrīb*; *Ḥāshiya al-Abyārī* and elsewhere.

CHAPTER TEN
DEFECTS, ALTERATIONS,
DISCREPANCIES AND INTERPOLATIONS

DEFECTIVE [MU'ALLAL]

مُعَلَّلٌ عِنْـدَهُمْ قَدْ عُرِفَا   وَمَا بِـعِـلَّـةٍ غَمُـوضٍ أَوْ خَفَـا

That which contains an obscure or hidden defect,
Is known to them as mu'allal

Amongst the scholars of Hadith the *mu'allal* is also called *mu'all* or *ma'lūl*.[204]

Linguistically it is the passive participle denoting someone who has a weakness.

Technically it is an expression for a Hadith in which an insightful Hadith scholar has discovered a debilitating defect which affects the soundness of a Hadith, although it outwardly appears to be free of it.

As explained [by Ibn Ḥajar] in *Sharḥ al-Nukhba*:

> [It is] one of the most complicated and delicate of the sciences of Hadith. No-one successfully engages it except someone whom Allah has granted deep understanding, expansive memory, and exhaustive knowledge of the different types of narrators, as well as a mastery of the chains and wordings of Hadith.
>
> For this reason, only a few of those engaged in this matter speak about it, such as 'Alī b. al-Madīnī, Aḥmad b. Ḥanbal, Imam al-Bukhārī, Ya'qūb b. Shayba, Abū Ḥātim, Abū Zur'a and al-Dāraquṭnī.

---

[204] As is the position of the verifying scholars [muḥaqqiqūn]. (*Ḥāshiya al-Abyārī*)

> Often the scholar [of this discipline] may be unable to express his reasoning for the claims he makes, much as is the case with a currency exchanger[205] when he examines *dinars* and *dirhams*.

Despite its hidden and obscure nature, the way that a subtle weakness is identified is thus: the perceptive Hadith master must gather all the chains of the Hadith, thoroughly going through the various *jawāmi'*, *masānīd* and *ajzā'*, and examine the ranks of each narrator, focussing on the strength of their memory and precision. He must scrutinise the route of the Hadith regarding the possibility that it may be the narration of a sole narrator and the lack of supporting narrations, or that it may contradict the narration of someone who is stronger than the original narrator, who has a better memory and is more accurate, or contradict a greater number of narrators. This critical scholar will then be guided to uncover the narrator's mistake in connecting a *mursal* or severed [*munqaṭi'*] [Hadith], or inserting one Hadith into another, or misattributing initial disconnection [*irsāl*] when it is in fact connected [*mawṣūl*], or as halted [*mawqūf*] when it is in fact raised [*marfū'*], or he will become aware of [any] *tadlīs* (misleading) which affects the soundness of the Hadith, such as substituting a weak narrator for a reliable one, or discrepancy [*iḍṭirāb*] within the Hadith, and so on. Such that he is overwhelmingly convinced by his conclusions so that he now pronounces the Hadith to be weak, or he may be wavering and therefore suspend judgement regarding the soundness of the Hadith, despite the Hadith having the appearance of being sound.

It is most common for the subtle weakness to be in the chain of narration, although it may also be in the wording itself. If it is found in the chain, then it may also be harmful to itself and to the wording, such as narrating a Hadith as *mursal* when it is in fact connected, or as *mawqūf* although it is *marfū'*.[206]

---

[205] The *ṣayrafī* (currency exchanger) was a person known for his understanding of the qualities of gold and silver and the different kinds of coins. The Hadith scholar is often compared to him—Ed.

[206] Such that the chain differs according to the same narrator, so that everyone from the group [of narrators] narrates it contradicting others,

It may not impair the wording that the connection [*ittiṣāl*] or raising [*raf*] becomes stronger, or that there occurs disagreement in specifying one of two reliable narrators, such as the Hadith, "Both the buyer and seller have a choice," in the case of Yaʿlā b. ʿUbayd narrating it from al-Thawrī, from ʿAmr b. Dīnār, from Ibn ʿUmar ﷺ.

The critics of this Hadith have stated explicitly that Yaʿlā made a mistake: it should be ʿAbdullah b. Dīnār, not ʿAmr b. Dīnār. Yaʿlā contradicted the other students of al-Thawrī [regarding this narration]. However, this weakness is not detrimental since both ʿAbdullah and ʿAmr are reliable.

As for a weakness which affects the wording of a Hadith, an example of this is the Hadith of Muslim by way of al-Awzāʿī from Qatāda, that he wrote to him, informing him that Anas ﷺ narrated, saying: "I prayed behind the Prophet ﷺ, Abū Bakr, ʿUmar and ʿUthmān ﷺ, and they would all begin [reciting] with *al-ḥamdu li-llahi rabb al-ʿālamīn*, without mentioning *bismillah al-raḥmān al-raḥīm*, at the beginning of their recitation or at the end."

Al-Shāfiʿī and others have attributed a weakness to the addition in this Hadith which negates [reading] the *basmala*, as seven or eight [narrators] have contradicted it. They agreed regarding beginning [reciting] with *al-ḥamdu li-llahi rabb al-ʿālamīn*, but did not mention [anything about] the *basmala*, meaning that they would begin with the Mother of the Qur'an[207] before reciting anything [i.e., another *Sūra*] after it.

As is mentioned in the narration of al-Dāraquṭnī, "They would begin [reciting a *sūra*] with the Mother of the Qur'an," not that they would leave out reciting the *basmala*. It seems that some of the narrators understood that beginning with *al-ḥamdu li-llahi rabb al-ʿālamīn* meant negating the *basmala*, stating clearly their understanding, which was erroneous.

[considering] it *mursal* when it is connected, and *mawqūf* [when it is] *marfū*.

[207] *Umm al-Qur'an* is another title for the Opening Chapter, *Sūra al-Fātiḥa* —Tr.

What substantiates this is that Anas did not narrate a negation of the *basmala*. Rather, when he was asked: "Did the Prophet ﷺ begin with *al-ḥamdu li-llahi rabb al-ʿālamīn* or *bismillah...*" he responded to the questioner by saying: "You ask me something that I cannot recall, and no-one has asked me this."[208]

A Hadith may contain a subtle weakness due to various types of criticisms such as lying, heedlessness, the flagrant wrongdoing of a narrator, or poor memory.

The ruling on the *muʿall*

A Hadith which contains a debilitating defect is rejected, given that it has been previously shown that it is one of the conditions of an acceptable Hadith that it be free of a damaging defect.

ORTHOGRAPHICALLY ALTERED
[*MUṢAḤḤAF WA-MUḤARRAF*]

A *muṣaḥḥaf* Hadith is that in which there is an alteration of one or more letters due to their dots, whilst the letters appear to remain the same, such as the altering of al-ʿAwwām b. Murājim to Muzāḥim.

A *muḥarraf* Hadith is that whose diacritical vowels are changed, such as changing *Yawm Kulāb*, with a *ḍamma* (u), to *Kilāb* with a *kasra* (i)—as in the Hadith of ʿArfaja.

The majority of the early scholars viewed the *muṣaḥḥaf* and *muḥarraf* as synonymous, although some differentiated between the two in the manner outlined above.

Both the *muṣaḥḥaf* and *muḥarraf* may occur in the chain of narration or in the wording.

---

[208] As narrated by Aḥmad and Ibn Khuzayma and al-Dāraquṭnī, the latter two saying it is *ṣaḥīḥ*.

An example of altering [*taṣḥīf*] in the wording is the Hadith, "The Messenger of Allah ﷺ cursed those who enunciate sermons like poetry." Some altered [the word *khuṭab* (sermons)] to 'firewood' [*ḥaṭab*].

The reason that *taṣḥīf* and *taḥrīf* occur is due to confusion when hearing, or in the script, or in meaning.

An awareness of these types of Hadith is extremely important in the sciences of Hadith, so that mistakes do not occur. For that reason the greatest scholars of Hadith were concerned about it and authored works clarifying *muṣaḥḥaf* and *muḥarraf* Hadith.

INCONSISTENT [*MUḌṬARIB*]

That which contains discrepancies in the chain or the wording,
Is muḍṭarib according to the experts in this science

The *muḍṭarib* Hadith is that which is narrated in various ways with differences that cannot be reconciled, by the same narrator, such that he narrates it on one occasion in a certain manner and narrates it again but contrary to his first narration. Or it may be that more than one narrator narrates a Hadith, but each one does so differing with the others.

The Hadith only becomes *muḍṭarib* unless the various narrations are considered to be of equal strength in terms of being *ṣaḥīḥ*, such that preference cannot be given to one narration, nor can they be reconciled.

However, if one of the narrations may be given preference due to the fact that the narrator is stronger in memory, or has spent a greater time with the one from whom he narrates, or due to other reasons which make a narration preponderant, then the Hadith is not considered to be *muḍṭarib*. Rather, the dominant narration is always given preference, and the abandoned narrations are considered to be anomalous [*shādh*] or denounced [*munkar*].

Similarly, a Hadith is not considered to be *muḍṭarib* if it possible to reconcile the various narrations, for example if the speaker used two or more different words to describe the same thing,[209] or if he intended to clarify two different rulings, as in the Hadith of Fāṭima bint Qays 🙏 in which she said: "The Prophet 🙏 was asked about the alms tax [*zakāt*] and said: 'With respect to wealth, there is a right over it other than *zakāt*.'" It is narrated by al-Tirmidhī like this.[210]

Ibn Mājah also narrated it from Fāṭima 🙏, except with the wording, "There is no right due on wealth except *zakāt*."

It is possible to interpret this discrepancy by saying that she narrated it with both wordings from the Prophet 🙏, and that the meaning of [the first narration, which mentions] the established right is that it is that which is recommended, and [the second narration which mentions] the negation denotes the obligation.[211]

---

[209] As is said regarding the different wordings transmitted from him 🙏 in the Hadith about the woman who gifted herself to the Prophet 🙏. It is mentioned in one narration, "I have married you off to her," and in another narration, "We have married you off to her," and in another narration, "We have given you access to her," and in another narration, "I have given you dominion over her."

Ḥāfiẓ al-Suyūṭī says: "The interpretation of these words is simple, since they all refer to one meaning." However, ʿAllāma al-Abyārī verified that there is *iḍṭirāb* in the wording, "...since it is unlikely that all of these wordings came from the Prophet 🙏 at the time of marriage, and it is not narrated that these refer to numerous instances. So it must be that what he 🙏 said was one of these wordings. If we decided upon one of these, that it was one of dominion [*tamlīk*], then this indicates that it (i.e., the contract) with it was sound. If we say the correct wording was not one of dominion, then the contract is not sound. Herein lies the *iḍṭirāb*." (*Ḥāshiya al-Abyārī*, p. 60)

[210] From the narration of Sharīk, from Abū Ḥamza, from al-Shaʿbī, from Fāṭima 🙏.

[211] Al-Sakhāwī says: "What supports this interpretation is the additional narration which states, 'then he 🙏 read [the verse], ❨...and gives from his wealth, despite his love for it...❩ (Qurʾan 2:177), as has been narrated in some chains.'

The discrepancy [*iḍṭirāb*] can exist due to there being a difference as to whether it is connected [*mawṣūl*] or *mursal*, or in the establishment of a narrator or his omission,[212] or in an affirmation or negation, or in other areas.

The *iḍṭirāb* can occur in the chain—and this is the more common—or in the wording of the Hadith. It can occur in both at the same time.[213]

Examples

As an example in the chain of narration, there is the Hadith of Abū Bakr ﷺ in which he said: "O Messenger of Allah ﷺ, I see that you have gone grey!" He ﷺ said: "[The Chapter of] Hūd and her sisters[214] have turned my hair grey."

Al-Dāraquṭnī said this is *muḍṭarib* as it has only been narrated by way of Abū Isḥāq al-Sabī'ī, and there are around ten different ways in which it has been narrated from him: some narrate it in a *mursal* form, some narrated it connected [*mawṣūl*]. Others have said it is from the narrations of Abū Bakr al-Ṣiddīq ﷺ, and others have said it is from Saʿd ﷺ, and others have said it is from the Mother of the Believers, ʿĀ'isha ﷺ.

In another wording of the Hadith, Abū Ḥamza said: 'I said to al-Shaʿbī: "If a person pays the alms-tax on his wealth, does his wealth become pure for him?" So he recited, ⟪*Piety is not that you turn your face...*⟫ up till the end of the [same] verse.' This is despite its weakness without *iḍṭirāb*, as Abū Hamza, the teacher of Sharīk, is somewhat weak."
(*Fatḥ al-Mughīth*, p. 101)

[212] Al-Sakhāwī, *Fatḥ al-Mughīth* (p. 99)

[213] Ḥāfiẓ al-Sakhāwī says: "There are many examples of *iḍṭirāb* in both the chain and wording. As for those in the chain only, which are the majority, they can be found in the *ʿIlal* of al-Dāraquṭnī, and our teacher used this and added to it in his book, *al-Muqtarib fī Bayān al-Muḍṭarib*."
(*Fatḥ al-Mughīth*)

[214] The term 'sisters' in Arabic is an idiomatic way of referring to similar entities, analogous to the first item mentioned. In this example, it refers to the Chapter of Hūd and other similar chapters of the Qur'an regarding their mention of the Day of Judgement and its terrors. The other chapters are: *al-Wāqiʿa* (Chapter 56), *al-Mursalāt* (Chapter 77), *al-Naba'* (Chapter 78) and *al-Takwīr* (Chapter 82)—Tr.

It is narrated from Abū Isḥāq, from Abū al-Aḥwaṣ, from Ibn Masʿūd ﷺ, and in other ways too, as al-Dāraquṭnī has explained. All the narrators are reliable and it is not possible to give preference to one narration over the other, and reconciling the narrations is impossible.[215]

An example of *iḍṭirāb* in the wording is the Hadith negating the saying of the *basmala*, previously mentioned in the discussion on the *muʿallal*. Al-Suyūṭī said: "Ibn ʿAbd al-Barr considered it to be weak on account of the *iḍṭirāb*. The *muʿallal* (defective) includes the *muḍṭarib*, as its weakness could be that [the *iḍṭirāb*]."[216]

The ruling on the *muḍṭarib*

The default position is that *iḍṭirāb* causes a Hadith to be weak, since it implies inaccuracy in the narrator or narrators, and as mentioned previously, accuracy [*ḍabṭ*] is a pre-condition for a sound [*ṣaḥīḥ*] or fair [*ḥasan*] Hadith.

It is possible for a *muḍṭarib* Hadith to be reconciled with it being *ṣaḥīḥ*, where the difference lies in the name of a single narrator, or in his father's name, or his ascription [*nisba*],[217] and the like, and yet he is reliable. The Hadith is considered to be sound and the difference in what was mentioned does not affect its soundness, even though it is called *muḍṭarib*. There are many examples of this in the two *Ṣaḥīḥ* books [of al-Bukhārī and Muslim].[218]

---

[215] [Al-Sakhāwī] *Fatḥ al-Mughīth*; [al-Suyūṭī] *al-Tadrīb*

[216] In the same way the Ḥanafīs regard the Hadith of the two pitchers [*qullatayn*] as weak on account of its *iḍṭirāb*, for it revolves around Walīd b. Kathīr. In the narration of Aḥmad, "If water is *qullatayn* [in volume], or three [pitchers], it does not become impure." In the narration of al-Dāraquṭnī, "If water reaches the amount of a *qulla*, it does not carry filth." In another narration of al-Dāraquṭnī, "If water reaches the amount of forty *qulla*, it does not carry filth."

[217] The name indicating his place of origin or tribe and the like, such as 'al-Bukhārī,' which ascribes the individual to Bukhara, a city in modern day Uzbekistan—Tr.

[218] *Al-Tadrīb* and elsewhere.

INTERPOLATED [*MUDRAJ*]

وَالْمُدْرَجَاتُ فِي الْحَدِيثِ مَا أَتَتْ   مِنْ بَعْضِ أَلْفَاظِ الرُّوَاةِ اتَّصَلَتْ

Interpolations in a Hadith appear in the form,
Of some words from narrators connectedly

The *mudraj* Hadith is the addition of a narrator, be it a Companion or anyone thereafter, in the wording or the chain of the Hadith. The narrator of the Hadith considers this addition to be a part of the Hadith itself due to there being no separation, but in reality it is not part of the Hadith.

The *mudraj* is of two types: that which is found in the wording, and that which is found in the chain.

Idrāj in the wording

There are three types of *mudraj* in the wording: at the beginning, in the middle or at the end, and the latter is the most common of the three.

An example where it occurs at the beginning of a Hadith is that which is narrated by al-Khaṭīb, from Abū Qaṭan, and Shabāba from Shu'ba, from Muḥammad b. Ziyād, from Abū Hurayra ﷺ who said: "The Prophet ﷺ said: 'Do your ablution thoroughly. Woe [*wayl*][219] to the heels from the Fire.'"

The words, "Do your ablution thoroughly," is an insertion from Abū Hurayra ﷺ, which is clear due to the narration in [*Ṣaḥīḥ*] al-Bukhārī, from Ādam, from Shu'ba, from Muḥammad b. Ziyād, from Abū Hurayra ﷺ who said: "Do your ablution thoroughly, for Abū al-Qāsim said: 'Woe [*wayl*] to the heels from the Fire.'" Al-Khaṭīb said: "Abū Qaṭan and Shabāba were mistaken in their narrations from Shu'ba, as we have mentioned. Numerous narrators have transmitted it from him, such as the narration of Ādam."

An example in the middle of the Hadith is found in the collections of the two *Ṣaḥīḥ* books [of al-Bukhārī and Muslim], from 'Ā'isha ﷺ, [who said:] "The Prophet ﷺ would devote himself

---

[219] A valley in Hell according to the more correct opinion—Tr.

[*yataḥannathu*]—'and that is worship'—in the Cave of Ḥirā' for nights on end...' The sentence, "and that is worship" was an insertion by al-Zuhrī to explain the meaning of *yataḥannathu*.

An example of where an insertion occurs at the end of a Hadith is what has been narrated from Abū Dharr ☙, raising it to the Prophet ☙ [*marfūʿan*], "By Allah, had you known what I knew, you would have laughed little and cried much, and you would not have taken pleasure in your wives in bed, and you would have gone out to the hilltops supplicating fervently. Would that I were a tree that had been cut down!"

The sentence, "Would that I were a tree that had been cut down [*tuʿḍad*]," is an insertion from Abū Dharr ☙, which the narration of al-Tirmidhī explains.

Idrāj in the chain

There are various types of insertions in the chain:

The first type is that in which the narrator narrates two different wordings, and each Hadith has a different chain. Some narrate the two Hadith with one of the two chains, or they narrate one of the two wordings with its particular chain and insert something into the Hadith that is actually from the other Hadith, which is not a part of the original Hadith.

An example of this is that which is narrated by Saʿīd b. Abī Maryam from Mālik, from al-Zuhrī, from Anas ☙, that the Prophet ☙ said: "Do not hate one another, do not envy one another, do not turn your backs on one another, and do not compete with one another..."

The part, "do not compete with one another," is an insertion by Ibn Abī Maryam from a separate Hadith narrated by Mālik from Abū al-Zinād, from al-Aʿraj, from Abū Hurayra ☙, from the Prophet ☙, which is, "Beware of suspicion for suspicion is the most false of all speech. Do not spy [on one another], do not compete with one another, and do not envy one another."

Both narrations are agreed upon [by al-Bukhārī and Muslim] by way of Mālik. However, the first Hadith does not contain the words, "Do not compete with one another." Rather, this is from the second [Hadith].

The second type is when some narrate a Hadith from a group of a people but there are differences in the chains of each narrator. However, he unites them all together in a single chain despite their differences, and then inserts the narration of the one who differed with the others along with them as if in unanimous agreement.

An example of this is that which is narrated by al-Tirmidhī from Bundār, from ʿAbd al-Raḥmān b. Mahdī, from Sufyān al-Thawrī, from Wāṣil, and Manṣūr from al-Aʿmash, from Abū Wāʾil, from ʿAmr b. Shuraḥbīl, from ʿAbdullah b. Masʿūd ﷺ who said: "I said: 'O Messenger of Allah, what is the greatest wrong action?' He ﷺ said: 'That one should set up a rival to Allah, while it is He Who created you...'"

This is how Muḥammad b. Kathīr al-ʿAbdī narrated it from Sufyān, in that which al-Khaṭīb narrated. This narration of Wāṣil is an insertion into the narration of Manṣūr and al-Aʿmash, since Wāṣil does not mention ʿAmr in it. Rather, he narrated it from Abū Wāʾil, from ʿAbdullah b. Masʿūd ﷺ. This is how Shuʿba, Mahdī b. Maymūn, Mālik b. Mighwal, and Saʿīd b. Masrūq narrated it from Wāṣil, as al-Khaṭīb has mentioned.

Yaḥyā b. Saʿīd al-Qaṭṭān clarifies the two narrations in his narration from Sufyān, and differentiates one from the other, as narrated by al-Bukhārī in his *Ṣaḥīḥ* from ʿAmr b. ʿAlī, from Yaḥyā, from Sufyān, from Manṣūr, and al-Aʿmash, both of whom [narrate] from Abū Wāʾil, from ʿAmr b. Shuraḥbīl, from ʿAbdullah ﷺ.

And from Sufyān, from Wāṣil, from Abū Wāʾil, from ʿAbdullah b. Masʿūd ﷺ, without mentioning ʿAmr b. Shuraḥbīl, as Ḥāfiẓ al-ʿIrāqī has clarified in his commentary.

The third type is when the narrator quotes the chain but something happens, so he says something of his own words, such that some of those listening believe that the narrator's own interjection is a part of the Hadith and they therefore narrate it including these words.

An example of this is that which is narrated by Ibn Mājah from Ismāʿīl b. Muḥammad al-Ṭalḥī, from Thābit b. Mūsā al-Zāhid, from Sharīk, from al-Aʿmash, from Abū Sufyān, from Jābir ﷺ, raising it to the Prophet ﷺ [*marfūʿan*], "Whoever prays much at night, his face is beautified during the day."

Al-Ḥākim says:

> Thābit entered whilst Sharīk was dictating, saying: "Al-A'mash narrated to us from Abū Sufyān, from Jābir 🙵 who said: 'The Prophet 🙵 said...'" Then he [Sharīk] fell silent so that his students could write down what he was saying, and he looked at Thābit and said: "Whoever prays much at night, his face is beautified during the day," intending Thābit by this statement, on account of his worldly detachment and scrupulousness. Thābit, however, believed that it was the wording for the chain that Sharīk had narrated and thereafter narrated it in this way.[220]

How to recognise *idrāj*

The *mudraj* Hadith is identified by another narration which clarifies to what extent interpolation [*idrāj*] took place, as in the Hadith, "Do your ablution thoroughly." Or it may be identified by explicit mention [*tanṣīṣ*] of that by the narrator himself, or by those scholars conversant in such matters. It may also be identified by it being impossible to have been said by the Prophet 🙵, as in the Hadith of Abū Hurayra 🙵, raising it to the Prophet 🙵 [*marfū'an*], "'The slave in bondage has two rewards.' By Him in Whose hand is my soul, were it not for struggle in the way of Allah, the pilgrimage, and service towards my mother, I would love to have died as a slave."

The statement, "By Him in Whose hand is my soul...," are the words of Abū Hurayra 🙵, as it is impossible for the Prophet 🙵 to desire to be a slave, and likewise because his mother at that time was not alive, such that he could serve her.

---

[220] Most authors of books on Hadith terminology mention this story in the section on fabrications. However, it is more appropriate to include it in the section on *mudraj*, as has been mentioned in *al-Tadrīb* [of al-Suyūṭī] and *Fatḥ al-Mughīth*, where [al-Sakhāwī] says, after narrating this story in the previously mentioned manner: "Based on this, it is one of the types of *mudraj*." Al-Ajhūrī transmitted from al-Ḥamawī that he used this story as an example of *mudraj* and said: "Ibn Ḥibbān considered this to be an example of *mudraj*, even though Abū Ḥātim considered it to be a fabrication."

The ruling on *idrāj*

If the *idrāj* is for explanation, then there is a degree of laxity, as was the way of al-Zuhrī and others. It is better for the insertions to be made clear.

If it is due to an unintended error or forgetfulness, then there is no blame on the one who made the error, except if this happens frequently in which case it would impair his accuracy as a narrator of Hadith.

However, if the *idrāj* is done intentionally, it is *ḥarām* depending on the type of *idrāj*, as this represents a type of deception and misleading [*tadlīs*].

Ibn al-Samʿānī said: "Whoever inserts something into a Hadith deliberately loses his integrity [ʿadāla], and is considered someone who ⟨*distorts the true meaning of words...*⟩ [Qur'an 4:46]. He is counted amongst the liars."

Ḥāfiẓ al-Suyūṭī says:

> *All of this is ḥarām and damaging [to a narrator],*
> *And in my opinion, explanations can be overlooked*

CHAPTER ELEVEN
COMPLEMENTARY AND CONTRASTING[221]

RULINGS ON ADDITIONAL RELIABLE NARRATORS [ZIYĀDA AL-THIQĀT]

This is when two reliable masters of Hadith [*thiqa ḥāfiẓ*] both narrate the same Hadith, though one of them has an addition not present in the other's narration. It may also be that one reliable master narrates the same Hadith twice, but on one occasion he narrates it with an addition not present in his other narration.

Scholars have various opinions regarding the ruling on whether this addition is accepted or rejected:

The first opinion is that is accepted without exception, regardless of whether it occurred from someone who narrated the Hadith with a shortcoming, or from someone else, and regardless of whether it relates to a legal ruling or not, and whether or it not it affects an established ruling, and whether it entails contradicting rulings established by a narration which does not contain the addition, or not.

This is the opinion of the majority of scholars of law and Hadith.[222]

The second opinion is that it is rejected completely.

The third opinion is that is accepted if it is also narrated by someone other than those who narrated it with an omission. It is not accepted from someone who narrated it once with an omission.

The fourth opinion, which Ibn al-Ṣalāḥ and others were satisfied with, is that there are three types of additions:

---

[221] The title of this chapter has not been drawn directly from the commentary, but was nevertheless found reflective of the subchapters gathered therein—Pub

[222] [Al-Nawawī] *Al-Taqrīb* and its commentary [*al-Tadrīb* by al-Suyūṭī]

1. That which does not contradict the narration without the addition. This type is accepted as it is a separate Hadith which a reliable narrator alone has narrated, as no one narrated it from his teacher.
2. That which contradicts what reliable narrators narrated. This type is rejected.
3. That which is in between the above two types, namely that it contradicts the narration which does not contain the addition, with a restriction to the absolute [taqyīd al-muṭlaq],[223] for example.[224]

He said in *al-Tadrīb*:

An example of this [third] type is the Hadith of the two Shaykhs[225] from Ibn Masʿūd ﷺ who said: "I asked the Messenger of Allah ﷺ: 'What is the best of actions?' He replied: 'Prayer at its correct time.'"

Al-Ḥasan b. Mukrim and Bundār added in their narrations of this Hadith, "...at the beginning of its time." Al-Ḥākim and Ibn Ḥibbān said this addition is sound.

[Another example is] the Hadith of the two Shaykhs from Anas ﷺ, "Bilāl was ordered to double [the phrases] in the call to prayer [adhān], but to tighten [them to one] in the pre-prayer call [iqāma]." Simāk b. ʿAṭiyya added, "...except the *iqāma*." Al-Ḥākim and Ibn Ḥibbān said this addition is sound.

The ruling of this type of addition is that it is accepted according to the correct opinion.[226]

Regarding this, Ḥāfiẓ al-Suyūṭī said:

---

[223] A term used in legal theory [uṣūl al-fiqh] which is when a specific word [khāṣṣ] with an absolute meaning [muṭlaq] becomes restricted by the presence of another legal text [naṣṣ]. The schools of law differ regarding the ruling which is produced as a result—Tr.

[224] The other example is something which renders a general application specific [takhṣīṣ al-ʿāmm]—Tr.

[225] This refers to Imam al-Bukhārī and Imam Muslim as the Hadith is found in both of their collections—Tr.

[226] [Al-Nawawī] *Al-Taqrīb*

Ibn al-Ṣalāḥ said—and this is the position relied upon [mu'tamad],

If it contradicts reliable narrators, it is rejected,
If not, then take this, by a clear consensus,

Or if it contradicts in an absolute [general] sense,
Then accept it, according to the more correct view

ELEVATED AND DESCENDING CHAINS [*ISNĀD 'ĀLĪ WA-NĀZIL*]

وَضِدُّهُ ذَاكَ الَّـذِي قَدْ نَزَلاَ   وَكُلُّ مَـا قَلَّـتْ رِجَالُهُ عَـلاَ

Everything that has few narrators is 'ālī,
And its opposite is nāzil

The chain of narration is a unique and lofty quality by which Allah singled out this Muhammadan community, may prayers and salutations be upon its Prophet, which does not exist in other communities. Abū 'Alī al-Jayyānī said: "Allah, the Exalted, has singled out this community with three things that were not given to previous communities: the chain of narration, lineages and grammatical inflection."

[Al-Suyūṭī] said in *al-Tadrīb*:

> "Evidence of this is that which is narrated by al-Ḥākim and others from Maṭar al-Warrāq regarding His words, exalted is He, ⟨*and vestiges of knowledge,*⟩[227] that it refers to the chain of narration of Hadith.

Ibn al-Mubārak said: "The chain of narration [*isnād*] is from the religion, and were it not for the *isnād*, anyone could have said whatever they pleased." Muslim narrated it in the introduction to his *Ṣaḥīḥ*.

Al-Thawrī said: "*Isnād* is the weapon of the believer."

Al-Nawawī has said it is a highly emphasised *sunna*, and seeking an elevated [short] chain of narration ['*uluww*] is *sunna*.

---

[227] Qur'an 46:4

Elevated ['ālī] and its types

An elevated chain ['ālī] is a chain which has few narrators and there are five types of it:

The first type is called absolute elevation [al-'uluww al-muṭlaq] and is defined by its proximity to our master the Messenger of Allah ﷺ with a small number of narrators in relation to another chain of narration of the same Hadith which has a greater number of narrators, or it may be in relation to other chains of narration in general.

This type is the greatest and most meritorious, as long as the chain is sound and free from those who are suspect. If, however, the chain contains a weakness, then this quality of brevity in the chain does not warrant attention, especially if the chain contains later liars claiming to have heard [narrations] from the Companions, such as Ibn Hudba, Ibn Dīnār, Nu'aym b. Sālim, Ya'lā b. al-Ashdaq and Khirāsh. Al-Dhahabī said [in Mīzān al-'Itidāl]: "Whenever you see a scholar of Hadith express joy in elevated chains containing these [narrators], then you should know he is a layperson."

The second type is defined by proximity to a particular Imam of Hadith who possesses a lofty characteristic, such as his memory, or accuracy and the like, in spite of the large number of narrators between this Imam and the Messenger of Allah ﷺ. That is like proximity to Imam Mālik, al-Shāfi'ī, al-Thawrī, al-Bukhārī or Muslim, and so on.

This type is called 'relative elevation' [al-'uluww al-nisbī], since it is elevated with regard to a particular master of Hadith. This type is second in superiority after the first type in terms of its value and merit, again on the condition that it be sound and free of any deficiency.

The third type is elevation with regard to a particular relied upon Hadith collection, such as the two Ṣaḥīḥ books [of al-Bukhārī and Muslim], the four Sunan [al-Tirmidhī, Abū Dāwūd, Ibn Mājah and al-Nasā'ī], the Musnad of Imam Aḥmad and the like.

This type has four sub-categories:

1. Concordance [muwāfaqa]

This is when a scholar of Hadith narrates a Hadith that is found in one of the relied upon Hadith collections with a chain of narrations that differs from that of the author, which eventually meets with the teacher of the book's author through a different chain than that of the author. If he were to narrate this through the same chain as the author, the number of narrators in the chain would be increased.

Ḥāfiẓ Ibn Ḥajar says in *Sharḥ al-Nukhba*:

> An example of this is where al-Bukhārī narrates a Hadith from Qutayba, from Mālik, which, if we were to narrate it through his (al-Bukhārī's) chain between me and Qutayba there would be eight narrators. If we were to narrate the Hadith by itself, for example, by way of Abū al-ʿAbbās al-Sarrāj from Qutayba, then between me and Qutayba there would be seven. Therefore, *muwāfaqa* occurred between us and al-Bukhārī by his own teacher, with the elevated chain going back to him (al-Bukhārī).

Ibn Daqīq al-ʿĪd called this type *ʿuluww al-tanzīl* since it is descending [*nāzil*] in relation to the Prophet 🕋 and elevated [*ʿuluww*] in relation to the book from which it is taken, and it is narrated in a way other than that of its author.

2.   Substitution [*badal*]

This is when a scholar of Hadith narrates a Hadith which is found in one of the relied upon collections of Hadith with his chain of narration, which contains the teacher of the teacher of the author of the book. Ḥāfiẓ Ibn Ḥajar said in *Sharḥ al-Nukhba*:

> It is as if this particular chain (i.e., the previously mentioned chain of al-Bukhārī) from Qutayba, from Mālik, and so on, reached us through a different chain, from al-Qaʿnabī.[228] Hence, al-Qaʿnabī is a substitute for Qutayba.

3.   Equivalence [*musāwā*]

This occurs when the number of narrators in the chain of a scholar of Hadith (until the end) is equal to the number of narrators in a chain belonging to the author of one of the Hadith collections.

------

[228] The teacher of al-Bukhārī.

Ḥāfiẓ Ibn Ḥajar says in *Sharḥ al-Nukhba*:

> For example, when al-Nasā'ī narrates a Hadith in which there are eleven narrators between him and the Prophet 鐵, and for the same Hadith we (the Ḥāfiẓ [Ibn Ḥajar] and others like him) have, through another chain, eleven narrators between us and the Prophet 鐵. Therefore, we are equal to al-Nasā'ī regarding the number, keeping in mind the differences with his particular chain.[229]

4.   *Muṣāfaḥa* (lit. handshake)

This is when a scholar narrates a Hadith with his chain of narration, the number of the narrators in the chain being one more than the number of narrators in the chain of a particular Hadith collection's author, and it as if the Hadith scholar met the author and narrated from him.

An example of this is the Hadith of 'Alī 鐵 concerning the prohibition of temporary marriage. Al-Nasā'ī narrates it, and there are ten narrators between him and the Prophet 鐵. Ḥāfiẓ al-'Irāqī narrates the same Hadith through a separate chain and it transpires that between his teacher [and the Prophet 鐵] the narrators are equal in number. As for al-'Irāqī himself, the number is not the same, rather there is *muṣāfaḥa*—therefore it is as if al-'Irāqī met al-Nasā'ī, between whom [the latter] and the Prophet 鐵 are ten narrators, and shook hands with him.[230]

This is what was meant by al-Nawawī in *al-Taqrīb* when he said:

> *Muṣāfaḥa* is when your teacher has this equivalence [*musāwā*], and so you have *muṣāfaḥa*... [Then he said:] If *musāwā* occurs with the teacher of your teacher, then your teacher has *muṣāfaḥa* with his teacher. If it [*musāwā*] occurs with the teacher of your teacher's teacher, then your teacher's teacher has *muṣāfaḥa* with his teacher.

---

[229] Ḥāfiẓ Ibn Ḥajar gathered ten Hadith of this type in a small treatise called *al-'Ashr al-'Ushariyya*. It was possible for this to occur in the time of Ibn Ḥajar and those prior to him, although in our times, due to the passage of time and the number of generations, it can no longer occur.
[230] Again, in our time this type is not possible.

This type is only called *muṣāfaḥa* because meeting is a means by which handshakes take place between two parties, as is the case in the Sacred Law.

The fourth type is when the reason for the chain being elevated is due to the narrator passing away before his teacher, compared to a different narrator passing away before the same teacher, regardless of whether the number of narrators in the chain is the same. He said in *al-Taqrīb*:

> What I narrate from three, from al-Bayhaqī, from al-Ḥākim is more elevated than what I narrate from three, from Abū Bakr b. Khalaf, from al-Ḥākim, due to the passing away of al-Bayhaqī being before that of Ibn Khalaf.

This elevation is due to the death of one teacher being before the death of another. Perhaps they considered the death of the narrator alone, rather than in relation to it being before the death of another teacher.

The scholars have differed regarding how much earlier it may be. Some have said fifty years after his death, meaning fifty years after the death of the teacher before he narrates from him. Ibn Mandah said: "It is by thirty years."

The fifth type is when the reason for the elevation is due to one of the narrators hearing it before another narrator, both of whom heard it directly from their teacher, or before another narrator heard it from a companion of the teacher; the first of which is more elevated.

An example of this is when two people hear a Hadith from the same teacher, although one heard it before the other, and this elevation may be reinforced if the teacher became confused [in old age] or became senile.

Another example is when a person hears a Hadith from his teacher, and someone else hears it from a companion of his teacher, and the first person hears it before the second.

Descent [*nuzūl*] and its types

Descent is the opposite of elevation and there are also five types. Each type corresponds to one of the five types of elevation.

The ruling on 'ālī and *nuzūl*

The elevated Hadith is superior and stronger than the descending [Hadith], as long as there is nothing in the descending chain of narration which restores what is in it from descending, in which case, it may reach a level greater than the elevated chain of narration.

This may occur when the narrators of the descending chain have better memories and are more accurate or more discerning [in *fiqh*] than the narrators of the elevated chain, or if the descending chain is connected by [the narrators'] direct hearing, and in the elevated chain it is merely by [their] being present, or being licensed [*ijāza*] or [being] presented [a copy of the Hadith] [*munāwala*],[231] or if the elevated chain is given the quality of elevation due to [the narrator] having heard it from his teacher, although this occurred before the teacher reached the level of excellence and accuracy, whereas the second, despite hearing it later, heard it from this teacher after he reached the level of accuracy and excellence.

In the three previously mentioned scenarios, the descending chain is superior, and this is called indirect elevation ['uluww *ma'nawī*]. Therefore, there are two types of elevation: elevated in meaning, as in these three examples, and direct elevation ['uluww *fī al-ẓāhir*], as previously mentioned.

Al-'Irāqī says:

> *Whenever [that which is descended] is blameworthy,*
> *It is so unless it is rectified,*
>
> *And soundness is elevation,*
> *Subject to investigation*

Ḥāfiẓ al-Silafī[232] says:

---

[231] These terms denote methods of receiving a Hadith, which are inferior to having heard it directly. This is discussed in the chapter on ways of bearing and transmitting Hadith [p. 194-203]—Tr.

[232] Aḥmad b. Muḥammad b. Aḥmad Abū Ṭāhir al-Silafī, with a *kasra* (i) on the *sīn* and a *fatḥa* (a) on the *lām*, whose name goes back to Silafa, a title of his grandfather. Ibn al-Sam'ānī said that he was reliable, scrupulous, precise and a master. He died in 576 H.

The fairness of a Hadith is not in the proximity of its narrators,
According to the critical scholars of this science

Rather, the elevation of a Hadith,
According to those proficient in memory and mastery,
Is in the soundness of the chain

If they are gathered in one Hadith,
Then take benefit, for this is the highest of things to be desired!

MUTUAL NARRATION [MUDABBAJ]

That which each contemporary narrates from his brother
Is mudabbaj, so know this is the truth and rejoice!

According to the scholars of Hadith, *mudabbaj* is that which each contemporary narrates from the other, regardless if they are Companions, Successors, their followers, or their followers' followers and so on.

An example amongst the Companions is Abū Hurayra narrating from ʿĀʾisha 🕮 and vice versa. An example amongst the Successors is al-Zuhrī narrating from ʿAṭāʾ, and ʿAṭāʾ narrating from al-Zuhrī. An example from the followers of the Successors is Mālik narrating from al-Awzāʿī and vice versa. An example from the followers of the followers of the Successors is Aḥmad narrating from Ibn al-Madīnī and vice versa.

There is no distinction between the cases where there is no intermediary between them or there is an intermediary between them, such as the narration of al-Layth from Yazīd b. al-Hād, from Mālik, and the narration of Mālik from Yazīd, from al-Layth.

The principle that unites this type and similar things, as mentioned in *al-Nukhba* and its commentary, is that the narrator and the one from whom he narrates share in a matter related to the narration, such as age and meeting, which is taking from the teachers.

This is the type known as *riwāya al-aqrān* (narrations from contemporaries), since he is narrating from a contemporary. If each—both contemporaries—narrates from the other, then this is known as *mudabbaj* and is more specific than the first type, so that every *mudabbaj* Hadith is a Hadith of *aqrān*, but not every *aqrān* Hadith is *mudabbaj*.

Ibn Ḥajar has clarified that *tadbīj*[233] is taken from the word for the cheeks of the face, which means that they are equal from both sides. The first to name this Hadith was al-Dāraquṭnī.

If the narrator narrates from someone younger than him, such as al-Zuhrī and Yaḥyā b. Saʿīd from Mālik, or from someone of lesser knowledge and rank, such as Mālik from ʿAbdullah b. Dīnār, and such as Aḥmad and Isḥāq from ʿUbaydullah b. Mūsā, or if someone narrates from another junior to him in terms of both [age and rank], such as the narrations of the four named ʿAbdullah [Ibn ʿUmar, Ibn ʿAbbās, Ibn Masʿūd and Ibn ʿAmr b. al-ʿĀṣ ﷺ] from Kaʿb, and the narrations of many of the scholars from their students, such as the narrations of al-Bukhārī from his student Abū al-ʿAbbās al-Sarrāj—all of the previously mentioned types are called the narrations of seniors from juniors [*al-akābir ʿan al-ṣaghāʾir*].

The basis for this is the narration of the Prophet ﷺ from Tamīm al-Dārī ﷺ regarding the *Jassāsa*[234] as found in *Ṣaḥīḥ Muslim* and elsewhere.

The narration of seniors from juniors includes narrations of fathers from their sons, and Companions from Successors.

If two narrators take from the same teacher, and one student passes away before the other, it is known as *al-sābiq wal-lāḥiq*, such as Abū ʿAlī al-Baradānī, who heard a Hadith from his student al-Silafī and narrated it from him, and passed away at the beginning of the fifth century [H.], and the last companion of al-Silafī was his grandchild Abū al-Qāsim b. Makkī, who passed

---

[233] *Tadbīj* is the verbal noun from which the word *mudabbaj* is derived. —Tr.

[234] The Beast that is described by Tamīm al-Dārī, who they found on an island after becoming shipwrecked for a month. In the lengthy narration, the Beast directs the questioners to the Dajjāl (the Antichrist), and therefore it has been suggested that the name *jassāsa* comes from the word for spy [*jāsūs*]—Tr.

away in 650 H. He therefore shared with Abū 'Alī in narrating from al-Silafī, and yet their deaths were one hundred and fifty years apart. Ḥāfiẓ Ibn Ḥajar said: "This is the most I have come across in this regard."

There are important benefits of knowing these types of Hadith. For example, the benefits of knowing the narrations of contemporaries [*aqrān*] are that the researcher of this type of Hadith is not under the impression that the mention of either of the two contemporaries is a mistake in the chain by one of the narrators.

Also, he understands that the word *'an* (from) in the chain is not a mistake, and that it is correctly the conjunctive particle *wāw* (and) which denotes that both narrators took from the same person before them in the chain.

Knowing the narrations of seniors from juniors keeps one safe from the fear of thinking there is a mistaken inversion in the chain [*inqilāb*], and that one not make false assumptions about the fact that the one who receives the Hadith is senior in age and rank to the one from whom he narrates, given that the norm is that the one narrated from is senior in age and rank.

Similarly, the benefit of knowing *al-sābiq wal-lāḥiq* narrations is that one is safe from thinking that someone between him and his teacher is missing from the chain of a later person, since when the researcher sees that the student who took from the teacher had died, he may think that there is a missing link between the narrator and his teacher.

RESEMBLANT AND DIVERGENT [*MUTTAFIQ WA-MUFTARIQ*]

وَضِدُّهُ فِيمَا ذَكَرْنَا الْمُفْتَرِقْ   مُتَّفِقٌ لَفْظاً وَخَطّاً مُتَّفِقْ

Muttafiq is that which concurs in pronunciation and writing,
And the opposite of this is muftariq

Anyone who is involved in the study of Hadith ought to have a comprehensive regard for knowing the types of *muttafiq* and *muftariq*. This is when the expression and writing concur yet the meanings differ, such that there are numerous things designated by it. It comes under the category of homophones [*mushtarak lafẓī*].[235] There are various types:

1. When the name of the person and that of his father is the same, such as Khalīl b. Aḥmad, of whom there are six, the first of being the teacher of Sībawayh.

2. When the name of the person and that of his father and grandfather are all the same, such as Aḥmad b. Ja'far b. Ḥamdān, of whom there are four and they are all contemporaries.

3. When the surname of relationship [*kunya*] and ascription [*nisba*] are the same, such as 'Imrān al-Jūnī, of whom there are two.

4. When the name of the person, the name of the father and the ascription are the same, such as Muḥammad b. 'Abdullah al-Anṣārī, of whom there are two.

5. When the surname of relationship [*kunya*] and the name of the father are the same, such as Abū Bakr b. 'Ayyāsh, of whom there are three.

6. When the name of the person and the surname of relationship [*kunya*] of the father are the same, such as Ṣāliḥ b. Abī Ṣāliḥ, of whom there are four and they are all Successors.

7. When the name or the surname of relationship [*kunya*] is the same.

---

[235] Possibly the author's expression could be imagined to mean that the *muttafiq* and the *muftariq* are two categories, but they are not. There is only one category which is named such because it concurs in both expression and writing but differs in that which it designates.

An example of this in relation to [the same] names is 'Abdullah, which refers to Ibn al-Zubayr when used in the context of Mecca. If in the context of Medina, it refers to Ibn 'Umar. In Kufa it refers to Ibn Mas'ūd, in Basra it refers to Ibn 'Abbās, in Khorasan it refers to to Ibn al-Mubārak, and in the Levant it refers to Ibn 'Amr b. al-'Āṣ, may Allah be pleased with them all!

As for the *muttafiq* and *muftariq* in relation to surnames of relationship [*kunya*], there are seven with the name Abū Ḥamza, all of whom are with a *ḥā'* and a *zāy*, except one which is with a *jīm* and a *rā'*,[236] and they all narrate from Ibn 'Abbās ﷺ.

8. When two [names] concur in *nisba* in terms of pronunciation, but differ in what is meant by it. For example, al-Ḥanafī refers to either a tribe or [the school of] Abū Ḥanīfa. Some of the people of Hadith differentiated between the two by adding a *yā'* (ī), saying *Ḥanīfī*, if it refers to the founder of the school.

The benefit of knowing the *muttafiq* and *muftariq* is that one is safe from confusion, since one could erroneously believe multiple people are the same person, whereas one of them is a reliable narrator and the other is weak.

SIMILAR AND DISSIMILAR [*MU'TALIF WA-MUKHTALIF*]

مُؤْتَلِفٌ مُتَّفِقُ الْـخَطِّ فَقَطْ   وَضِدُّهُ مُخْتَلِفٌ فَاخْشَ الْغَلَطْ

Mu'talif concurs in writing alone,
And its opposite is mukhtalif, so beware of erring!

---

236 *Jamra*—Tr.

This is when the orthography and script are the same, although the pronunciation is different, whether the difference is in terms of diacritics [*naqt*] or vowelling [*shakl*].[237] The most perilous is when this occurs in names of narrators.

There is no way to know this other than by transmission and narrations from the people of knowledge—it cannot be known from the preceding or following parts of the speech. Therefore, the student of Hadith ought to be concerned about knowing this in order to avoid an alteration of one or more letters due to their dots, in names, ascriptions [*nisba*], titles and surnames of relationship [*kunya*].

The first to author an independent work on this topic was Ḥāfiẓ ʿAbd al-Ghanī b. Saʿīd al-Miṣrī, and the last was Ḥāfiẓ Ibn Ḥajar.

There are two types:

The first type, which is the most common, is that which has no particular governing rule to be referred to because of its regular occurrence—and this is only known through sound transmission and memorisation, such as Usayd in the diminutive form, and Asīd in the augmentative form, and Ḥayyān and Ḥibbān.

The second type has a rule due to it being uncommon.

Sometimes it can be a general rule, such as the name Sallām —all of them have a doubled *lām* except the Companion ʿAbdullah b. Salām, his sister's son Salām, the grandfather of Abū ʿAlī al-Jubbāʾī the Muʿtazilī, the grandfather of al-Nasafī, the grandfather of al-Sīdī, the father of al-Bīkandī, Salām b. Abū al-Ḥuqayq, and Salām b. Mishkam al-Yahūdī.

On other occasions, the rule can be specific to the two *Ṣaḥīḥ* collections and the *Muwaṭṭaʾ*, such as saying that there is no-one called so-and-so in these three books except for so-and-so, for example, Khāzim—with a *khāʾ*, Muḥammad b. Khāzim Abū Muʿāwiya. Aside of him, there is no other Khāzim in these three books, rather they are Ḥāzim, such as Abū Ḥāzim al-Aʿraj and Jarīr b. Ḥāzim.

---

[237] They are two terms for a single category, contrary to what the author's expression might cause one to imagine, i.e., that they are distinct.

Denounced and Affirmed [*Munkar wa-Ma'rūf*]

تَعْدِيـلُهُ لاَ يَحْـمِلُ التَّفَرُّدَا   وَالْـمُنْكَرُ الْـفَرْدُ بِهِ رَاوٍ غَدَا

Munkar is narrated by a sole narrator,
Whose rank does not allow for a solitary narration

Munkar is a solitarily narrated Hadith which contradicts that of someone who is reliable [*thiqa*], and which is far from being accurate and precise. An example of this from [Ibn Ḥajar's] *Sharḥ al-Nukhba* is that which is narrated by Ibn Abī Ḥātim by way of Ḥubayb—in the diminutive form—b. Ḥabīb al-Muqrī', from Abū Isḥāq, from al-'Ayzār b. Ḥurayth, from Ibn 'Abbās ﷺ, from the Prophet ﷺ, "Whoever establishes the prayer, fulfils his charitable obligations, makes pilgrimage to the House, fasts in the month of Ramaḍān and receives his guest well will enter Paradise."

Abū Ḥātim said: "This (Hadith) is *munkar* because there are upright narrators other than Ḥubayb who narrate this from Abū Isḥāq in a halted [*mawqūf*] form (meaning from Ibn 'Abbās ﷺ) and this is well-known."

Then Ḥāfiẓ [Ibn Ḥajar] said in *Sharḥ al-Nukhba*:

> Due to this it is known that the *shādh* (anomalous) and *munkar* share general and particular matters from one point of view, since both entail that they contradict [other more reliable reports], but differ in that the narrator of the *shādh* is reliable or truthful [*ṣadūq*], whereas the narrator of the *munkar* Hadith is weak. Those who equate the two are forgetful [of this distinction].[238]

Ma'rūf is that in which a weightier person contradicts someone who is weak. The ruling on the *munkar* Hadith is that it is weak and rejected. One only uses the opposing narration, the *ma'rūf*, in an argument and as proof.

---

[238] In *Laqṭ al-Durar*, he [al-'Adawī] says: "He meant Ibn al-Ṣalāḥ by this, since he equated them, making no distinction between the two, inasmuch as he [Ibn al-Ṣalāḥ] said: '*Munkar* means *shādh*...'"

A benefit

He [al-Suyūṭī] says in *al-Tadrīb*: "We find in their expressions, 'The most *munkar*[239] narration of so-and-so is this Hadith,' even if that Hadith is not weak."

Ibn ʿAdī says:

> The most *munkar* narration of Burayd b. ʿAbdullah b. Abī Burda is, "When Allah desires good for a nation, He takes their Prophet [back to Him] before them."
>
> …(He said:) This chain is fair and its narrators are all reliable, and some have even included it in their *Ṣaḥīḥ* collections.'

This Hadith is in *Ṣaḥīḥ Muslim*. Therefore the usage of the word *munkar* is interpretable to denote its linguistic connotation rather than its technical usage, just as Ḥāfiẓ Ibn Kathīr says in *Ikhtiṣār ʿUlūm al-Ḥadīth*:

> And when the only one who narrates the Hadith has integrity, is accurate and has a strong memory, his narration is legally [*shar'an*] accepted and not called *munkar*, even it is considered to be so linguistically.

---

[239] The literal meaning connotes something reprehensible or objectionable. Therefore, the term is used here in comparison to other superior narrations of that individual—Tr.

CHAPTER TWELVE
ABANDONED, FABRICATED, CONTRADICTION AND ABROGATION

ABANDONED [*MATRŪK*]

مَتْرُوكُـهُ مَا وَاحِدٌ بِـهِ انْـفَرَدْ   وَأَجْمَعُواْ لِضَعْفِـهِ فَهْوَ كَرَدّ

Matrūk is narrated by a single narrator,

Whose weakness in status there is consensus upon,
Thus it is like a rejected [tradition][240]

Matrūk is that which is narrated by a single narrator who is suspected of lying in Hadith, or who is a flagrant sinner in word or deed, or who is greatly inattentive or excessively prone to make mistakes [*kathīr al-wahm*]. For example, the Hadith of Ṣadaqa al-Daqīqī from Farqad, from Murra, from Abū Bakr ﷺ, and the Hadith of ʿAmr b. Shamir from Jābir al-Juʿfī, from al-Ḥārith al-Aʿwar, from ʿAlī ﷺ.

Thus, everyone whom the scholars of Hadith unanimously accuse of lying, flagrant sin, great inattentiveness or mistakes, their narrations are *matrūk*.

The ruling on the *matrūk* Hadith is that it cannot be considered due to its severe weakness, and cannot serve as proof, neither independently nor as a corroborative narration.

---

[240] *Radd* here means rejected [*mardūd*], and some consider the *kāf* ('as') here to be superfluous. The meaning is then that the *matrūk* Hadith is rejected. Some have considered the *kāf* to be fundamental, and the meaning is to liken the *matrūk* to the fabricated [*mawḍūʿ*], which is rejected. The meaning therefore being that it is similar to the rejected Hadith, that is to say the fabricated [Hadith], albeit lesser in weakness than it.

FABRICATED [*MAWḌŪʿ*]

وَالْكَذِبُ الْمُخْتَلَقْ الْـمَصْنُوعُ   عَلَى النَّبِي فَذَلِكَ الْـمَوْضُوعُ

The concocted and manufactured lie,
Against the Prophet ﷺ is called mawḍūʿ

Mawḍūʿ is that which an individual contrived, and an invented lie which he attributed to the Messenger of Allah ﷺ.

Ways of recognising fabrication

Fabrication can be recognised in a number of ways:

1. By the admission of the fabricator himself, such as the admission of ʿUmar b. Ṣubḥ. Al-Bukhārī said in *al-Tārīkh al-Awsaṭ*: "Yaḥyā al-Yashkurī narrated to me from ʿAlī b. Jarīr and said: 'I heard ʿUmar b. Ṣubḥ saying: "I fabricated a sermon of the Prophet ﷺ."'"

   Similarly, Maysara al-Fārisī confessed to fabricating narrations regarding the virtues of the Qur'an, and narrations on the merits of ʿAlī ﷺ. Confessing is also connected to similar phenomena, such as when a fabricator narrates a Hadith from a teacher and is asked about his [teacher's] date of birth and then mentions the teacher's date and it transpires that the teacher died before the fabricator [was born], and additionally that no-one else has narrated this Hadith. Although the fabricator did not confess to it, his acknowledgement of his date of birth is treated as being the same as a confession of fabrication.

   An example of this, as al-ʿIrāqī said, is that Maʾmūn b. Aḥmad al-Harawī claimed that he had heard from Hishām b. ʿAmmār, so Ḥāfiẓ Ibn Ḥibbān asked him: "When did you enter the Levant?" He replied: "In the year 250 H." Ibn Ḥibbān then said: "The Hishām that you narrate from died in the year 245 H." He replied: "That is another Hishām b. ʿAmmār!"

2. When the meaning is flimsy, regardless of whether it is also flimsy in expression.

    Al-Rabi‘ b. Khaytham said: "Hadith has a luminance like that of the day which you can recognise, and darkness like the dark of night which you repudiate." Ibn al-Jawzī said: "The skin of the student of knowledge creeps because of the denounced [*munkar*] Hadith, from which for the most part his heart flees."

    If the expression alone is flimsy, then this is not by itself evidence of fabrication, since he may have narrated it in meaning [and not verbatim], such that he changed a beautiful wording to another which is flimsy. If the wording is flimsy and then he claimed that these are the actual words of the Prophet ﷺ, then this is evidence that the narrator is a lying fabricator.

3. There is a contextual indication [*qarīna*] concerning the narrator that the Hadith is fabricated.

    This was the case with Ghiyāth b. Ibrāhīm when he visited [the Caliph] al-Mahdī and found him playing with a dove. On the spot, he then attributed a chain [*isnād*] to the Prophet ﷺ that he said: "There is no prize-giving [for a competition] except in archery,[241] camels[242] or horses,"[243] "or wings," and he added "or wings" to the Hadith, and al-Mahdī knew that he had lied for his sake, so he [al-Mahdī] ordered for the dove to be slaughtered.

    Another example of this is what al-Ḥākim narrated from Sayf b. ‘Umar al-Tamīmī who said: "I was with Sa‘d b. Ṭarīf when his son came from the Qur’an school [*kuttāb*] crying. He said: 'What happened?' [The son] replied: 'The teacher hit me.' He [Sa‘d b. Ṭarīf] said: 'I shall disgrace them today. ‘Ikrima narrated to me from Ibn ‘Abbās ﷺ, raising it to the Prophet ﷺ [*marfū‘an*],

---

[241] *Naṣl*: lit. arrowhead—Ed.
[242] *Khuff*: lit. camel-hoof—Ed.
[243] *Ḥāfir*: lit. horse's hoof—Ed.

"The teachers of your children are the worst of you, the least merciful towards orphans and the harshest towards the poor.""""

He says in *al-Tadrīb*: "Among the circumstantial evidence [of fabrication] is that the narrator is a *Rāfiḍī*[244] while the Hadith concerns the virtues of the People of the Prophetic Household [*Ahl al-Bayt*]."

4. That the narration contradicts a definitive [*qaṭʿī*] principle from the Qur'an or the mass-transmitted Sunna, or definitive consensus [*ijmāʿ qaṭʿī*], or rational evidence—and that the narration does not allow for an interpretation that would reconcile it with that which contradicts it. If it does allow for an interpretation, then it is not [necessarily fabricated].

5. That the report relates to a significant matter which a great number would have transmitted in a large gathering, and yet only one person narrates it.

6. That someone who searches for it investigates it but does not find it among eminent scholars or in books.

7. That the narration contains an excessive threat for a relatively minor misdeed, or a tremendous promise for a less insignificant good deed. Such a type is very common amongst the Hadith of the storytellers.

Al-Suyūṭī says:

> *The worst of reports are fabrications,*
> *So beware of a scholar who knows it, mentioning it,*
>
> *However that may be,*
> *Except to describe it as fabrication*
>
> *Fabrication is known by:*
> *Confession and what he cites*

---

[244] Those Shiʿa who disparage certain Companions of the Prophet ﷺ, or most of them, and his wife, Lady ʿĀʾisha ﷺ—Tr.

> *Or by feeble expression,*
> *Or by evidence within it*
>
> *And it contradicts something definitive,*
> *With no room for interpretation*
>
> *Or that what is narrated [by one],*
> *When the circumstances suggest*
>
> *It should [be narrated by many],*[245]
> *Or it is not found amongst the people [of Hadith]*
>
> *And that which carries a great threat or a promise,*
> *For a lesser or minor sin*

Reasons for fabrication

There are many reasons that fabricators manufactured Hadith, and we shall mention the most important reasons here:

1. In order to corrupt religion amongst people, as the heretics [*zanādiqa*] did when they fabricated fourteen thousand Hadith, as mentioned by al-ʿUqaylī.

   One of them was ʿAbd al-Karīm b. Abī ʿAwjāʾ, who was killed and crucified during the time of [the Caliph] al-Mahdī. Ibn ʿAdī said: "When he was captured, his neck was struck. He said: 'I have fabricated amongst you fourteen thousand Hadith in which I forbade the permissible and permitted that which is forbidden.'"[246]

   One of them was Muḥammad b. Saʿīd al-Shāmī al-Maṣlūb (the crucified). He narrated from Ḥumayd, from Anas ﷺ, raising it to the Prophet ﷺ [*marfūʿan*], "I am the seal of the Prophets. There will be no Prophet after me, except if God wills." He fabricated this exception ["except if God wills"] in order to summon to his own claim to prophecy and disbelief.

---

[245] The meaning here is that a sign of a fabricated Hadith is something which refers to an event that ought to have been witnessed (and therefore narrated) by many people, yet is only narrated by one person—Tr.

[246] [Al-Suyūṭī] *Tadrīb al-Rāwī*, p. 210]

2. In order to promote one's ideology. As Ibn Abī Ḥātim narrates that a Shaykh of the Seceders [*Khawārij*] would say after repenting: "Be careful who you take your religion from, for if we desired a certain thing, we would make it into a Hadith."

3. Where the fabricator does so in order to ingratiate himself with leaders and emirs and justify their actions, as happened in the earlier mentioned story of Ghiyāth b. Ibrāhīm with al-Mahdī.

4. In order to gain money and a livelihood, such as Abū Saʿīd al-Madāʾinī.

5. In order to gain other-worldly reward by fabricating, according to the claim of the fabricator, as an ignorant group of people did who fabricated narrations in order to encourage others to perform good deeds, anticipating a reward in the afterlife, despite their erroneous claims.

He [al-Suyūṭī] says in *al-Tadrīb*:

As an example of fabrication that was done desiring a [religious] reward, there is the narration of al-Ḥākim with his chain up to ʿAmmār al-Marwazī, that it was said to Abū ʿIṣma Nūḥ b. Abī Maryam: "Did you get the narration from ʿIkrima and from Ibn ʿAbbās regarding the virtues of individual chapters of the Qurʾan, whereas the companions of ʿIkrima don't have anything of this sort!" He [Abū ʿIṣma] said: "I saw people had turned away from the Qurʾan, and had become preoccupied with the *madhhab* (school of law) of Abū Ḥanīfa and *al-Maghāzī* of Ibn Isḥāq, so I fabricated this Hadith in hope of reward." It would be said of Abū ʿIṣma, "Nūḥ, the comprehensive compiler." Ibn Ḥibbān said: "Rather, he compiled everything except the truth!"

6. Fabrication in order to gain fame by having wondrous narrations [that no-one else had].

A benefit

He [al-Suyūṭī] says in *al-Tadrīb*:

> There are Hadith that have been narrated regarding the virtues of various chapters—some of which are sound, some are fair and others are weak, but not fabricated. The Qur'anic commentary of Ḥāfiẓ 'Imād al-Dīn b. Kathīr is the most reliable in this regard, since the majority of what he mentions is not fabricated, even if there are some oversights. I have compiled a brief treatise on this topic called *Khamā'il al-Zuhar fī Faḍā'il al-Suwar*.
>
> You should know that the chapters of the Qur'an which have sound narrations regarding their virtues are the following: *al-Fātiḥa* and *al-Zahrawān* [*al-Baqara* and *Āl 'Imrān*], *al-An'ām*, the Seven Lengthy chapters [*Sab' al-Ṭuwal*],[247] *al-Kahf, Yā Sīn, al-Dukhān, al-Mulk, al-Zalzala, al-Naṣr, al-Kāfirūn, al-Ikhlāṣ* and *al-Mu'awwidhatān* [*al-Falaq* and *al-Nās*]. Apart from that nothing else is sound.

This [last] statement is [true] in the majority of cases.[248]

The ruling on fabrication

By consensus of the Muslims whose opinion is to be reckoned with, fabrication in all its forms is categorically forbidden. However, the *Karrāmiyya*—a group of innovators who ascribed to Muḥammad b. Karrām the theologian—differed in this. They permitted the fabrication of Hadith in order to encourage good deeds and discourage acts of disobedience, but not those which have any relevance to legal rulings in terms of reward and punishment. They interpreted the Hadith, "Whoever lies against me intentionally, let him prepare his seat in Hellfire," by saying, "We merely lie *for* him, not *against* him."[249]

---

[247] This refers to the first seven chapters of the Qur'an, namely: *al-Baqara, Āl 'Imrān, al-Nisā', al-Mā'ida, al-An'ām, al-A'rāf* and *Yūnus*. This is according to one opinion—Tr.

[248] I.e., the list provided is not exhaustive, and other narrations exist regarding virtues of other chapters of the Qur'an—Tr.

[249] They also adduced as proof that which has been narrated through other chains of narration, "Whoever lies against me intentionally *in*

There is no doubt that this is a mistake on the part of the one who does it, which stems from ignorance, since encouraging [good] and warning [against evil] form a part of legal rulings. The majority of *Ahl al-Sunna* (Sunni orthodoxy) concur that to lie intentionally about the Prophet ﷺ is one of the major sins, given the severe threat that has been transmitted, for example, the Hadith narrated by the two Shaykhs [al-Bukhārī and Muslim] and others, "Whoever lies against me intentionally, let him prepare his seat in Hellfire."

Abū Muḥammad al-Juwaynī was emphatic about this, declaring those who lied against the Prophet ﷺ intentionally to be disbelievers, and that it is permissible to spill their blood. The majority of scholars do not declare them disbelievers unless they consider it to be permissible. Rather, they are considered to be flagrant wrongdoers whose narrations are to be rejected in their entirety, and are all rendered invalid in an argument and as proof.

The ruling on the *mawḍūʿ*

The scholars are in complete agreement that a fabricated narration cannot be used in any way, since it constitutes a forged lie.

The ruling on narrating fabricated Hadith

It is prohibited to narrate fabrications knowing that they are fabricated in any sense—regardless of whether they relate to legal rulings, stories, encouraging good deeds and discouraging evil deeds and the like, except if one clarifies that they are fabrications, due to the Hadith in [*Ṣaḥīḥ*] Muslim, "Whoever narrates a Hadith from me which is considered to be a lie, is one of the liars." And if a person is not aware that it is a fabrication, then he is not sinful for narrating it, although he will have fallen short in researching it.[250]

---

order to misguide people." However, the masters of Hadith have concurred that this addition is false. On the assumption that it was sound, it would be for emphasis [and not restrictive].

[250] Regarding the soundness of the Hadith, and in the collections of fabrications.

And for a scholar to narrate a fabrication in order to clarify that it is a fabrication is an act for which he is rewarded.

Books of fabrications

The scholars have authored many works clarifying fabricated Hadith, and we shall mention the most famous extant ones:

1. *Al-Mawḍūʿāt al-Kubrā* by Ibn al-Jawzī

However, he did not investigate thoroughly nor did he consider them carefully, to the extent that he mentions numerous *ṣaḥīḥ* and *ḥasan* narrations in his book as being fabrications. Some of the *ʿulamā* therefore considered him to be mistaken.

Ḥāfiẓ Ibn Ḥajar wrote a book called *al-Qawl al-Musaddad fī al-Dhabbi ʿan Musnad Aḥmad* in which he mentions twenty-four Hadith from the *Musnad* of Imam Aḥmad [b. Ḥanbal] which Ibn al-Jawzī mentioned in *al-Mawḍūʿāt*.

Ḥāfiẓ al-Suyūṭī wrote a book called *al-Qawl al-Ḥasan fī al-Dhabbi ʿan al-Sunan* in which he mentioned around one hundred and twenty Hadith which Ibn al-Jawzī included in *al-Mawḍūʿāt*, some of which are found in *Sunan Abū Dāwūd*, some in *Sunan al-Tirmidhī*, some in *Sunan al-Nasāʾī*, some in *Sunan Ibn Mājah*, some in *Musnad al-Dārimī*, some in *al-Mustadrak* of al-Ḥākim and some from *al-Anwāʿ wal-Taqāsīm* of Ibn Ḥibbān. The strangest thing is that Ibn Jawzī includes a Hadith in *al-Mawḍūʿāt* which Muslim narrated in his *Ṣaḥīḥ*.

Ibn Ḥajar clarifies that the only narration he found in *al-Mawḍūʿāt* of Ibn al-Jawzī from either of the two *Ṣaḥīḥ* collections which he [Ibn al-Jawzī] classified as a fabrication is the Hadith of Muslim, "If you live a lengthy life, you will soon see a people going out in the morning in the displeasure of Allah and returning in the evening under the curse of Allah. In their hands will be [whips like] the tails of cows." He said: "This is an act of gross oversight by Ibn al-Jawzī."

2. *Tadhkira al-Mawḍūʿāt* by Ḥāfiẓ Abū al-Faḍl al-Maqdisī
3. *Al-Maqāṣid al-Ḥasana* by Ḥāfiẓ al-Sakhāwī. I possess this in manuscript form.

4. *Tamyīz al-Ṭayyib min al-Khabīth*
   by Ibn al-Daybaʿ al-Shaybānī

5. *Al-Laʾālīʾ al-Maṣnūʿa fī al-Aḥādīth al-Mawḍūʿa*
   by Ḥāfiẓ al-Suyūṭī

This is a summary of *al-Mawḍūʿāt al-Kubrā* of Ibn al-Jawzī along with clarifications of where he inaccurately declared narrations to be fabrications, which are *ṣaḥīḥ*, *ḥasan* or *ḍaʿīf*, but not fabrications.

6. *Tadhkira al-Mawḍūʿāt* by ʿAllāma Muḥammad b. Ṭāhir b. ʿAlī al-Hindī al-Fattānī. It includes *Qānūn al-Mawḍūʿāt wal-Ḍuʿafāʾ* by the same author in the appendix.
7. *Al-Mawḍūʿāt al-Kubrā wal-Ṣughrā* by Shaykh ʿAlī al-Qārī
8. *Al-Luʾluʾ al-Marṣūʿ*
   by Abū Maḥāsin al-Qāwuqjī al-Ḥasanī al-Mashīshī
9. *Al-Mawḍūʿāt* by al-Ṣaghānī
10. *Asnā al-Maṭālib* by Shaykh Muḥammad b. al-Sayyid Darwīsh, better known as al-Ḥūt

11. *Kashf al-Khafā wa-Muzīl al-Iltibās* by ʿAllāma al-ʿAjlūnī

It is a comprehensive work of the narrations that people commonly mention. It is a valuable book which clarifies the narrations that people commonly mention, including [those that are] *ṣaḥīḥ*, *ḥasan*, *ḍaʿīf* and fabrications, with a great deal of research and investigation.

CONTRADICTORY NARRATIONS [*MUKHTALIF AL-ḤADĪTH*]

It is when two narrations contradict each other in their literal meanings. Regarding its ruling, it requires investigation:

1. If it is possible to reconcile both narrations in a correct way, one does not turn away from them, rather they can be acted upon at the same time.

For example, the Hadith, "There is nothing contagious," and his ﷺ saying, "Flee from a leper as you would from a lion." Both are narrated in one Hadith.

These two narrations have been reconciled by saying that these illnesses are not contagious by their nature, but Allah has made an ill person engage with a healthy person a means for infecting someone else with his illness. This can be suspended, as with all means, since it only has an effect due to the power of Allah, the Exalted, if this was preceded by the will of Allah for that. Otherwise, it causes no effect inherently.

There are other ways to reconcile them. This is an example relating to natural law. As for religious legal rulings, there is the example of the Hadith, "If water reaches the amount of two pitchers [*qullatayn*], it does not carry filth," with the Hadith, "Allah created water to be purifying; nothing renders it impure except whatever alters its taste, colour or smell."

Regarding the first Hadith, the literal meaning suggests that two pitchers [of water] are pure regardless of whether the water changes or not. The literal meaning of the second narration suggests the purity of that which does not itself change, regardless of whether it amounts to two pitchers or less. The general meaning of each one is qualified by the other, as mentioned in *al-Tadrīb* [of al-Suyūṭī].

2. If the there are two narrations that contradict one another, without any way to reconcile them, then if we know that one abrogates the other in any of the various ways which indicate abrogation, we take the abrogating Hadith.

3. If abrogation cannot be established, we take the preponderant one.

There are numerous detailed methods in which the preponderant [narration] can be demonstrated which are mentioned in the books of legal theory [*uṣūl al-fiqh*] and elsewhere. Al-Ḥāzimī mentions fifty different ways in his book *al-Iʿtibār*. Al-ʿIrāqī mentions one hundred and ten. Al-Suyūṭī summarised them and reduced them to seven types, each type containing numerous ways.

First, preference given because of the circumstances of the narrator, such as when there are numerous narrators, or there is an elevated chain, or because of the *fiqh* (understanding) of the narrator, and so on.

Second, preference given to the method of receiving the Hadith, such as preferring direct narration [*taḥdīth*] over reading to a teacher [*ʿarḍ*], preferring *ʿarḍ* to receiving by writing [*kitāba*], presentation [*munāwala*], or finding the Hadith written down [*wijāda*].

Third, preference given due to the method of narrating, such as preferring narration verbatim to narration in meaning. Also [preference given] to those which mention the reasons for which the Hadith came about [*sabab al-wurūd*],[251] over those in which no mention of that is made, since the former indicates the concern of the narrator.

Fourth, preponderance due to the time it came about, such as the preponderance of Medinan over Meccan.

Fifth, preponderance according to the type of utterance used in the narration, such as the preponderance of [something] specific [*khāṣṣ*] over [something] general [*ʿāmm*], and absolute [*muṭlaq*] over that which was mentioned due to a reason, and the preponderance of that which is literal [*ḥaqīqa*] over that which is metaphorical [*majāz*].

Sixth, preponderance due to a legal ruling, such as the preponderance of that which is evidence of prohibition over that which is evidence of permissibility.

Seventh, preponderance due to an external factor, such as the preponderance of that which conforms to the literal meaning of the Qurʾan or another Hadith.

---

[251] The study of the Qurʾan has a science known as *asbāb al-nuzūl* (the reasons for revelation), which deals with the reasons for which verses were revealed. Hadith has an equivalent science, known as *asbāb al-wurūd*—Tr.

4.   If there is no way to give precedence to either of the two
Hadith using any of the previously mentioned ways, then
judgement must be suspended [*tawaqquf*].

This art is one of the most important of all sciences of Hadith
that the scholar must know. Only those Imams who gather
Hadith, jurisprudence and legal theory, and who are immersed in
deriving precise meanings, are concerned with it.

The most important works

Imam al-Shāfiʿī wrote on this subject, in fact it is said that he
was the first to do so. Ibn Qutayba then authored a work titled
Taʾwīl Mukhtalif al-Ḥadīth in which he mentioned good points, as
well as other than that, due to his shortcomings in it. Then Ibn
Jarīr [al-Ṭabarī] compiled something on this topic. Al-Ṭaḥāwī
authored his work *Muskhil al-Āthār*, which is a tremendously
useful book spanning several volumes, in which he provides
convincing answers.

Ibn Khuzayma was one of the proficient in this science, so
much so that he said: "There are no two Hadith which completely
contradict each other. If anyone finds anything of that nature, let
him bring it to me so that I can resolve it!"

ABROGATING AND ABROGATED [*AL-NĀSIKH WAL-MANSŪKH*]

Abrogation is defined as the legislator [*shāriʿ*] replacing an
earlier legal ruling with a later one. The meaning of 'replacing' is
the removal of its application to those with legal responsibility
[*mukallafīn*]. An exception to this is that which was originally
permissible [and then became prohibited],[252] since its removal is
not called abrogation.

An example of abrogation is that which Muslim narrated from
Burayda 🙏, raising it to the Prophet 🙏 [*marfūʿan*], "I used to
forbid you from visiting graves, but now you should visit them."

---

[252] Such as the prohibition of alcohol, which was originally permissible
but then became prohibited in three Qurʾanic stages, first becoming
disliked and eventually completely forbidden—Tr.

How abrogation is identified
Abrogation is identified in a number of ways:

1.   By explicit mention by the legislator [*shāriʿ*]

Such as the Hadith of al-Tirmidhī, "I used to forbid you sacrificial meat beyond three nights so that the prosperous could give to those less prosperous, but now you should eat what you like, feed others and keep some."

Likewise, the Hadith, "I used to forbid you drinks except from tanned leather vessels, but now you may drink from any type of vessel, but do not drink intoxicants."

2.   By confirmation of a Companion of a later ruling

Such as the statement of Jābir ⬥, "The latter of two commands from the Prophet ⬥ was to leave off doing ablution for anything that fire has touched." Abū Dāwūd and al-Nasāʾī narrated it.

As for a Companion saying "this abrogates that," the majority of scholars of legal theory do not accept this, since this constitutes independent reasoning [*ijtihād*], in which one may make an error. As for his confirmation of a latter explicit statement, then he is transmitting, and he is someone who is reliable and whose narrations are accepted.

Al-ʿIrāqī said:

> The approach of the people of Hadith is clearer and more well-known, which is that regardless of whether it entails a confirmation of the latter event or passing a judgement of abrogation, it is the same, since abrogation is not reached through *ijtihād* and opinion [*raʾy*]. Rather, it is reached through knowledge of historical records. The Companions were too scrupulous for any one of them to pronounce a legal judgement as being abrogated without knowing the later abrogating event.

3.   Abrogation known through chronology

Such as the Hadith of Shaddād b. 'Aws 🙽, raising it to the Prophet 🙽 [*marfū'an*], "The practitioner and patient of cupping invalidate their fast [by doing so]." Narrated by Abū Dāwūd and al-Nasā'ī. Al-Shāfi'ī said: "This is abrogated due to the Hadith of Ibn 'Abbās, 'that the Prophet 🙽 underwent cupping whilst in a state of *ihrām*[253] and while fasting.'" Muslim narrated the Hadith with its chain [*isnād*].

Ibn 'Abbās only accompanied the Prophet 🙽 while he was in a state of *ihrām* during the Farewell Pilgrimage in the tenth year. In some variants of the narration of Shaddād 🙽 he said that this occurred at the time of the Conquest [*al-Fath*] [of Mecca] in the eighth year H.[254]

4.   Abrogation known by the evidence of consensus
Al-Suyūtī says:

A *sahīh* example of this is that which is narrated by al-Tirmidhī from the Hadith of Jābir 🙽, in which he said: "When we performed *hajj* with the Prophet 🙽, we would call out the *talbiya*[255] on behalf of women and we would perform the stoning [ritual] on behalf of children."

Al-Tirmidhī says: "The people of knowledge unanimously agree that no-one is able to perform the *talbiya* on behalf of a woman."

---

[253] *Ihrām* is the state which one enters before performing either of the two pilgrimages—Tr.

[254] That which is narrated by al-Dāraqutnī is also evidence of abrogation, that the Prophet 🙽 passed by Ja'far b. Abī Tālib 🙽 who underwent cupping while fasting, so he 🙽 said: "This one has invalidated the fast." Afterwards, the Prophet 🙽 made an allowance for the fasting person to undergo cupping [without invalidating the fast]. The Prophet 🙽 would undergo whilst fasting. All of its narrators are reliable.

[255] The invocation that is read during the rites of the pilgrimage—Tr.

The importance of knowing this subject

Knowing the abrogating and abrogated narrations is one of the most important sciences, and one of the most delicate and difficult [at the same time]. Al-Zuhrī said: "Knowledge of the difference between the abrogating and abrogated Hadith exhausted the jurists and left them powerless."

Al-Shāfiʿī displayed a particular degree of expertise in this, so much so that Imam Aḥmad said to Ibn Wārah, who had just come from Egypt: "Did you record[256] the books of al-Shāfiʿī?" He said: "No." [Imam Aḥmad] said: "Then you have been negligent. We never knew the *mujmal*[257] from the *mufassar*,[258] or the abrogating from the abrogated, before we sat with al-Shāfiʿī."

Al-Ḥāzimī narrated with a chain that ʿAlī ﷺ passed by a storyteller and said: "Can you differentiate between the abrogating and the abrogated?" He replied: "No." [ʿAlī ﷺ] said to him: "Then you will perish and you will cause others to perish."

He also narrated with a chain that Ḥudhayfa ﷺ was asked about a matter and said: "The only one who should issue legal edicts is someone who can differentiate between the abrogating and the abrogated." So they said: "Who knows this?" He [Ḥudhayfa ﷺ] said: "ʿUmar ﷺ."

Therefore, detailed research regarding the science of abrogation comes under the remit of legal theory and the like, as Ibn Kathīr and others have clarified, because the jurist is someone who derives rulings from Hadith and therefore requires expertise in this field. As for the scholar of Hadith, his role is to transmit and narrate what he hears of Hadith in the manner he heard it. If he embarks on anything beyond that it is praiseworthy and virtuous.

---

[256] This refers to the fact that books at that time would be copied, often by the person himself (as opposed to a scribe) and therefore what is ultimately being asked is whether Ibn Wārah had read the books of Imam al-Shāfiʿī—Tr.

[257] A classification of a word or expression which lacks clarity in its utterance and meaning and requires additional information that cannot be qualified by the intellect—Tr.

[258] A classification of word or expression which is clear in its denotation, that accepts the possibility of abrogation during the Prophetic era of legislation.—Tr.

KNOWING WHOSE NARRATIONS ARE ACCEPTED
AND WHOSE ARE REJECTED

The narrations of someone who is reliable in his religion and in his narration are accepted: that is someone who has integrity [*'adl*] is accurate [*ḍābiṭ*].

The person who has integrity [*'adl*] is someone who is an adult Muslim of sound mind and free from flagrant sin [*fisq*]—which is perpetrating major sins or persisting in minor sins—and is free of contraventions of social norms [*murū'a*].

Murū'a refers to engaging in things considered to be good and distancing oneself from those things considered to be lowly, such as eating whilst walking and unnecessarily urinating in the street.

Accuracy [*ḍabṭ*] is proficiency [*itqān*] in what one narrates; meaning one is vigilant and alert, not heedless. He narrates from memory, is accurate in his writing if he cites from a book, is knowledgeable about the meaning of what he narrates, and is aware of what would change the meaning from what was intended, if he narrates in meaning.

The narrator's integrity [*'adāla*] is established by having a good and praiseworthy reputation, such as the four Imams and others, or by the Imams, or two of them, or even one, declaring someone to have integrity.

His accuracy is established when his narrations concur with the reliable and proficient masters [*al-thiqāt al-mutqinīn*]. Occasional contradictions do not affect this. However, if this occurs frequently, a person's narrations are rejected due to his inaccuracy.

Narrating from people of creedal innovation [*ahl al-bid'a*]

The narrations of an innovator are rejected if his innovation is of the kind that makes him a disbeliever, in that it involves rejecting a matter of the religion that is known by necessity [*ma'lūm min al-dīn bil-ḍarūra*], or believing the opposite of this, and so on, for example anthropomorphists and those who believe that Allah is ignorant of minutiae [*al-juz'iyyāt*].

If his innovation does not remove him from the fold of Islam, but he regards lying as legitimate, then his narrations are also rejected. However, if he does not regard lying as legitimate, his narrations are accepted as long as he does not summon others to his heterodoxy, since if he summons others, this embellishment of his creedal deviance may lead him to corrupt his narrations.

Imam al-Nawawī has given preference to this detail, saying: "It is the clearest and most balanced approach, and it is the opinion of many, or even the majority."

Ḥāfiẓ Abū Isḥāq al-Jūzjānī further qualified the condition of not calling to his heterodox beliefs, adding that he must not narrate Hadith which give credence to his innovation.

Ibn Ḥajar said: "What he [al-Jūzjānī] said is well-balanced, since the reason for rejecting the narrations of someone who calls [others to his innovations] is also contained in it [i.e., in his qualification]."

Levels of *jarḥ wa-ta'dīl*

In his book *Taqrīb al-Tahdhīb* Ḥāfiẓ Ibn Ḥajar clarified the levels of *jarḥ wa-ta'dīl* (narrator evaluation), enumerating them as twelve:

1. The Companions ﷺ.
2. Those whose praise has been emphasised by the use of the superlative form [*af'al*], such as "the most reliable of people," or by uttering a quality repeatedly, such as "reliable! reliable! [*thiqa! thiqa!*]," or in meaning, such as "reliable! a master! [*thiqa! ḥāfiẓ!*]"
3. When a singular quality is mentioned, such as 'reliable' [*thiqa*], 'proficient' [*mutqin*] or 'affirmed' [*thabt*], or 'a person with integrity' [*'adl*].

4. A degree slightly below the previous one, such as 'truthful' [*ṣadūq*], or 'there is no issue with him' [*lā ba's bihi* or *laysa bihi ba's*].

5. A degree below the fourth, which is indicated by such words as "truthful but with a poor memory" [*ṣadūq sayyi' al-ḥifẓ*], or "truthful but prone to error" [*ṣadūq yahim*], or "he has some mistakes" [*lahu awhām*], or "he makes mistakes" [*yukhṭi'*], or "he changed later in life" [*taghayyara bi-ākhirihi*].

   An addition to this category is someone who has been affected by innovated beliefs such as an inclination to Shi'ism [*tashayyu'*], or rejection of predestination [*qadar*],[259] or antinomianism [*irjā'*].[260]

6. Someone who only narrated a few Hadith, but there is nothing that has been affirmed for him that could be a cause for his narrations to be rejected. This is indicated by the words, "acceptable if accompanied by supporting narrations" [*maqbūl ḥaythu yutāba'*]. If a reason is found to reject his narrations, then without [supporting narrations] he is "weak in narrating" [*layyin al-ḥadīth*].

7. Someone from whom more than one person narrates, but no-one has declared him to be reliable. This is indicated by the words 'concealed' [*mastūr*] or 'status unknown' [*majhūl al-ḥāl*].

8. Someone who has not been declared reliable by anyone qualified to do so, while some have declared him to be weak, albeit without presenting proof. This is indicated by the word 'weak' [*ḍa'īf*].

9. Someone from whom only one person narrates, and who hasn't been declared reliable by anyone. This is indicated by the word 'unknown individual' [*majhūl al-'ayn*], meaning he is unknown to the scholars of Hadith.

---

[259] The *Qadariyya* were a sect who believed in unrestricted free will and rejected the idea of pre-destination—Tr.

[260] The *Murji'a* were a sect who believed that one's faith is not harmed by good or evil deeds—Tr.

[An antinomian is someone who is "against [*anti*] the law [*nomos*]," believing that people who have *īmān* are not harmed by wrong action —Ed.]

10. Someone who hasn't been declared reliable by anyone [qualified or not], and he has been declared weak with an impairment that is mentioned. This is indicated by the word 'abandoned' [*matrūk*] or '[his] Hadith are abandoned' [*matrūk al-ḥadīth*] or 'erroneous in narrating' [*wāhī al-ḥadīth*] or 'disregarded' [*sāqiṭ*].

11. Someone suspected of lying. It is said about [such a person: 'suspect' [*muttaham*] or 'suspect of lying' [*muttaham bil-kadhib*], which means he is suspected of deliberately lying,[261] or he lies when narrating but not deliberately and purposefully, although this happens with such frequency that he is suspected of doing so deliberately.[262]

12. Someone who is referred to as a liar or fabricator, such as when they say 'compulsive liar' [*kadhāb*] or 'consistent fabricator' [*waḍḍāʿ*] or 'astonishing liar' [*mā akdhabahu*].

The narrations of those from the second and third ranks are accepted, and the majority of them appear in the two Ṣaḥīḥ collections.

The narrations of those from the fourth rank are likewise accepted, although at a secondary level. They are those that are declared to be *ḥasan* by al-Tirmidhī, although Abū Dāwūd remained silent about them.

If the Hadith of those from the fifth and sixth rank is narrated through multiple chains and is strengthened by supporting narrations, it is considered to be fair due to supporting narrations [*ḥasan li-ghayrihi*]. If not, they are rejected [*mardūd*].

Those from the seventh to the final rank are considered to be weak, although they differ in their levels of weakness.

---

[261] As may be noted here and elsewhere, unlike in English, the word for 'lying' in Arabic does not always denote lying intentionally. Therefore, the scholars have differentiated between intentional and unintentional lying—Tr.

[262] Additionally, someone "accused of lying" may refer to someone who is known to lie in day-to-day life but not known to fabricate narrations. However, the mere possibility that he is known to lie is sufficient for his narrations to be rejected—Tr.

Expressions used by particular scholars of Hadith

1. Imam al-Bukhārī

Sometimes al-Bukhārī used certain expressions with a particular meaning in mind, such as his saying regarding a narrator, 'They were silent regarding him' [*sakatū 'anhu*] or 'it requires investigation' [*fīhi naẓar*], meaning that his narrations are abandoned [*matrūk al-ḥadīth*] and that he is of the lowest level. However, al-Bukhārī was gentle in his use of expressions in critiquing.[263] Likewise, the saying of al-Bukhārī, '[his] Hadith are denounced' [*munkar al-ḥadīth*], by which he referred to persistent fabricators, as Ibn al-Qaṭṭān transmitted from him, saying: "Al-Bukhārī said: 'Whenever I say, "[his] Hadith are denounced" [*munkar al-ḥadīth*], it is not permissible to narrate from him.'"

2. Yaḥyā b. Ma'īn

He said: "If I say 'there is no issue with him' [*laysa bihi ba's*], he is reliable [*thiqa*]."

3. Imam al-Shāfiʿī

His saying, "Someone who I do not suspect, informed me" [*akhbaranī man lā attahim*], is as if he said, "The reliable person informed me," as opposed to al-Dhahabī who says: "It is merely negation of suspicion—it does not demonstrate his proficiency [*itqān*], nor that it is a proof [*ḥujja*]."

4. General scholars of Hadith

When a scholar of Hadith says, "The reliable person informed me," and the like, without naming the individual, it does not suffice as a testimony of his integrity, because he may be reliable according to this particular scholar but, had he named him, other scholars may have negatively critiqued him. It is said: it [his testimony] is accepted as if he had named him. If the one who says it is an independent jurist [*mujtahid*], such as, for example, one of the Imams, it is sufficient for those who follow his school of law [*madhhab*], according to some of the scholars.

---

[263] We find some scholars very harsh in their choice of terminology when describing liars, such as saying 'deceiver' [*dajjāl*], a term which most commonly denotes the Antichrist—Tr.

When is *jarḥ wa-taʿdīl* accepted?

The people of knowledge have differed as to whether vague *jarḥ wa-taʿdīl* (narrator evaluation) is accepted, i.e., when the reasons are not mentioned.

1. Some take the position that such conclusions are not acceptable without providing a reason for omitting the name, in both cases [*jarḥ* and *taʿdīl*].

2. Some have stipulated that the reason must be given for omitting the name when it comes to declaring [someone's] integrity [*taʿdīl*], but not for being critical [*jarḥ*].

3. Some accept a vague declaration of integrity [*taʿdīl mubham*, when the name is not mentioned], but have stipulated that a detailed reason must be given for being critical [*jarḥ*]. Ibn al-Ṣalāḥ, al-Nawawī and others held this position.

4. Some have accepted both *jarḥ* and *taʿdīl* when vague, if the critic is a scholar in the field of narrator evaluation, and knowledgeable of the reasons for being critical of or endorsing [narrators], and possesses insight and is accepted in his belief and deeds. Al-Suyūṭī said: "This is the position of Qāḍī Abū Bakr [b. al-ʿArabī], which he transmits as being that of the majority."

5. Ibn Ḥajar chose the position that whoever is negatively criticised [*juriḥ*] in general terms [without explanation], yet one of the Imams of Hadith regarded him as reliable, then criticism of him is not accepted from anyone unless it is explained, since his reliability has been established and cannot be negated unless there is a clear reason. If, however, there has been no testimony regarding his integrity, unqualified criticism of him is accepted if a qualified person makes it. This is reasonable, because if no-one has testified to his integrity, he is in the realm of being unknown, and acting upon the word of the critic is better than ignoring it.

Contradictions between *jarḥ* and *ta'dīl*

If, for a certain narrator, there is both detailed criticism and testimony to his integrity, the negative criticism takes precedence the positive testimony, even if those who testify to his integrity are greater in number.

Al-Suyūṭī said: "This is the more correct position according to the scholars of jurisprudence and legal theory." Al-Khaṭīb cites this as being the position of the majority of the 'ulamā', because the one who was critical of him had additional information which the one who regarded him as having integrity [*mu'addil*] did not possess, and because he affirms the person who regarded him as having integrity with respect to what he informed about the external state of the narrator, unless he informs about an inner state which was hidden from him.

The jurists have stipulated the above unless the person who regards the narrator as having integrity [*mu'addil*] says, "I know the reason the critic believed him to be unacceptable, but he repented from this," in which case the testimony of his integrity takes precedence over the negative criticism. It is also said that if there is a greater number of positive testimonies then the testimony of his integrity is accepted.

The above applies to two contradictory conclusions of two scholars. If we find two contradictory positions from one scholar, as happened with Ibn Ma'īn and Ibn Ḥibbān, then the latter of the two positions is taken if this is known. If not, then we suspend judgement.

Aspersions that have been transmitted about some of the Imams

It has been the case that some of the 'ulamā' have cast aspersions on some Imams, or narrators of Hadith who are exemplary in their reliability, integrity and acceptability. This may occur for various reasons:

These aspersions against some the Imams could be borne out of one's fanaticism for his school, or because of matters of dispute regarding legal reasoning, or it could be due to worldly competitiveness.

These aspersions are given no heed, as long as the one who is being aspersed is known for his integrity and accuracy, and his piety and God-consciousness.

'Allāma al-Subkī says under the heading, 'A Principle in *Jarḥ wa-Taʿdīl*':

> Someone whose Imamate and integrity are reliably established, and who has been greatly praised and declared to be praiseworthy and veracious, [and who has been] rarely criticised, and there is an indication of the reason for which he has been criticised, such as fanatical devotion to his school or otherwise, then we do not pay any heed to such criticism towards him and we act upon the basis of him having integrity. Were this not the case,[264] and were we to take the position that critical comment has precedence, then none of the Imams would be safe, since there is no Imam who has not been the subject of aspersions from critics, and those who have done so have perished.

> Ḥāfiẓ Ibn ʿAbd al-Barr has included in his book on knowledge [*Jāmiʿ Bayān al-ʿIlm wa-Faḍlihi*] a chapter on the ruling of scholars' statements regarding one another. He begins with a Hadith of al-Zubayr ꜯ, raising it to the Prophet ꜯ [*marfūʿan*], "A disease of the nations of the past has crept amongst you: envy and hatred." He narrates with his chain of narration from Ibn ʿAbbās ꜯ that he said: "Be attentive to the knowledge of scholars, but do not believe what they say about each other, for by the One in Whose hand is my soul, they differ among themselves more than young children."[265] It is narrated from Mālik b. Dīnār that he said: "The words of scholars and reciters are taken in every matter except what they say about one another."[266]

Then 'Allāma al-Subkī said, after citing many other sayings:

---

[264] I.e., "were we to take on board such criticism"—Tr.
[265] *Al-Tuyūs fī zurūbihā*: lit. goats in their barn—Tr.
[266] *Al-Ṭabaqāt al-Kubrā* (vol. 1, p. 187)

As we have mentioned earlier, the criticism of the one who negatively criticises is not accepted, even if he has justifications for this, with respect to the one whose acts of obedience outweigh his acts of disobedience, and those who praise him are more numerous than those who disparage him, and those who declare him veracious are more numerous than those who criticise his rank, if there is an indication that could logically be interpreted as an attack on the one he criticised, whether this is because of fanaticism for a school, or a worldly rivalry, as occurs between peers, or the like.

So we say, for example, that we do not pay any attention to what Ibn Abī Dhi'b said regarding Mālik, nor what Ibn Ma'īn said regarding al-Shāfi'ī, nor what al-Nasā'ī said regarding Aḥmad b. Ṣāliḥ—since all these are well-known Imams. The one who criticises them is like someone who comes with a narration that is unusual in having a single narrator at some point in its chain [gharīb]—if it [the criticisms] was correct, there would have been an ample number of people to convey it,[267] and therefore we can be certain that it is false.

When faced with negative criticism, we must also consider any differences in creed, with respect to the one criticising as well as the subject of this criticism. It may be that they differ in this and criticism arises as a result [of that]. Al-Rāfi'ī refers to this when he says: "Those who are evaluating narrators [muzakkūn] should be free of hatred and fanatical adherence to their school, lest they declare someone who has integrity to be otherwise, or overlook the flaws of a flagrant sinner [which would affect his status as a narrator]. This has happened to many of the great Imams..."

In his book, al-Iqtirāḥ, Shaykh al-Islam Taqī al-Dīn b. Daqīq al-'Īd hinted at this when he said: "The honour of a Muslim is one of the pits of Hell upon whose brink two groups of people stand: the scholars of Hadith and judges."

'Allāma al-Subkī said:

---

[267] Given the fame and repute of such scholars, any criticism would be transmitted by larger numbers instead of through an anomalous report—Tr.

An example of what we mentioned previously was people saying of al-Bukhārī that Abū Zurʿa and Abū Ḥātim abandoned him due to the issue of the utterance.[268] May Allah save the Muslims! Is it conceivable for anyone to say "Al-Bukhārī is abandoned!" whilst he is the standard-bearer of this science and at the forefront of *Ahl al-Sunna wal-Jamāʿa*?

He then went on to say:

> Similarly, some anthropomorphists said regarding Abū Ḥātim b. Ḥibbān "...We drove him out of Sijistan because he denied that Allah may have a limit [*ḥadd*]." Who is more deserving of being driven out? The one who imposes limits upon his Lord or the one who declares his Lord transcendent above physical form! There are many such examples.

He [al-Subkī] said:

> Our teacher al-Dhahabī, may Allah have mercy upon him, is of this type. He is a person of knowledge and religiosity, yet he attacked *Ahl al-Sunna wal-Jamāʿa* excessively. Therefore, it is not permissible to rely on him (with regard to those he cast aspersions upon who opposed his school).

Every aspersion that stems from partisanship for a school or differences in relation to matters of independent reasoning [*ijtihād*] or rivalry, then no consideration is given to any of these.

As has been mentioned in the biography of Muḥammad b. al-Muthannā in *Tahdhīb al-Tahdhīb* [by Ibn Ḥajar], ʿAmr b. ʿAlī was asked about Muḥammad b. al-Muthannā and Bundār. He said: "They are both reliable. Everything they say is to be accepted from them, except what they say regarding one another."

He [al-Laknawī] said in his commentary:

---

[268] This refers to an event in the life of Imam al-Bukhārī in which he was accused of heterodox beliefs regarding the nature of the Qurʾan—Tr.

Note well! Those who evaluate narrators must have integrity and be cognisant of the reasons for *jarḥ wal-taʿdīl*, and must be equitable and sincere. They must not be partisan or bigoted, and impressed with their own opinions, for no notice is to be taken of someone who is fanatical, such as al-Dāraquṭnī who criticised the teacher of Ibn Humām, the magnanimous Imam Abū Ḥanīfa, as being weak in Hadith. Is there anything more despicable than this?

Abū Ḥanīfa was a scrupulous master, untainted and God-conscious, and fearful of Allah. He was well-known for having miraculous marks of honour [*karāmāt*]. In what way could he ever be considered weak?

Sometimes they say that he was preoccupied with jurisprudence, so he has no expertise in Hadith. Look with a fair eye, how ugly is that which they say! Rather, it is more appropriate that Hadith be taken from the jurist, since legal rulings are based upon them so there is no way other than for him to be grounded in it.

At other times they say that he never met the Imams of Hadith, but that he only took from Ḥammād ﷺ. This too is false, since he narrates from a great number of Imams such as Imam Muḥammad al-Bāqir, al-Aʿmash and others, and given that Ḥammād was a great vessel of knowledge, taking from him would suffice him from taking from others. Furthermore, this is a sign of his scrupulousness and the perfection of his knowledge and piety, since he did not have many teachers in order not to be overburdened with fulfilling their rights, out of fear of falling short.

On other occasions, they say that he was a person of analogical deduction [*qiyās*] and opinion [*raʾy*] and he did not act upon Hadith, such that Abū Bakr b. Abī Shayba, may Allah have mercy upon him, included a chapter in his work *al-Muṣannaf* on refuting him, entitling it, 'The Chapter of Refuting Abū Ḥanīfa.' Again, this is the result of bigotry.[269]

Then he transmits in the previously mentioned commentary something astonishing, [namely] that Abū Ḥanīfa ﷺ said: "Whatever comes from the Messenger of Allah ﷺ I submit to, and what comes from his Companions, I will not abandon." And he

---

[269] *Fawātiḥ al-Raḥamūt* (vol. 2, p. 154)

did not render specific [*takhṣīṣ*] something that is [meant] in a general sense [*ʿāmm*] in the Qurʾan, using analogical deduction or using a singular report [*khabar wāhid*]. He did not act upon *maṣāliḥ mursala*[270] and he accepted *mursal* [Hadith][271] and acted upon them, opposing al-Shāfiʿī therein, and [al-Shāfiʿī] did not cast aspersions on him for it, rather he accepted that from him. May Allah be well pleased with them all.

Then he said:

> The truth is that all these statements which emanated from them against the noble Imām [Abū Ḥanīfa], the model for mankind, was due to bias and fanaticism. They do not warrant any attention—the light of Allah will not be extinguished due to their mouths. Therefore, remember [this] and remain steadfast!
>
> The reason for them falling into this heinous matter is that they had poor understanding, using the very literal senses of the words of the Hadith without exercising aiming to understand the inner meanings, let alone the finer points from which those of mediocre intellects are deprived of. This proficient Imam was assisted by Divine assistance, deeply engrossed in the seas of meaning.

It is mentioned in the book *al-Rafʿ wal-Takmīl* by the Imam and Hadith scholar, Shaykh ʿAbd al-Ḥayy al-Laknawī, regarding Abū Ḥanīfa:

> Imam ʿAlī al-Madīnī said: "Al-Thawrī, Ibn al-Mubārak, Ḥammād b. Zayd, Hishām, ʿAbbād b. al-ʿAwwām, Wakīʿ and Jaʿfar b. ʿAwn all narrate from Abū Ḥanīfa. He is upright without there being any issue affecting him. Shuʿba held him in high esteem."

---

[270] A term used in legal theory [*uṣūl al-fiqh*] to denote a prohibition or commandment which serves to bring about a benefit or ward off a harm, the basis for which does not stem directly from a legal text, but is rather based on the overall aims of the law—Tr.

[271] See p. 110-115 for the chapter on the *mursal* Hadith

Yaḥyā b. Maʿīn said: "Our companions are remiss with respect to Abū Ḥanīfa and his colleagues." Someone said to him: "Did he lie?" He said: "No."

Aspersions that arise from fanaticism regarding differences between schools are not to be heeded and have no bearing, in the same way that aspersions that arise from differences in Prophetic Sunni understandings and movements have no bearing.

Bearing Hadith and Relaying them

The conditions for bearing Hadith

The majority of Hadith scholars did not stipulate reaching the age of puberty as a condition for bearing Hadith, neither did they stipulate Islam or integrity. Rather, they considered the bearing of a child, a flagrant wrongdoer and a disbeliever to be valid, if they relayed what they carried after reaching puberty, [converting to] Islam and [gaining] integrity.

Some prohibited accepting narrations of Hadith borne by a child, although the majority saw this [position] as being flawed. The majority educed the validity of the Hadith borne by a child from the fact that the overwhelming majority of Muslims accepted the Companions' narration of events by such as al-Ḥasan and al-Ḥusayn, ʿAbdullah b. al-Zubayr, Ibn ʿAbbās, al-Nuʿmān b. Bashīr, al-Sāʾib b. Yazīd, al-Miswar b. Makhrama and others ﷺ, without differentiating between what they received as as a child or after reaching puberty.

Similarly, the people of knowledge would bring children to gatherings of Hadith, and they would rely upon their narrations after they reached puberty. Likewise, they would use the Hadith agreed-upon [by al-Bukhārī and Muslim] of Jubayr b. Muṭʿim to prove the validity of a non-Muslim bearing a Hadith if they relayed it after becoming Muslim. He heard the Prophet ﷺ recited the Chapter of the Mountain [*Sūra al-Ṭūr*] in the dusk prayer, which he witnessed as a ransomed prisoner of war from the Battle of Badr prior to becoming Muslim. In the narration of al-Bukhārī, [he says:] "That was the first time faith settled in my heart."

If that which a non-Muslim has carried is accepted if he narrates what he received after Islam, then what a flagrant wrongdoer has carried should be accepted all the more, if he narrated it after gaining integrity.

The age at which receiving a Hadith is accepted

Scholars differ regarding the age at which a child is effectively able to receive Hadith and his direct audition [*samā'*] will be considered *ṣaḥīḥ*. Qāḍī 'Iyāḍ, may Allah have mercy upon him, has transmitted that the people of the science have defined the earliest at which direct hearing can be *ṣaḥīḥ* is five years of age. Ibn al-Ṣalāḥ said:

> The people of Hadith have settled upon this position, such that they record that a child of five years or above may say that he heard it directly. If he is younger than five, then he merely attended or was brought to attend.

Their proof for this is that which al-Bukhārī and others narrated from the Hadith of Maḥmūd b. al-Rabīʿ ﷺ that he said: "I recall [*'aqaltu*] of the Prophet ﷺ the spurt of water that he took from a bucket and squirted in my face when I was a boy of five." Imam al-Bukhārī named the chapter based on this, "When the child's direct hearing [of a Hadith] is *ṣaḥīḥ*."

Some said that it is valid at four years of age, and others said at ten years of age. Al-Nawawī and Ibn al-Ṣalāḥ said:

> The correct opinion is the age of discernment [*tamyīz*]. If he understands when addressed and replies, then he is at the age of discernment and his direct hearing [of a Hadith] is *ṣaḥīḥ*, even if this occurs before the age of five. If he is not able to, then he is not, whether he is five or even fifty years of age.

Al-Qasṭallānī says in *al-Minhāj* that what Ibn al-Ṣalāḥ has chosen is accurate and the proper approach.

Ways of bearing and transmitting Hadith

The first way is directly hearing the wording of the teacher by dictation or by direct narration [*taḥdīth*] without dictation, each of which is from the memory of the teacher or his book. This is the highest and most exalted way of receiving Hadith.

The formulas that are used in this type of narration where the person who heard [the Hadith] directly says in his narration: "I heard" [*samiʿtu*], "he informed us" [*akhbaranā*], "he narrated to us" [*ḥaddathanā*], "he reported to us" [*anbaʾanā*], "I heard so-and-so" [*samiʿtu fulān*], "so-and-so said to us" [*qāla lanā fulān*], or "so-and-so mentioned to us" [*dhakara lanā fulān*].

They differ as to which one of these expressions is superior, as is explained in detail in *al-Taqrīb* and its commentary [*al-Tadrīb*].

The second way is reading to a teacher. Most of the scholars of Hadith called this 'presenting' [*ʿarḍ*], given that the reader presents to his teacher what he reads, in the same way as the student of Qurʾan presents his reading of the Qurʾan to the teacher.

This is regardless of whether the student himself is reading to the teacher, or someone else is reading and he is listening, and regardless of whether the reading is from a book or from memory, and whether the teacher has memorised the material being read out to him or not, on the condition that the teacher retains the original material or someone else who is reliable [*thiqa*] retains it in his presence.

Narration based on this method of receiving Hadith by reading is sound without dispute if it fulfils the previously mentioned conditions, based on the opinions of those whose views are considered. This is indicated by the Hadith of Ḍimām b. Thaʿlaba ﷺ and others.

The scholars differ as to whether this method is equal to the first method of directly hearing from the words of the teacher, or whether one method is superior [over the other].

The first opinion, that they are equal, has been transmitted from Mālik, his companions and his teachers from the scholars of Medina, and likewise the majority of the scholars of Ḥijāz and Kufa, and from al-Bukhārī and others. Al-Rāmahurmuzī cites this from ʿAlī and Ibn ʿAbbās ﷺ.

The superiority of directly hearing [Hadith] over reading them out is the opinion of the majority of the scholars of the East. Al-Nawawī says that this is correct.

The superiority of reading [Hadith] out to directly hearing [them] is attributed to Abū Ḥanīfa, Ibn Abī Dhi'b and others, and is a narration from Mālik.

Regarding the formulas used for this type, the most cautious in narrating is to say "I read to so-and-so" or "It was read to him and I was listening." Thereafter, any expression alluding to hearing but qualified by reading, such as "I heard so-and-so read to" and "He narrated to us [by] being read to," or "He informed us [by] being read to."

There is a difference opinion regarding the use of "he narrated to us" or "he informed us"—Ibn al-Mubārak, Yaḥyā al-Tamīmī, al-Nasā'ī, Aḥmad b. Ḥanbal and others forbade it. Some allowed its usage, such as al-Zuhrī, Mālik, Ibn 'Uyayna, al-Bukhārī, and the majority of the scholars of the Ḥijāz and of Kufa, such as Abū Ḥanīfa and his two companions [Muḥammad and Abū Yūsuf], al-Thawrī and others.

A group forbade the use of "he narrated to us" but permitted the use of "he informed us." Al-Nawawī said that this is the school of al-Shāfi'ī, Muslim and the majority of the scholars of the East, and it became overwhelmingly widespread amongst the people of Hadith.

The third way is by being licensed [*ijāza*], which is, as 'Allāma al-Shumunnī said, permission to narrate by word or in writing, and customarily denotes informing summarily [*al-ikhbār al-ijmālī*], meaning it constitutes his informing about that which he grants permission to him to narrate from him.

It is has four essential elements:

1. The one licensing [*al-mujīz*]
2. The one licensed [*al-mujāz*]
3. That which is licensed [*al-mujāz bihi*]
4. The license itself [*al-ijāza*]

There are various types:

1. Licensing someone specific for something specific

Such as the one licensing saying, "I grant you permission for al-Bukhārī," or "for everything included in my collection [*fihris*]." Narrating this way is permissible according to the majority of scholars of Hadith and others, as opposed to some scholars of Hadith and jurists who forbade it, such as Shuʿba and others.

2. Licensing someone specific for something unspecified

Such as saying, "I license everything I have heard [*masmūʿātī*] to you." The majority permit narration on this basis and the obligation of acting upon it.

3. Licensing someone unspecified
     using a general expression

Such as one saying, "I license all [*jamīʿ*] of the Muslims," or "everyone [*kullu aḥad*]," or "the people of my time [*ahl zamānī*]." There is a difference of opinion regarding this amongst later scholars. If he specifies the general license using a restrictive description, such as "I license the students of knowledge from such-and-such a place," then it is closer to being permitted than if it were unrestricted, *a fortiori*.

[Al-Suyūṭī] mentions in *al-Tadrīb* a party of Imams of the scholars who permitted this type absolutely [*muṭlaqan*].

Ibn Kathīr said:

> A group of experts and scholars accepted this including al-Khaṭīb, and he transmitted that from his teacher Qāḍī Abū al-Ṭayyib al-Ṭabarī, and Abū Bakr al-Ḥāzimī transmitted it from his teacher Abū al-ʿAlāʾ al-Hamadānī, and other Hadith scholars of the Maghreb.

4. Licensing someone specific in ambiguous books,
     or specific books to someone who is unknown

An example of the first type is saying, "I license you in the book *al-Sunan*" even though he narrates numerous books of *Sunan*, or "I license you some of what I have heard" but without being specific.

An example of the second type is saying, "I license Muḥammad b. Khālid al-Dimashqī such-and-such a book," yet there are a number of people who go by this name. This type of license is invalid, but if there is an indication of the intention of the one licensing, then the license is valid.

5.   Licensing someone who doesn't exist

Such as saying, "I license the unborn offspring of so-and-so." He says in *al-Taqrīb*:

> Later scholars have disagreed regarding the soundness of this. If it is appended to someone who exists, such as "I license so-and-so and whoever is born to him," or "to you and to your progeny," then it is more likely to be permitted.

Abū Bakr b. Abī Dāwūd, one of the scholars of Hadith, acted upon this second type, and al-Khaṭīb permitted the former, and the latter with all the more reason.

6.   Licensing something that the one licensing did not acquire by directly hearing or licensing [*ijāza*] for the one licensed to narrate something from him[272]

Qāḍī ʿIyāḍ said: "I have not seen anyone speak of this, but I saw some of the later scholars engage in it." Later he endorsed the position that it is forbidden. Imam al-Nawawī said: "This is correct."[273]

7.   Licensing what the teacher has been licensed with

Such as saying, "I license you my licenses [i.e., that which I have been permitted to narrate]." Some prohibited this.

Al-Nawawī said: "The correct opinion, which is the practice, is that it is permissible." The following experts [*ḥuffāẓ*] were categorical regarding its permissibility: al-Dāraquṭnī, Ibn ʿUqda, Abū Nuʿaym and Abū al-Fatḥ Naṣr al-Maqdisī.

---

[272] This is when one licenses something one does not possess at all, or where the one licensing does so regarding something he will possess in the future. In each case, there is no existing license at the time when he is licensing someone else—Tr.

[273] I.e., that it is not permitted—Tr.

The fourth way is presentation [*munāwala*], which is when the teacher gives a book to his student containing the narrations that he has heard directly. There are two types: that which is accompanied by license [*maqrūna bil-ijāza*] and that which is not [*mujarrada*].

The former is when the teacher gives the student his original copy of those things which he heard, or a copy corresponding to it [which has been compared against the original], and says to him, "This is what I heard," or "These are my narrations from so-and-so, so you may narrate them from me," or "I license you to narrate his narrations from me," then gives him the book to keep, or to make a copy of and to check against his own, and then return it.

There are various scenarios of this type which are expounded upon in the lengthy works. It is below the level of hearing directly or reading [to a teacher] according to the correct opinion, as mentioned in *al-Taqrīb* and elsewhere.

As for simply giving alone [without license], it entails giving the book, but is qualified by [the teacher] saying, "This is what I have heard" or "These are some of my Hadith," but without saying, "So you can narrate them from me" or "I license you to narrate them from me," and the like.

Al-Nawawī said: "It is not permitted to narrate this type, according to the correct opinion of the jurists and scholars of legal theory. The scholars of Hadith also criticised those who permitted it."

Al-Khaṭīb cited from a group of scholars that they viewed it as valid to narrate using this type.

Ibn al-Ṣalāḥ said:

> Narration of this type (by presentation [*munāwala*] without license [*mujarrada*]) is preferred over the teacher merely informing because of the presentation in it, as this contains notification of authorisation to narrate.

This means that if some scholars permit narrating from the teacher by merely informing, then *a fortiori*, they should permit the narration from presentation without license, as he [al-Suyūṭī] clarified in *al-Tadrīb*.

Regarding the expressions used in this type of Hadith transmission—through licensing [*ijāza*] and presentation [*munāwala*]—Imam al-Nawawī cited in *al-Taqrīb* that the majority of scholars and researchers forbade using the expressions "he narrated to us" and "he informed us" when narrating through licensing and presentation. Rather, the appropriate expression which explains the method ought to be used, such as "he narrated to us by licensing," or "by licensing and presentation," or "he informed us by licensing," or "by licensing and presentation," or "by authorisation," or "in that which he authorised me for," or "in that which is valid for me to narrate," or "in that which he licensed me *or* presented to me," and the like.

The fifth way is by writing. This is when the teacher writes that which he heard for someone who is present, or to someone who is absent to whom he then sends it, regardless of whether the teacher writes it himself or instructs someone else to write it. It is sufficient for the person written to recognise the handwriting as that of the teacher or of the scribe on behalf of the teacher. It is a condition that the scribe must be reliable.

Writing can be accompanied by licensing, such as saying, "I grant you license in that which has been written for you," or "that which I wrote to you," and the like of those expressions which denote licensing. It is similar in its soundness and strength to presentation accompanied by license [*munāwala maqrūna bil-ijāza*].

As for transmission through writing without specific license, such as by saying, "So-and-so wrote to me saying: 'So-and-so narrated to us,'" Imam al-Nawawī said:

> As for [writing] without license, many forbade narrating based on it, amongst them Qāḍī al-Māwardī al-Shāfiʿī in *al-Ḥāwī*. Many of the early and later scholars permitted it. He [al-Māwardī] said: "This is the sound and well-known opinion amongst the people of Hadith. It is mentioned in their works, 'So-and-so wrote to me, saying: "So-and-so narrated to us."' The meaning here is as being described. It is acted upon by them and is considered to be connected, given that it implies permission."

Regarding the phrases used for this type, he says in *al-Taqrīb*:

> It is sound to say when narrating, "So-and-so wrote to me, saying: 'So-and-so narrated to us,'" or "So-and-so informed us in correspondence," or "by writing," or "in writing," or the like, such as "He narrated to us in writing."
>
> ...(He said:) It is not permitted to use "He narrated to us" and "He informed us," although al-Layth, Manṣūr and other scholars of Hadith, including the greatest of them, permitted it.

The sixth way is through informing [*iʿlām*], which is when the teacher informs the student that the Hadith or book is what he heard directly from so-and-so, confining himself to this without authorising the student to narrate it from him.

Al-Nawawī said:

> Many scholars of Hadith, jurisprudence and, legal theory as well as the Ẓāhirīs permitted narrating this way (without *ijāza*). ...(Then he said:) The correct opinion is that which was stated by more than one of the Hadith scholars, and indeed others, that it is not permitted to narrate in this way. However, it is obligatory to act upon this (i.e., that which was narrated by the teacher, which he heard, if the chain is *ṣaḥīḥ*).

The seventh way is by bequest [*waṣiyya*] which is when, at the time of death or when travelling, the teacher bequeaths to a person a book that that teacher narrates. Some of the predecessors [*salaf*] permitted the bequeathed to narrate this book from the one bequeathing, drawing similarities between this and presentation and narration by informing.

Qāḍī ʿIyāḍ sought to support this opinion, by saying that giving a bequest to the bequeathed constitutes a type of authorisation, and due to its similarity with presenting by reading [*ʿarḍ*] and presentation in writing [*munāwala*]. Ibn al-Ṣalāḥ said that this [understanding] is improbable. Al-Nawawī said: "This is a mistake and the correct position is that it is not permitted."

The eighth way is finding [*wijāda*], which is when someone discovers Hadith in the handwriting of the one who narrated them, regardless of whether he was his contemporary or not, and the one who found these Hadith did not hear these particular ones from that person, and he has no license from him for them, but he says, "I found or I read such-and-such in the handwriting of so-and-so." He then shows the chain of narration and wording if he is confident that it is indeed his handwriting or his book. If not, then he should say, "It has reached me from so-and-so," or "I found from him" and the like, or "I read in a book that so-and-so informed me of that it was in the handwriting of so-and-so," or "I believed it to be the handwriting of so-and-so," or "the compilation of so-and so," or "it is said to be the handwriting of so-and-so,' or "the compilation of so-and-so," and other similar expressions which denote some kind of document with a chain [*isnād*].

If he transmitted something from a document, then he should not say, "So-and-so said," using a phrase that indicates decisiveness [*ṣīgha al-jazm*], unless he is certain about the soundness of the copy in that it was checked against the author's original book, or against another copy which had been checked against the original.

If none of this applies, then one should say, "It has reached me from so-and-so" or "I found in a copy of his book," and the like, without the use of decisive affirmation.

Al-Nawawī said:

> Most people in these times have been liberal in their use of decisiveness in this context, without thorough investigation. However, the correct approach is what we have mentioned. If the one reading is an expert who would be aware of omissions or alterations, we would hope that his decisive affirmation is permissible. Many authors seem to be at ease with this in their narrations (i.e., what they find in the books of the people of knowledge).

In the *Musnad* of Imam Aḥmad [b. Ḥanbal], there are many narrations which his son ʿAbdullah transmits from him in which he says: "I found in the handwriting of my father in his book," and then mentions a Hadith, but which he does not narrate from his father by way of direct narration [*taḥdīth*] nor direct informing [*ikhbār*], not using the particle 'from' [*'an*], which may give the impression of having heard it directly, despite the fact that 'Abdullah was the narrator of his father's books and his student.

Some narrators were lax in this and they would narrate what they found in the handwriting of their contemporaries or their teachers, using the phrase "from so-and-so" [*'an fulān*].

Ibn al-Ṣalāḥ said:

> This is an ugly form [*qabīḥ*] of deception [*tadlīs*] if they intend to give the impression that they heard it directly. Some would speak in general terms and would transmit that using the phrases "So-and-so narrated to us" or "So-and-so informed us." The scholars disapproved of this strenuously.

Al-Suyūṭī said: "No reliable person permits this."

As for the ruling on acting upon narrations that have only been found [in books], it has been transmitted from the majority of scholars of Hadith and Mālikī jurists and others that they did not permit it. It is said that al-Shāfiʿī and his peers amongst his companions permitted it. Some of the scholars who investigate matters and verify them carefully [*muḥaqqiqūn*] from amongst the Shāfiʿī scholars and others firmly believed that it is obligatory to act upon it if there is confidence in what the reader has found —such that he is certain that this report or Hadith is in the handwriting of the teacher whom he knows, or is confident of the book's attribution to the author, and that the author was reliable and the chain of narration is sound or fair. In this case it must be acted upon.[274]

---

[274] It should be noted that the discussion around the obligation of whether a Hadith is to be acted upon or not, regardless of whether mentioned in this particular context or elsewhere, does not literally mean it must be acted upon. Rather, what is meant is that the Hadith in question now warrants a separate discussion about its application, since not every Hadith, however sound it may be, is to be acted upon. The discussion moves into the sphere of jurisprudence and legal theory [*uṣūl al-fiqh*] with regard to its application—Tr.

Imām al-Nawawī said: "This is the correct opinion upon which there is no difference in these times."

Ibn al-Ṣalāḥ said: "For if the practice concerning it was to be restricted to the [direct] narration [from the teacher], the door of action would be barred because of the impossibility of its conditions."

Ḥāfiẓ 'Imād al-Dīn b. Kathīr adduced the following Hadith as proof for acting upon narrations acquired by finding, which was narrated by Ibn 'Arafa in his compilation [juz'], and narrated through multiple chains, that the Prophet ﷺ said: "Which creation is the most wondrous in faith?"

They said: "The angels."

He ﷺ said: "How could they not believe when they are with their Lord?"

They said: "The Prophets."

He ﷺ said: "How could they not believe when they are given revelation?"

They said: "Us."

He ﷺ said: "How could you not believe when I am amongst you?'

They said: "Then who, O Messenger of Allah?"

He ﷺ said: "A people who will come after you, who will encounter written pieces of paper and believe in them."

Al-Bulqīnī said: "This is a beautiful inference."

WAYS OF STUDYING HADITH

There are three ways of studying Hadith according to the people of knowledge:

1.   Reading aloud uninterruptedly [sard]

This is when the teacher reads one of the books of Hadith or the student reads to the teacher without pausing for linguistic or juristic discussions, or those concerning the names of narrators and the like.

2. Unlocking meanings and resolving issues
    [*ṭarīq al-ḥall wal-baḥth*]

It is that after reading out a Hadith, they stop at unfamiliar words, and derive understanding of the linguistic constructions, [stop at] rare names which appear in the chains of narration, resolve questions about the apparent causes of [the Hadith's] occurrence, and solve problems using moderate detail, after which the reading of the Hadith is resumed.

3. Profound study [*im'ān*]

This is when the teacher comments on every word in the noble Hadith, explaining it in light of the various scholarly disciplines, in the same was as he would speak about unfamiliar words and difficult constructions. He produces linguistic proofs from poetry, clarifying the construction of the etymology, investigates the circumstances of the narrators, and extracts legal rulings based on the textual evidences within the Hadith.

The ruling on reading Hadith with *tajwīd*

Imam Muḥammad b. Muḥammad al-Budayrī al-Dimyāṭī says:

> As for reading Hadith with *tajwīd* in the same manner one would the Noble Qur'an, adhering to the rules of the vowelless *nūn* [*nūn sākina*], nunation [*tanwīn*], lengthening [*madd*] and shortening and the like, it is recommended, as some have clarified.
>
> However, I asked my teacher, the seal of the verifying scholars [*muḥaqqiqīn*], Shaykh ʿAlī al-Shabrāmulissī—may Allah cover him in mercy—regarding my reading *Ṣaḥīḥ al-Bukhārī* to him in this way, and he replied that it is obligatory. He mentioned that he had found this opinion transmitted in a book called *al-Aqwāl al-Shāriḥa fī Tafsīr al-Fātiḥa*.
>
> The reason he gave for this was that *tajwīd* is one of the beauties of speech, it is of the language of the Arabs and it is of the eloquence of a speaker. All of these meanings are united in him ﷺ, so whoever narrates his Hadith must pay due care to that which he ﷺ pronounced.[275]

---

[275] [Al-ʿAdawī] *Laqṭ al-Durar*

Given that the station of Hadith narration [*taḥdīth*] is lofty and awe-inspiring because in it is a form of *khilāfa* (succession) in narrating from the Messenger of Allah ﷺ, for that reason the people of knowledge drew particular attention to specific etiquettes relating to the Hadith narrator and the student of Hadith. God willing, we shall mention some of those etiquettes here.

Etiquette of the scholar of Hadith

He must verify his intention and make it sound, purify his heart from inessential matters of the world and its filth, and from the self's objectives and its frivolities, such as love of leadership and reputation.

His objective in that should be dissemination of Hadith and conveyance from the Messenger of Allah ﷺ, anticipating therein his reward from Allah ﷻ, not desiring any worldly goods—for indeed actions are only according to intentions.

Sufyān al-Thawrī said: "I said to Ḥabīb b. Abī Thābit: 'Narrate to us.' He said: 'Not until the intention is there.'"

Someone said to Abū Aḥwaṣ Sallām b. Salim: "Narrate to us." He said: "I do not have an intention." They said to him: "You will be rewarded for it." He then said [reciting a couplet of poetry]:

> *They tempt me with much good,*
> *But would that I were saved,*
>
> *With enough for my needs,*
> *With nothing against me, or for me*

Imam al-Nawawī said:

> There is a difference of opinion regarding the age in which one is deserving of narrating Hadith. The correct opinion is that whenever there is a need for what he has,[276]

---

[276] This means that if despite his young age he is the only one to possess a certain Hadith, then he is considered to be worthy of narrating that Hadith—Tr.

people will sit with him regardless of age. One ought to withhold from narrating Hadith if one fears confusion due to old age, senility or blindness. This differs from person to person.

The scholar of Hadith ought to have a beautiful character, a good way about him and a good nature. It is more appropriate not to narrate Hadith in the presence of someone more deserving than himself with regard to age, knowledge or the like.

It is recommend if someone wants to attend a gathering of Hadith narration to perform ablution or *ghusl*, and that he clean and perfume himself. He should use the teeth cleaning twig [*miswāk*] and comb his beard and sit still with calmness, dignity and respect.

Al-Bayhaqī mentions that Mālik would do this and was asked why. He said: "I love to venerate the Hadith of the Messenger of Allah ﷺ, and I do not narrate Hadith other than in a state of purity while being settled." He would dislike narrating in the street or whilst standing.

Al-Bayhaqī narrated from a number of the predecessors [*salaf*] that they would dislike narrating Hadith whilst not in a state of purity, and from Ibn al-Musayyib that he was asked about a Hadith whilst reclining during an illness, so he sat up and narrated it. Someone said to him: "I wanted you not to impose hardship on yourself!" He then said: "I dislike narrating from the Messenger of Allah ﷺ whilst reclining."

It is narrated that Mālik said: "Gatherings of knowledge should be attended in a state of humility, tranquillity and dignity."

It is disliked for him to stand up for someone else. It is said that if the reader of Hadith stands up for someone else then he has a misdeed recorded for him.

One ought to be silently attentive and calm in the gatherings of Hadith. If someone raises their voice, then the Hadith narrator should rebuke him for this, as Imam Mālik would do, saying: "Allah ﷻ says: ❨*O you who believe! Do not raise your voices over the voice of the Prophet.*❩ Thus, whoever raises their voice when his ﷺ Hadith are being read out, it is as if they raised their voice above his ﷺ actual voice."

The Hadith narrator should face all of the attendees, and open and conclude the gathering with praise of Allah, the Exalted, and sending prayers upon the Prophet ﷺ, and with a prayer that is appropriate to the occasion, after someone with a beautiful voice reads something from the magnificent Qur'an.

Al-Ḥākim narrates from Abū Saʿīd ؓ that he said: "When the Companions of the Messenger of Allah ﷺ gathered they would discuss knowledge and recite a chapter from the Qur'an."

The teacher should not read the Hadith uninterruptedly in a way that prevents understanding. Mālik would not hurry and he would say: "I love to gain understanding of the Hadith of the Messenger of Allah ﷺ."

This is because of what has been narrated in *Ṣaḥīḥ Muslim* from ʿĀʾisha ؓ, "He ﷺ would not speak uninterruptedly in the way that you do." Al-Bayhaqī had an addition [to this,] "His speech was distinct,[277] which the hearts would comprehend."

It is recommended for the Hadith teacher to hold a weekly gathering in which to allow dictation of Hadith and to appoint someone who is vigilant to dictate, and if needed, someone to convey the Hadith if the gathering is large. If the gathering becomes large and increases, he should appoint additional people to dictate according to the need.

When Abū Muslim Ibrāhīm b. ʿAbdullah b. Muslim al-Kajjī—by ascription to *kajj* which means 'plaster,' but it is also said his name was al-Kashī referring to his great-grandfather—would dictate in the courtyard of Ghassān, there were seven who would convey the dictation, each of whom would make his voice reach his nearest colleague. Forty thousand bottles of ink would be present in the gathering, excluding general attendees.

The one conveying the dictation should hush the people present and then say to the teacher who is dictating, "Which teachers did you mention?" or "Which Hadith did you mention? May Allah have mercy upon you," or "May Allah be pleased with you" or the like.

---

[277] I.e., it was clear and apparent. ([Ibn al-Athīr] *Al-Nihāya*)

Furthermore, the one conveying the dictation should send prayers upon the Messenger ﷺ in a loud voice after the one who is dictating, and likewise each time the name of the Messenger ﷺ is mentioned. Similarly, when the name of a Companion is mentioned, he should say, "May Allah be pleased with him."

It is good for the Hadith scholar to praise his teacher in a befitting manner when he is narrating, such as ʿAṭāʾ who said: "The scholar and sea [of knowledge], Ibn ʿAbbās ﷺ, narrated to me..."

Likewise, Masrūq would say: "The truthful one, daughter of the truthful one, the beloved of the beloved of Allah, the exonerated one ﷺ [ʾĀʾisha bint Abū Bakr al-Ṣiddīq], narrated to me..."

Shuʿba would say: "The chief of the jurists, Ayyūb, narrated to me..."

Wakīʿ would say: "Sufyān al-Thawrī, the leader of the believers in Hadith, narrated to me..."

One should not refer to someone by a name he dislikes, except if it is to distinguish him from others, such as Ghundar, al-Aʿmash and al-Ḥannāṭ,[278] even if the person dislikes this name.

Etiquette of the student of Hadith

The student of Hadith should have a sincere intention for Allah ﷻ in his seeking knowledge, and he should be wary of using it as a means to obtain worldly goals, given the severe rebuke and emphatic threats that have been mentioned about this.

He should inculcate in himself noble character and beautiful etiquette, and should stop at nothing to achieve this, seeking success, guidance and ease from Allah, the Exalted.

He should begin by listening to the most prominent teachers of his own lands directly, [and take from] their chains of narration, knowledge, repute and religion. Once he has finished with their requirements and directly heard their elevated chains, he should travel abroad, as was the custom of the prominent masters of Hadith, in order to benefit from their elevated chains

---

[278] Which mean the corpulent one, the one with a lazy eye and the wheat-seller respectively—Tr.

and from reminders and gatherings of knowledge [of those abroad], and also to benefit from their specific virtues. Jābir b. ʿAbdullah al-Anṣārī ﷺ travelled to ʿAbdullah b. Unays ﷺ for an entire month for the sake of a single Hadith.

There are many evidences of the legitimacy of that and its plentiful reward, so much so that Sayyidī Ibrāhīm b. Adham ﷺ said: "Allah will repel trials from this community due to the travels undertaken by the people of Hadith."

The student of Hadith should act upon the Hadith he has heard on acts of worship, virtuous acts and etiquettes, qualities of character and the like. That is the *zakāt* on the Hadith he has collected and a means of preserving them.

Bishr al-Ḥāfī ﷺ would say: "People of Hadith, pay the *zakāt* on Hadith: five from every two hundred Hadith."[279]

ʿAmr b. Qays al-Malāʾī would say: "When something of tradition reaches you, act upon it even if only once, and you will be one of its people."

Wakīʿ said: "If you want to preserve Hadith then act upon them."

The student of Hadith should venerate his teacher, since he derives benefit from him, and should believe in his status and prominence, striving to please him and being wary of displeasing him. He should not inconvenience him by taking too much of his time. He should seek his advice about matters which come to him and about what he is occupied with and how he occupies himself with it. He should have patience with his teacher's harshness.

Al-Aṣmaʿī said: "Whoever does not endure the humbling of knowledge for a moment will remain in the humbling of ignorance forever."

He should not waste his time in seeking numerous teachers merely for the sake of having many and because of their reputation. He should neither be arrogant nor shy away from taking knowledge from those below him in lineage, age or the like. Mujāhid said: "Neither the shy nor the arrogant attain knowledge."

---

[279] This is an allusion to the legislated alms tax obligatory on Muslims who meet certain criteria which is to the value of 2.5%, which reflects in the amount in the quotation—Tr.

'Umar b. al-Khaṭṭāb said: "Whoever is embarrassed, his knowledge will lack substance."

Our mother, Lady 'Ā'isha ☙, said: "The best of women were the women of the Anṣār: modesty never prevented them from seeking understanding [*fiqh*] of the religion."

Wakī' said: "A man does not attain nobility until he writes from those better than him, those equal to him and those less than him."

The student of Hadith should acquaint himself with the ṣaḥīḥ, ḥasan and ḍa'īf of Hadith, along with their meanings, linguistic understandings, grammatical constructions, names of the narrators, investigating all of that and verifying it carefully, having a concern for knowing the problematic narrations thoroughly, both in memorisation and in writing.

He should prefer the two *Ṣaḥīḥ* collections over the other *Sunan* collections, and then the most important *Musnad* and *Jāmi'* collections, the books of Hadith defects [*'ilal*] and the names of narrators, and the accurate spelling of names, along with the unfamiliar words contained in the Hadith, and so on.

He should discuss those things which he has committed to memory and research with the people of knowledge.

Our master 'Alī ☙ said: "Remind each about these Hadith, for if you do not, they will be obliterated."

Ibn Mas'ūd ☙ said: "Remind each about these Hadith, because their life is through mutual reminder."

Ibn 'Abbās ☙ said: "Mutual reminder about knowledge for an hour is superior to giving life to the night [by standing in prayer]."

Abū Sa'īd al-Khudrī ☙ said: "Mutual reminder about Hadith is superior to reading the Qur'an."

CONCLUSION

وَقَدْ أَتَتْ كَالْجَوْهَرِ الْـمَكْنُونِ   سَمَّيْـتُهَا مَنْظُومَةَ الْـبَيْقُونِي

فَوْقَ الـثَّلَاثِيـنَ بِأَرْبَعٍ أَتَـتْ   أَقْـسَامُهَا تَمَّتْ بِخَيْرٍ خُتِمَتْ

It has indeed arrived like a hidden pearl,
I titled it: The Bayqūnī Poem

Its categories amount to thirty-four,
Completed, with goodness they are sealed!

'Pearl' [*jawhar*] means a large pearl. 'Hidden' [*maknūn*] means concealed due to it being precious and rare. He compared the poem to a hidden pearl due to its value and the types of sciences of Hadith it contains.

He then clarified that the categories of Hadith mentioned amount to thirty-four in number, given that the *mudallas* (misleading) and *maqlūb* (inverted) are two categories [each]. This resolves the problem that may arise, [namely] there being only thirty-two categories mentioned here. This is due to the fact that the majority of manuscripts mention "the number of categories amount to," although some copies mention "the number of verses amount to," so there is no problem in reality.

We have not come across a clear and detailed biography for the author, may Allah have mercy upon him, after researching and reviewing the books of biographies and history, in spite of him being famed for knowledge and his merit. However, we did come across a concise summary of his biography. Dr. Sayed Moazzem Hossain, professor at the University of Dhaka in India,[280] said:

> ʿUmar b. Muḥammad b. Futtūḥ al-Bayqūnī al-Dimashqī al-Shāfiʿī, who passed away in the year 1080 H., has a poem known as the *Bayqūniyya* in the science of Hadith terminology. Many commentaries on it havebeen written.[281]

---

[280] Present-day Bangladesh—Tr.
[281] In his introduction to *Maʿrifa ʿUlūm al-Ḥadīth* of al-Ḥākim (p. 19).

Dear Reader,

In this commentary of mine, I have mentioned the definition of every category within the sciences of Hadith, and the relevant rulings and categories, and the related principles and additional points, in a way that is succinct and summary.

I occasionally have brought some lines from the poem earlier, or mentioned them later, in order to facilitate the beginning student's study, those who possesses no prior knowledge of this science and its terminology, especially as people's aspirations have decreased and their enthusiasm for it has waned.

I remind whoever may hasten to criticise and challenge to refrain until he has carefully and calmly reviewed the source materials, because I have a model in 'Allāma al-Zurqānī, who said at the end of his commentary:

> *Open the door of apology for it,*
> *If a meaning becomes corrupt*
>
> *And interpret anything,*
> *Which gives the impression,*
> *Of being mistaken, if it occurs*

I conclude my commentary with the best of conclusions:

❴*O Allah accept this from us.*
You are the All-Hearing and All-Knowing.❵[282]

And:

❴*Your Lord is free of all deficiency, the Lord of might*
and free of what they describe. Salutations be upon the Messengers,
and all praise is due to Allah, the Lord of the Worlds.❵[283]

This was completed on Wednesday, 23rd Dhū al-Ḥijja, 1372 H.

---

[282] Qur'an 2:127
[283] Qur'an 37:180-182

BIBLIOGRAPHY

'Abd al-Barr, Yūsuf b. 'Abdullah b., *Jāmi' Bayān al-'Ilm wa-Faḍlihi*
'Absī al-Kūfī, 'Ubaydullah b. Mūsā al-, *Musnad*
'Adawī, 'Abdullah b. Ḥusayn al-,
———*Ḥāshiya Laqṭ al-Durar bi-Sharḥ Nukhba al-Fikar*
'Ajlūnī, Ismā'īl b. Muḥammad al-, *Kashf al-Khafā' wa-Muzīl al-Iltibās*
'Allān al-Ṣiddīqī, Muḥammad 'Alī b.,
———*Al-Futūḥāt al-Rabbānī 'alā al-Adhkār al-Nawawī*
'Aynī, Badr al-Dīn al-, *'Umda al-Qārī Sharḥ Ṣaḥīḥ al-Bukhārī*
Abyārī al-Shāfi'ī, 'Abd al-Hādī Najā b. Riḍwān al-,
———*Nīl al-Amānī fī Tawḍīḥ Muqaddima al-Qasṭallānī li-Sharḥihi 'alā Ṣaḥīḥ
     al-Bukhārī (Ḥāshiya al-Abyārī)*
Ajhūrī, 'Aṭiyya al-, *Ḥāshiya 'alā Sharḥ al-Zurqānī 'alā al-Bayqūniyya*
Ālūsī, Maḥmūd b. 'Abdullah al-Ḥusaynī al-, *Tafsīr Rūḥ al-Ma'ānī*
Anṣārī, Zakariyyā al-, *Sharḥ Alfiyya al-'Irāqī*
———*Fatḥ al-Bāqī*
Aṣbahānī, al-, Ismā'īl Abū al-Qāsim al-, *Al-Targhīb wal-Tarhīb*
Athīr, Mubārak b. Muḥammad b. al-, *Al-Nihāya fī Gharīb al-Ḥadīth*
Baqā' al-Kaffawī, Ayyūb b. Mūsā Abū al-,
———*Al-Kulliyāt, Mu'jam fī al-Muṣṭalaḥāt wal-Furuq al-Lughawiyya*
Barqānī, Aḥmad b. Ghālib Abū Bakr al-,
———*Mustakhraj Ṣaḥīḥ al-Bukhārī*
Bayhaqī, Aḥmad b. al-Ḥusayn Abū Bakr al-, *Al-Madkhal*
———*Al-Sunan al-Kubra*
Bayqūnī al-Dimashqī al-Shāfi'ī, Umar b. Muḥammad b. Futtūḥ al-,
———*Al-Manẓūma al-Bayqūniyya*
Bukhārī, Muḥammad b. Ismā'īl al-, *Ṣaḥīḥ al-Bukhārī*
———*Al-Tārīkh al-Awsaṭ*
Dāraquṭnī, 'Alī b. 'Umar al-, *Al-'Ilal al-Wārida fī al-Aḥādīth al-Nabawiyya*
Dārimī, Abū Sa'īd al-, *Al-Sunan*
Dāwūd al-Sijistānī, Sulaymān b. al-Ash'ath b. Abī, *Al-Sunan*
Dhahabī, Shams al-Dīn al-, *Mīzān al-'Itidāl*
Dayba' al-Shaybānī, Abū Abdullah 'Abd al-Raḥmān b.,
———*Tamyīz al-Ṭayyib min al-Khabīth*
Fattānī, Muḥammad b. Ṭāhir b. 'Alī al-Hindī al-, *Tadhkira al-Mawḍū'āt*
———*Qānūn al-Mawḍū'āt wal-Ḍu'afā'*

Ḥajar al-ʿAsqalānī, Shihāb al-Dīn Abū al-Faḍl Aḥmad b.,
——Al-ʿAshr al-ʿUshariyya
——Fatḥ al-Bārī Sharḥ Ṣaḥīḥ al-Bukhārī
——Nukhba al-Fikar fī Muṣṭalaḥ Ahl al-Athar
——Nuzha al-Naẓar fī Tawḍīḥ Nukhba al-Fikar (Sharḥ al-Nukhba)
——Al-Qawl al-Musaddad fī al-Dhabbi ʿan Musnad Aḥmad
——Taqrīb al-Tahdhīb
——Tahdhīb al-Tahdhīb
Ḥajar al-Haytamī al-Makkī, Shihāb al-Dīn Abū al-ʿAbbās Aḥmad b.,
——Sharḥ al-Arbaʿīn al-Nawawiyya
Ḥākim al-Naysābūrī, Muḥammad b. ʿAbdullah al-,
——Maʿrifa ʿUlūm al-Ḥadīth [Ed. Dr. Sayed Moazzem Hossain]
——Al-Mustadrak ʿalā al-Ṣaḥīḥayn
Ḥanbal, Aḥmad b., Musnad
Ḥāzimī, Abū Bakr Muḥammad al-,
——Al-Iʿtibār fī al-Nāsikh wal-Mansūkh min al-Āthār
Ḥibbān, Muḥammad b., al-Anwāʿ wal-Taqāsīm
——Ṣaḥīḥ
Ḥūt, Muḥammad b. al-Sayyid Darwīsh al-, Asnā al-Maṭālib
ʿĪd, Taqī al-Dīn b. Daqīq al-, Al-Iqtirāḥ fī Bayān al-Iṣṭilāḥ
ʿIrāqī, Zayn al-Dīn Abū al-Faḍl ʿAbd al-Raḥmān al-,
——Al-Alfiyya fī ʿUlūm al-Ḥadīth
——Fatḥ al-Mughīth bi-Sharḥ al-Alfiyya
ʿIyāḍ, Abū al-Faḍl Qāḍī, Al-Ilmāʿ fī Ḍabṭ al-Riwāya wa-Taqyīd al-Sāmiʿ
Ismāʿīlī, Abī Bakr Aḥmad b. Ibrāhīm al-, Mustakhraj Ṣaḥīḥ al-Bukhārī
Jawzī, Abū al-Faraj b. al-, Al-Mawḍūʿāt al-Kubrā
Jazāʾirī al-Dimashqī, Ṭāhir al-, Tawjīh al-Naẓar ilā Uṣūl al-Athar
Jurjānī, Sayyid Sharīf al-, Al-Taʿrīfāt
Kattānī, ʿAbd al-Ḥayy al-, Al-Tarātīb al-Idāriyya
Kattānī, Muḥammad b. Jaʿfar, Al-Risāla al-Mustaṭrafa li-Bayān Mashhūr
    Kutub al-Sunna al-Musharrafa
Kathīr, ʿImād al-Dīn b., Ikhtiṣār ʿUlūm al-Ḥadīth
——Al-Tafsīr
Kirmānī, Shams al-Dīn al-, Sharḥ Ṣaḥīḥ al-Bukhārī (Sharḥ al-Kirmānī)
Khaṭīb al-Baghdādī, Abū Bakr al-, Al-Jāmiʿ li-Ādāb al-Shaykh wal-Sāmiʿ
——Al-Kifāya fī ʿIlm al-Riwāya (al-Kifāya al-Rāwī)
——Sharaf Aṣḥāb Ahl al-Ḥadīth
Khuzāʿī, Nuʿaym b. Ḥammād al-, Musnad
Khuzayma, Abū Bakr Muḥammad b., Ṣaḥīḥ

Laknawī, ʿAbd al-Ḥayy al-, *Al-Ajwiba al-Fāḍila*
——*Fawātiḥ al-Raḥamūt bi-Sharḥ Musallam al-Thubūt*
——*Al-Rafʿ wal-Takmīl*
Mājah al-Qazwīnī, Muḥammad b. Yazīd b., *Sunan*
Mālik b. Anas, *Al-Muwaṭṭaʾ*
Maqdisī, Abū al-Faḍl al-, *Tadhkira al-Mawḍūʿāt*
Maqdisī, Ḍiyāʾ al-Dīn al-, *Al-Mukhtāra*
Mayāniji, ʿUmar b. ʿAbd al-Majīd al-,
——*Mā Lā Yasaʿu al-Muḥaddith Jahluhu*
Māwardī al-Shāfiʿī, Abū al-Ḥasan ʿAlī al-,
——*Al-Ḥāwī al-Kabīr fī Fiqh Madhhab al-Imām al-Shāfiʿī*
Mubārakfūrī, Abū ʿAlāʾ Muḥammad,
——*Tuḥfa al-Aḥwadhī bi-Sharḥ Jāmiʿ al-Tirmidhī*
Mudābighī, Ḥasan b. ʿAlī b. al-,
——*Ḥāshiya ʿalā Sharḥ al-Haytamī ʿalā al-Arbaʿīn al-Nawawiyya*
Musarhad al-Baṣrī, Musaddad b., *Musnad*
Muslim b. al-Ḥajjāj al-Naysābūrī, *Ṣaḥīḥ*
Munāwī, Zayn al-Dīn b. ʿAbd al-Raʾūf al-,
——*Fayḍ al-Qadīr Sharḥ al-Jāmiʿ al-Ṣaghīr*
Mundhirī, Zakī al-Dīn ʿAbd al-ʿAẓīm al-, *Al-Targhīb wal-Tarhīb*
Nasāʾī, al-, Abū Ḥafṣ ʿUmar b. ʿAbd al-Majīd al-, *Sunan*
Nawawī, Muḥyī al-Dīn, *Al-Adhkār*
——*Al-Arbaʿīn*
——*Al-Irshād ilā ʿIlm al-Isnād*
——*Sharḥ Ṣaḥīḥ Muslim*
——*Al-Taqrīb wal-Taysīr li-Maʿrifa Sunan al-Bashīr al-Naẓīr*
Nuʿaym al-Aṣbahānī, Aḥmad b. ʿAbdullah Abū-, *Tārīkh Aṣbahān*
Qārī, ʿAlī al-, *Al-Mawḍūʿāt al-Kubrā wal-Ṣughrā*
——*Ḥāshiya Irshād al-Sārī fī Sharḥ Ṣaḥīḥ al-Bukhārī*
Qasṭallānī, Aḥmad b. Muḥammad al-,
——*Minhāj al-Ibtihāj li-Sharḥ al-Jāmiʿ al-Ṣaḥīḥ li-Muslim b. al-Ḥajjāj*
——*Irshād al-Sārī fī Sharḥ Ṣaḥīḥ al-Bukhārī*
Qāsimī al-Dimashqī, Jamāl al-Dīn al-,
——*Qawāʿid al-Taḥdīth min Funūn Muṣṭalaḥ al-Ḥadīth*
Qaṭṭān, Abū al-Ḥasan b. al-, *Al-Wahm wal-Īhām*
Qāwuqjī al-Ḥasanī al-Mashīshī, Abū Maḥāsin al-, *Al-Luʾluʾ al-Marṣūʿ*
Qayyim al-Jawziyya, Shams al-Dīn b., *Jalāʾ al-Afhām*
Qutayba, Abū Muḥammad ʿAbdullah b., *Taʾwīl Mukhtalif al-Ḥadīth*
Rāmahurmuzī, Abū Muḥammad al-,
——*Al-Muḥaddith al-Fāṣil bayn al-Rāwī wal-Wāʿī*

Rāhūyah, Isḥāq b., *Musnad*
Ruhāwī, ʿAbd al-Qādir al-, *Al-Arbaʿīn al-Buldāniyya*
Ṣaghānī, Ḥasan b. Muḥammad al-, *al-Mawḍūʿāt*
Sakhāwī, Shams al-Dīn Muḥammad al-,
——*Fatḥ al-Mughīth bi-Sharḥ Alfiyya al-Ḥadīth (Sharḥ Alfiyya al-ʿIrāqī)*
——*Al-Maqāṣid al-Ḥasana*
——*Al-Qawl al-Badīʿ fī al-Ṣalāti ʿalā al-Ḥabīb al-Shafīʿ* ﷺ
Ṣalāḥ al-Shahrazūrī, Abū ʿAmr ʿUthmān b. al-,
——*Muqaddima fī ʿUlūm ʿIlm al-Ḥadīth*
Ṣayrafī, Abū Bakr al-, *Sharḥ Risāla al-Shāfiʿī fī ʿIlm Uṣūl al-Fiqh*
Shāfiʿī, Muḥammad b. Idrīs al-, *Al-Risāla fī ʿIlm Uṣūl al-Fiqh*
Shayba, ʿUthmān b. Abī, *Musnad*
Shayba, Abū Bakr b. Abī, *Al-Muṣannaf*
Ṣanʿānī, Muḥammad b. Ismāʿīl al-Amīr al-,
——*Tawḍīḥ al-Afkār li-Maʿānī Tanqīḥ al-Anẓār*
Subkī, Taqī al-Dīn al-, *Al-Ṭabaqāt al-Kubrā*
Suyūṭī, Jalāl al-Dīn al-, *Al-Alfiyya*
——*Al-Azhār al-Mutanāthira fī al-Akhbār al-Mutawātira*
——*Al-Durr al-Munaẓẓam*
——*Khamāʾil al-Zuhar fī Faḍāʾil al-Suwar*
——*Al-Laʾālīʾ al-Maṣnūʿa fī al-Aḥādīth al-Mawḍūʿa*
——*Al-Qawl al-Ḥasan fī al-Dhabbi ʿan al-Sunan*
——*Tadrīb al-Rāwī (Sharḥ al-Taqrīb)*
Ṭabarānī, Sulaymān b. Aḥmad al-, *Al-Muʿjam al-Awsaṭ*
——*Al-Muʿjam al-Kabīr*
——*Al-Muʿjam al-Ṣaghīr*
Ṭabarī, Abū Jaʿfar Muḥammad b. Jarīr al-, *Tahdhīb al-Āthār*
Taftāzānī, Saʿd al-Dīn al-, *Sharḥ al-Arbaʿīn al-Nawawiyya*
Ṭaḥāwī, Abū Jaʿfar Aḥmad b. Muḥammad al-, *Maʿānī al-Āthār*
——*Muskhil al-Āthār*
Tirmidhī, al-Ḥakīm al-, *Al-ʿIlal*
Tirmidhī, Muḥammad b. ʿĪsā al-, *Sunan*
Umawī, Asad b. Mūsā al-, *Musnad*
ʿUwāna al-Isfarāyīnī, Abū, *Mustakhraj Ṣaḥīḥ Muslim*
Zarkashī, Badr al-, *Nukat ʿalā Muqaddima Ibn al-Ṣalāḥ*
Zurqānī, Muḥammad b. ʿAbd al-Bāqī b. Yūsuf al-,
——*Al-Mawāhib al-Laduniyya*
——*Sharḥ al-Bayqūniyya*
——*Sharḥ al-Mawāhib*

INDEX

al-ʿāda, conventionally 100-101fn

ʿadāla, ʿadl, integrity 48, 50-51, 53, 55,
57-58, 66-67fn, 73-74, 111-112,
114, 120- 121, 147, 163, 180-181,
184-188, 190, 192-193

al-ʿadāla al-bāṭina, inward integrity
67fn, 121

al-ʿadāla al-ẓāhira, outward integrity
67fn, 121, 135

ʿālī, elevated 49, 150-155, 175, 208

ʿāmm, general 46, 77fn, 119, 150, 161,
162, 174-175, 185, 191, 196;
see also *takhṣīṣ al-ʿāmm* and
ʿumūm wa-khuṣūṣ min wajh

ʿan fulān, from so-and-so 108,
116-118fn, 131fn, 133, 198, 200-202

ʿaqāʾid, creed 61, 75, 77, 188;
see also *ahl al-bidʿa*

ʿāqil, sound mind 51, 180

ʿaqlan, rationally
62fn, 85, 101, 112, 167,

ʿarḍ, presenting by reading
30, 174, 194, 200

ʿazīz, rare 49, 65, 95, 97-98, 100

al-aʾimma al-muḥaqqiqīn, verifying
Imams 75

adhān, call to prayer 85, 149

āḥād, singular narration 39, 63, 95;
see also *khabar wāḥid*

aḥkām, sing. *ḥukm*, rulings of law 75

Ahl al-Bayt, the Prophetic Household
167

ahl al-bidʿa, people of creedal
innovation 181

Ahl al-Sunna, Sunni orthodoxy
171, 189

ajwad, best 72; see also *jayyid*

akhbaranā, 'he informed us' 93, 108,
194-195, 199-200

akhbaranī man lā attahim, 'someone
who I do not suspect, informed
me' 217

akhbārī, historian 37

al-akābir ʿan al-ṣaghāʾir, seniors
narrating from juniors 157-158

Amīr al-Muʾminīn, Leader of the
Believers 28, 38

anbaʾanā, 'he reported to us' 194

aqrān, contemporaries
104, 107, 109fn, 118, 124-125,
156-159, 201-202

arsala al-ḥadīth fulān, 'so-and-so
narrated the Hadith by *irsal*' 115

aṣaḥḥ, most sound 65, 94,
see also *ṣaḥīḥ*

aṣaḥḥ al-asānīd, most sound chain
56fn

asbāb al-wurūd, Hadith
contextualization 175fn

asbāb al-nuzūl,
reasons for revelation 82, 175fn

athar, traditions 37-37, 83

awhām, mistakes 182;
see also *kathīr al-wahm*

āya, verse 39

badal, substitution 152

bāligh, postpubescent 51

basmala, refers to *bismillah al-raḥmān
al-raḥīm* 43-46, 137-138, 142

dajjāl, deceiver 184fn; see also *kadhāb*

dirāya, comprehension 26, 30, 37

dunyā, worldly life 85-86

ḍaʿīf, weak 29, 48, 64, 69,
72, 73-74, 97, 133, 182

ḍaʿf qarīb muḥtamal, a slight weakness
68fn

ḍābiṭ, ḍabṭ, accurate, accuracy
49-50, 53-59, 66-67, 73-75, 105,
114, 120, 122, 131, 133, 136, 142,
147, 151, 155, 162-163, 180, 187

ḍabṭ kitāb, accuracy of the book 53

ḍabṭ ṣadr, accuracy of the heart 53

ḍabṭ tāmm, complete accuracy
54, 66fn-67, 131, 133

ḍarūrī, unequivocal 62

dhakara lanā fulān, 'so-and-so
mentioned to us' 194

faḍāʾil, meritorious acts 75-77

fard, solitary [narration]
65, 129-134, 162

fard muṭlaq, absolute solitary
130-134
fard muqayyad, particular solitary
130-134
fard nisbī, syn. *fard muqayyad*
farḍ, obligatory 130fn
fāsiq, fisq, flagrant sinner, flagrant sin
51-52, 67-68, 74, 164, 180, 188
al-ʿFatḥ, the Conquest of Mecca 178
fīhi naẓar, 'it requires investigation'
184
fiqh, jurisprudential understanding
25-26, 115, 135, 155,
175, 204, 207, 210

ghafla, heedlessness
53-54, 67, 75, 127, 138, 180
gharīb, unusual [narration] 49, 63, 65,
94-97, 100, 125, 131, 134, 188
ghayr maḥfūẓ, not protected from
corruption 96; see also *maḥfūẓ*
ghayr tāmm al-ḍabṭ, imperfect
accuracy 54, 59
ghusl, ritual bath 69, 130, 206

ḥaddathanā, 'he narrated to us'
93, 108, 194-195, 199-200
ḥarām, forbidden
40fn, 80, 127, 168, 170, 147
Ḥawḍ, the fountain on the Day of
Judgement 109fn
ḥāfiẓ pl. *ḥuffāẓ*, master [of Hadith]
37-38, 63-64, 70, 93-94, 127,
136, 148, 151, 171fn, 181, 208
ḥākim, master [of Hadith] 38
ḥamdala, praising God 43-46
ḥaqīqa, literal 173-175, 191
ḥaqīqa al-riwāya,
reality of the narration 30
ḥasan, fair 29, 48, 50, 54, 59-60,
64-73, 75, 97, 123fn, 131, 133,
142, 156, 163, 170, 183, 202
ḥasan al-isnād, fair chain 70
ḥasan gharīb, fair but unusual 133
ḥasan li-dhātihi, intrinsically fair
48, 50, 54, 59, 66fn, 67, 72
ḥasan li-ghayrihi, fair due to
supporting narrations
48, 50, 54, 59, 67-68, 183
ḥasan ṣaḥīḥ, fair and/or sound
70-71, 123fn
ḥujja, master [of Hadith] 38

ḥujja, proof 61, 81, 184
ḥukman, implicit 79-80
ḥukm al-marfūʿ, the ruling of being
raised 82; see also *marfūʿ*
ḥukm al-mawqūf, the ruling of being
halted 82; see also *mawqūf*

ʿibādāt, worship 61, 209
ʿilla pl. *ʿilal*, defect 37, 49-50, 54, 57-58,
66, 73, 75, 135, 138, 122, 210;
see also *muʿall*
ʿilla qādiḥa, detracting defect
49-50, 54, 66
al-ʿilm al-ḍarūrī, unequivocal
knowledge 102
al-ʿilm al-naẓarī, knowledge after
reflection 102
al-ʿilm al-yaqīnī al-ḍarūrī, unequivocal
certain knowledge 102
ʿilm yaqīn naẓarī, certain knowledge
after reflection 61, 62fn

iʿjāz, inimitability 38, 41
iʿlām, informing 200
iʿtibār, investigation 129
idrāj, interpolation
143-144, 146-147; see also *mudraj*
idṭirāb, discrepancy; 136, 140,
141-142; see also *muḍṭarib*
ighrāb, confusing the narrator 127
ijāza, license 30, 90, 155, 195-201
ijmāʿ, scholarly consensus
62, 65, 150, 164, 167, 170, 178
ijmāʿ qaṭʿī, definitive consensus 167
iḥtijāj, utilize as proof 54, 61, 69, 72,
74, 108, 111-113, 120, 124, 131,
133, 162, 164, 171; see also *ḥujja*
iḥrām, state during pilgrimage 178
ijtihād, independent reasoning
177, 186, 189
ikhbār, direct informing 30, 36, 117,
195, 198, 202; see also *khabar*
al-ikhbār al-ijmālī,
informing summarily 195
ilāhī, Divine [narration]
38, 42, 87; see also *qudsī*
ilhām, inspiration 41-42
imʿān, profound study 204
īmān, faith 182fn
inqilāb, inversion 158; see also *maqlūb*
inqiṭāʿ, severed 30; see also *munqaṭiʿ*
inshāʾ, origination 39

iqāma, pre-prayer call 84, 125, 149
irjā', antinomianism 260;
    see also *Murji'a*
irsāl, initial disconnection
    54, 115, 107, 136; see also *mursal*
irsāl ẓāhir, apparent initial
    disconnection 107
isnād, see *sanad*
Isrā'īliyyāt, Judaeo-Christian
    traditions 55, 85fn
istiqrā', detailed investigation 112
itqān, proficiency 128fn, 180, 184;
    see also *mutqin*
ittiṣāl, connected 30, 51, 137;
    see also *muttaṣil*
ittiṣāl al-sanad,
    connected chain 50, 57, 66, 73

al-jahl bi-'ayn al-rāwī aw bi-ḥālihi,
    unknown narrator or status 74
jamā'a, group 59, 98-100, 118fn,
    122, 124, 136fn, 145
jāmi' pl. *jawāmi'*, collection of
    various topics of Hadith
    31, 129, 136
jarḥ, criticism 67fn, 138, 185-188
jarḥ wa-ta'dīl, narrator evaluation
    30, 38, 107fn, 181, 185-192
Jassāsa, the Beast 157
jawhar, pearl 211
jayyid, good 72
jayyid ḥasan, 72; syn. *ḥasan ṣaḥīḥ*
juz' pl. *ajzā'*, a compilation of Hadith
    from only one narrator
    32, 33, 64, 129, 136, 203
al-juz'iyyāt, minutiae 181

kadhāb, liar 52, 97, 101fn, 147,
    151, 171, 183-184fn
kadhib, lying 67-68, 74, 77, 101fn,
    138, 164, 166, 181, 183
karāmāt,
    miraculous marks of honour 190
Karrāmiyya, a sect 170
kathīr al-wahm,
    prone to mistakes 67, 77, 164
kitāba, writing 175, 195, 199-200
kunya, surname of relationship
    86, 109, 159-161

khabar, narration 37, 83
khabar wāḥid, singular report 191;
    see also *āḥād*
khafī, hidden 104, 135-136,
khalīfa, *khilāfa*, caliph, succession
    27-28, 38, 205
khāṣṣ, specific 46, 71-73, 75, 90-91,
    102, 132-133, 149fn, 157, 161, 175,
    191, 196, 199; see also *takhṣīṣ*
Khawārij, Seceders 169
khawārim al-murū'a, contravention of
    social norms 51, 180
khirrīj, reference 58

lā ba's bihi, 'there is no issue with
    him' 182
lafẓ, *lafẓī* form 41, 101
layyin al-ḥadīth, weak in narrating 182
laysa bihi ba's, 'there is no issue with
    him' 182, 184

mā akdhabahu, an astonishing liar
    183; see also *kadhāb*
ma'lūl, syn. *mu'all*, defective 54,
    75, 135-138, 142; see also *'illa*
ma'lūm min al-dīn bil-ḍarūra, a matter
    of the religion that is known
    by necessity 181
ma'nā, *ma'nawī*, meaning 88, 101-102,
    139, 155, 166, 175, 180
ma'nā kulli, general meaning 102
ma'rūf, affirmed 72, 162-163
madhhab, school of law 53fn, 61fn,
    149, 160, 169, 184, 186-189, 192
majāz, metaphorical 175
majhūl pl. *majāhīl*, unknown 48, 53, 67,
    74, 106, 109, 112, 121, 182, 185
majhūl al-'ayn, unknown person
    121, 182, 196
majhūl al-ḥāl, unknown status 182
majhūl al-ḥāl ẓāhiran wa-bāṭinan,
    outwardly and inwardly
    unknown state 121
majhūl al-ḥāl bāṭinan lā ẓāhiran,
    inwardly unknown outwardly
    known state 121
majrūḥ, flawed 107
makhraj, source 36, 56, 60
maḥfūẓ, preserved 72, 122-124
maknūn, hidden 211
manṭiq, logic 74, 98

maqbūl, accepted 30, 33, 44fn, 48,
   50-51, 61, 71-72, 96fn, 105, 108,
   111, 114, 120, 148-149, 163, 177,
   180-181, 183, 192-193
maqbūl ḥaythu yutāba', 'acceptable
   if accompanied by supporting
   narrations' 182
maqlūb, inverted 48fn, 124-128, 211
maqrūna bil-ijāza,
   accompanied by license 198
maqṭū', cut-off 37, 49, 79-83, 115
   see also *inqiṭā'*
mardūd, rejected 30, 33, 48, 51-54,
   73, 105, 107, 121, 124, 131, 138,
   148-150, 162, 164fn, 171, 180-183
mardūd al-riwāya, someone whose
   narrations are rejected 107
marfū', *raf'*, raised 37, 49, 54,
   79-90, 110, 114, 136-137
marfū' mursal, raised after being
   initially disconnected 82
maṣāliḥ mursala, public interest 191
mashhūr, well-known
   49, 56, 63, 65, 95, 97fn,
   98-100, 124, 126-127
mastūr, concealed 67, 68fn, 73, 121,
   182; see also *majhūl al-ḥāl
   bāṭinan lā ẓāhiran*
matn pl. *mutūn*, wording
   36-38, 47, 55fn, 70, 79, 84, 91,
   94-96, 102, 112fn, 119-120,
   122-126, 129-130, 132,
   135-144, 146, 166
matrūk, abandoned
   74-75, 125, 139, 164, 183-184
matrūk al-ḥadīth, someone whose
   narrations are abandoned 183-184
mawḍū', pl. *mawḍū'āt*, fabricated 45fn,
   65, 76-77, 146fn, 164-173, 183-184
mawqūf pl. *mawqūfāt*, halted 37, 49,
   54, 79, 81-90, 114, 136-137fn
mawqūf muttaṣil, connected after
   being halted 82
mawṣūl, connected 44fn, 90, 141;
   syn. *muttaṣil*
muttaṣil, connected 30, 44fn, 48,
   50-51, 54, 57, 66, 73-74, 79-80,
   82-83, 89-90, 103, 105, 107-108,
   110, 113-114, 117-118, 122,
   136-137, 141, 143, 155, 199
mu'addil, someone who has integrity
   186; see also *'adāla*

mu'all, mu'allal, defective 49, 54, 75,
   135-138, 142; see also *'illa*
mu'allaq, suspended
   48, 66, 74, 103, 115-116
mu'āmalāt, transactions 61
mu'an'an, transmitted using 'from'
   48, 57, 103, 117-118
mu'ḍal, problematic
   48, 74, 103, 105-106
mu'jam pl. *ma'ājim*, a book of
   Hadith arranged according
   to the names of teachers 31
mu'tamad, relied upon
   50, 75, 89, 102, 150
mu'an'an, transmitting using 'that'
   48, 74, 103, 118
mu'talif, similar 160-161
mubham, unclear 48, 74, 119-120
mudabbaj, *tadbīj*, mutual narration
   156-158
mudallas, misleading 48, 67-69,
   103, 106-109, 117-118,
   136, 147, 202, 211
mudallis, someone engaged in *tadlīs*
   who narrates something that is
   mudallas 103, 107-109, 117
mudraj, interpolated 143-147
muḍṭarib, inconsistent
   49, 75, 136, 139-142
mufassar, a clear expression 258
muftariq, divergent 158-160
muḥaddith, scholar of Hadith 37
muḥaqqiqūn, verifying scholars
   63, 75, 117fn, 135, 202, 204;
muḥarraf, orthographically altered
   138-139
mujarrada, *munāwala* without license
   198; see also *ijāza*
mujawwad, articulate 72
al-mujāz, the one licensed 195;
   see also *ijāza*
al-mujāz bihi, that which is licensed
   195; see also *ijāza*
al-mujīz, the one licensing 195;
   see also *ijāza*
mujmal, an unclear expression 179
mujtahid, independent jurist 71, 184;
   see also *ijtihād*
mukallaf pl. *mukallafīn*, legally
   responsible person 51, 176
mukharrij, *mukhrij*, someone who
   references narrators 36

mukhtalif, dissimilar 160-161

mukhtalif al-ḥadīth, contradictory
    narrations 173-176

mumayyaz, discerning 51

munāwala, presentation
    155, 175, 198-200

munkar pl. *manākīr*, denounced
    68, 72, 74, 97, 139, 162-163, 166

munkar al-ḥadīth, someone whose
    narrations are denounced 184

munqaṭiʿ, severed 30, 48, 74, 83, 89,
    103-107, 114-115, 117, 136

mursal, initially disconnected 44fn,
    48, 54, 67, 74, 82, 103-104, 110-115,
    122, 136, 137fn, 141, 191

murūʾa, see *khawārim al-murūʾa*

muṣaḥḥaf, orthographically altered
    138-139

musalsal, concatenated 49, 63, 91-94

musalsal bil-ḥuffāẓ al-mutqinīn,
    narrated through a chain
    consisting of proficient are
    masters of Hadith 63

musāwā, equivalence 152-153

mushabbah, likened 72

mushtarak lafẓī, homophones 159

musnad pl. *masānīd*, a book of Hadith
    arranged according to the names
    of Companions 29, 31, 129, 136

musnad pl. *masānīd*, supported
    89-90, 110, 113

musnid, narrator with a chain 37

mustadrak pl. *mustadrakāt*, a book
    of Hadith that complements
    another collection 32

mustafīḍ, abundant 49, 95, 100

mustakhraj pl. *mustakhrajāt*, a book of
    Hadith that complements
    references of another collection
    32-33, 118, 123

mutābaʿa, supportive
    59, 72fn, 129, 130fn

mutābaʿ ʿalayhi,
    that which is *mutābaʿa* 129

mutābiʿ, someone who narrates
    mutābaʿa 67, 68, 129

mutakallam fīhi, someone who is
    criticized 58, 63

muṭlaq, absolute
    54, 94fn-95, 111, 130,
    149-150, 151, 175, 196

mutqin pl. *mutqinīn*, proficient
    54, 59, 63, 128fn 180-181, 184

mutawakkil pl. *mutawakkilūn*, people
    of reliance on God 86

mutawātir, mass-transmitted 39, 41,
    49, 56, 61, 63, 65, 95, 100-102, 167

mutayaqqiẓ, mindful 53

muttafaq ʿalayhi, agreed upon 55

muttafiq, resemblant 158-160

muttaham bil-kadhib, suspect of lying
    67, 77fn, 93fn, 151, 164, 183

muwāfaqa, concordance 151-152

muzakkūn, narrator evaluators 188

Nabawī, Prophetic [tradition] 36

nāqiṣa, deficient 129

naqliyya, transmitted 85

naqṭ, diacritics 161

naṣṣ, legal text 149fn

nāsikh, abrogated 176

nāzil, nuzūl, descending, descent
    49, 150-156

nisba, ascription 142, 159-161

nukat, notes 34

qabīḥ, ugly 202

qadar, predestination 182;
    see also *Qadariyya*

qadīm, eternal 36

qāla lanā fulān, 'so-and-so said to us'
    194

qarīna, contextual indication 82, 166

qāṣira, deficient 129

qaṭʿ, qaṭʿī definitive 61, 167-168

Qadariyya, a sect 182

qawī, strong 72

qiyās, analogical deduction 190

qudsī, Divine [narration] 38-43, 87

raʾy, opinion 177, 190

rabbānī, Divine [narration] 38, 42;
    see also *qudsī*

rafʿ, see *marfūʿ*

radd, see *mardūd*

Rāfiḍī, Shiʿa Rejecter 167

riqāq, softening hearts 31, 75

riwāya, narration 26, 37

riwāya al-aqrān, narrations from
    contemporaries 157

sabab al-wurūd, reasons for Hadith
175

al-sābiq wal-lāḥiq, when one student
of a particular teacher passes
away before another student
157-158

sakatū ʿanhu, 'they were silent
regarding him' 184

salaf, predecessors 28, 37, 200, 206

salāma min al-ʿilla al-qādiḥa, free of
defects that detract from the
narrator's reputation 50, 57,
66, 73; see also *ʿilla*

salāma min al-shudhūdh, free of
anomalies 50, 57, 66, 73;
see also *shādh*

samāʿ, direct audition 30, 103, 117, 193

sanad, chain of narration 32, 36, 47,
55, 106-107, 113-118, 144, 150

sāqiṭ, disregarded 109, 183

sard, reading aloud uninterruptedly
203

sayyiʾ al-ḥifẓ, poor memory 68fn, 182

sunna, Prophetic example 28, 30, 37,
39-40, 82, 84-85, 150, 167;
pl. *sunan*, a book of Hadith
arranged according to topics
of jurisprudence 31, 151, 210

sūra, chapter of the Qurʾan 39, 137

ṣabiyy, child 51-52

ṣadūq, truthful 71, 162, 182

ṣadūq al-amīn, truthful and
trustworthy 67

ṣadūq sayyiʾ al-ḥifẓ, truthful but
with a poor memory 182

ṣadūq yahim, truthful but
prone to error 182

Ṣaḥābī, pl. *Ṣaḥāba*, Companion
31-32, 37, 49, 67, 79-88, 96,
101, 110-114, 120, 156, 157,
177, 181, 202,

ṣaḥīḥ, sound 29-30, 48, 50-67, 69-72,
76, 78, 94-97, 108, 112fn, 113,
116-118, 123fn, 131, 133, 136,
139, 142, 149, 151, 155-156,
161, 170, 178, 193

ṣaḥīḥ li-dhātihi, intrinsically sound
54, 59-60, fn66

ṣaḥīḥ li-ghayrihi, sound due to
supporting narrations 54, 59-60

ṣalāt, prayer 31, 39, 86

ṣalāt, ṣalāwāt, sending Prayers upon
the Prophet ﷺ 43, 45-47fn

ṣāliḥ, valid 72

samiʿtu, 'I heard' 88, 93, 194-195

ṣayrafī, currency exchanger 136

ṣīgha al-jazm, a phrase that indicates
decisiveness 78, 116, 201

ṣīgha al-tamrīḍ, a phrase that
indicates weakness 78

ṣiḥḥa, soundness 55-57, 62, 72, 78,
116, 135-136,142, 155-156, 171;
see also *ṣaḥīḥ*

ṣiyām, fasting 31

Shaykh, pl. *shuyūkh*, teacher
31-32, 51-52, 58, 106, 109, 112fn,
129, 152-155, 157, 158, 165, 194,
198-200, 204, 207-209

shādh pl. *shudhūdh*, anomalous
49, 50, 54, 57-58, 66, 72-73, 75,
122-124, 131, 139, 162, 188fn

shāhid pl. *shawāhid*, corroboration
67-68, 72fn, 129-130, 164

shakl, vowelling 161

sharʿan, legally 163

shāriʿ, legislator 176-177

shuhra, being well-known 53, 59

shuhra qawiyya, well-known to a high
degree 56; see also *mashhūr*

taʿdīl, declaring someone's integrity
185; see also *ʿadāla*

taʿdīl mubham, vaguely declaring
someone's integrity 185

tābaʿa, supporting 122;
see also *mutābaʿa*

Tābiʿī pl. *Tābiʿīn*, Successor 29, 37,
49, 79, 80-82, 87-88, 110-114,
118, 120, 130-131, 156-157, 159

tābiʿ al-Tābiʿīn, followers of the
Successors 81, 156

tadbīj, see *mudabbaj*

tadlīs, misleading 67-69, 106-109, 118,
136, 147, 202; see also *mudallas*

tadlīs al-isnād, misleading in the chain
106-107

tadlīs al-shuyūkh, misleading with the
teachers 106, 109

taghayyara bi-ākhirihi, 'he changed
later in life' 182

taḥammul, receiving Hadith 30

taḥdīth, direct narration 30, 117, 175, 194, 202, 205

taḥrīf, orthographical alteration 139; see also *muḥarraf*

tajwīd, rules of recitation 204

takhṣīṣ al-ʿāmm, rendering a general application specific 149fn; see also *khāṣṣ* and *ʿāmm*

tāmm, complete 54, 129

tamyīz, discernment 193; see also *mumayyaz*

tanṣīṣ, testifying, explicitly mention 53, 146, 177

tanzīhi dhāt, transcendent essence [of Allah] 42

targhīb, encouragement 76

tasāhul, laxity 75

tashayyuʿ, inclination to Shiʿism 182

taṣḥīf, orthographical alteration 139; see also *muṣaḥḥaf*

taṣrīḥan, explicit 79, 80

tawaqquf, suspend judgment 65, 176

tawātur, mass-transmission 39, 56, 61, 63; see also *mutawātir*

ṭabaqa, pl. *ṭabaqāt* level 98

ṭahāra, purification 31

ṭālib, student 36-37, 48, 109, 146, 157-158, 161, 180, 194, 198, 200, 203, 208-210

taqyīd al-muṭlaq, restriction to the absolute 149

ṭaraf, sing. *aṭrāf*, books in which only the beginning of Hadith are collected 32-33

ṭarīq, route 36, 59, 105, 133, 136; see also *sanad*

ṭarīq al-ḥall wal-baḥth, unlocking meanings and resolving issues 204

thabt, *thābit*, affirmed 72, 128, 181, 186

thiqa pl. *thiqāt*, reliable narrator 44fn, 49, 54, 59-60, 71, 75, 89, 95, 97, 105, 108, 112, 114, 120, 122-124, 130-133, 136-137, 142, 148-150, 160, 162, 177, 180-185, 194, 199

thiqa! thiqa!, 'reliable! reliable!' 181

thiqa ḥāfiẓ, reliable master of hadith 64, 70, 148

thiqa! ḥāfiẓ!, 'reliable! a master!' 181

al-thiqāt al-mutqinīn, reliable and proficient masters 54, 180

thubūt al-ʿadāla, integrity affirmed 50, 57, 66, 73; see also *ʿadāla*

thubūt al-ḍabṭ, accuracy affirmed 50, 57, 66, 73; see also *ḍabṭ*

ʿudūl, sing. *ʿādil*, with integrity 120; see also *ʿadāla*

ʿulamāʾ, sing. *ʿālim*, scholars 172, 186; see also *ʿilm*

ʿuluww, elevation 32, 150, 152; see also *ʿālī*

ʿuluww fī al-ẓāhir, direct elevation 155

ʿuluww maʿnawī, indirect elevation 155

al-ʿuluww al-muṭlaq, absolute elevation 151

al-ʿuluww al-nisbī, relatively elevation 151

ʿuluww al-tanzīl, descending elevation 152

ʿumūm wa-khuṣūṣ min wajh, sharing in one quality and differing in another 97

uṣūl al-fiqh, legal theory 51-52fn, 61, 102fn, 111, 149fn, 191fn, 202fn

umma, nation 61-63

waḍḍāʿ, consistent fabricator 183

wāhī al-ḥadīth, erroneous in narrating 183

waḥy, revelation 39-42, 44, 82, 113

waṣiyya, bequest 200

wijāda, finding 175, 201-203

yablughu bi, 'he reaches by means of it' 87

yanmīhi, 'he attributes it' 87

yarfaʿuhu, 'he raises it' 87

yukhṭiʾ, 'he makes mistakes' 182

yarwī bil-maʿnā, narrating the meaning 53

ẓāhir, apparent 104,

Ẓāhirīs, a school of law 200

zakāt, alms tax 31, 123, 140, 209

zanādiqa, heretics 168

ẓann, probability 62

al-ẓann al-qawī, high probability 61

ziyāda al-thiqa, additional reliable narrator 44fn, 114fn, 148

An Explanation of the Bayqūnī Poem
In Hadith Terminology

شرح المنظومة البيقونية في مصطلح الحديث

Sharḥ al-Manẓūma al-Bayqūniyya fī Muṣṭalaḥ al-Ḥadīth

By Imam ʿAbdallah Sirājuddīn al-Ḥusaynī

Translated by
Imran Rahim

Edited by
Abdassamad Clarke

LOOH PRESS
SUNNI PUBLICATIONS